A TRAIL FOR

PUBLICATIONS OF THE FINNISH LITERATURE SOCIETY 601

a TRAIL for SINGERS

FINNISH
FOLK
POETRY:
EPIC

EDITED BY

Matti Kuusi

TRANSLATED BY

Keith Bosley

FINNISH LITERATURE SOCIETY · HELSINKI
1995

Finnish Folk Poetry. Epic,
ed. and transl. by
Matti Kuusi, Keith Bosley and
Michael Branch
with both Finnish and
English poems was
published in 1977.

ISBN 951-717-865-4

Designed by Urpo Huhtanen and Mika Launis

Printed by/ Raamattutalo
Pieksämäki, Finland

C O N T E N T S

TO THE READER 11

TRANSLATOR'S NOTE 15

PRONUNCIATION 19

1 PROLOGUE 20
2 THE CREATION I 22
3 THE CREATION II 23
4 THE CREATION III 24
5 THE CREATION IV 25
6 THE WOUND 27
7 THE TASKS 29
8 THE SMITH 30
9 FIRE 31
10 THE SINGING MATCH I 33
11 THE SINGING MATCH II 35
12 THE SAMPO I 37
13 THE SAMPO II 43
14 THE SAMPO III 44
15 THE SAMPO IV 47
16 THE COURTSHIP I 51
17 THE COURTSHIP II 54
18 THE COURTSHIP III 58
19 THE GIFT I 60
20 THE GIFT II 63
21 THE GOLDEN BRIDE I 65
22 THE GOLDEN BRIDE II 67
23 THE KANTELE I 69
24 THE KANTELE II 71
25 THE KANTELE III 72
26 THE VOYAGE I 74
27 THE VOYAGE II 77
28 THE SPELL I 80
29 THE SPELL II 82
30 THE VISIT TO TUONELA 85
31 SUN AND MOON I 87
32 SUN AND MOON II 88
33 SUN AND MOON III 90
34 LEMMINKÄINEN I 93
35 LEMMINKÄINEN II 97
36 LEMMINKÄINEN III 102
37 KAUKAMOINEN I 104
38 KAUKAMOINEN II 109
39 THE BOND I 112
40 THE BOND II 113

41 THE ORPHAN I 115
42 THE ORPHAN II 117
43 THE ORPHAN III 119
44 THE INCEST I 121
45 THE INCEST II 122
46 THE SOWER I 123
47 THE SOWER II 125
48 THE BEAR 127
49 THE OAK I 128
50 THE OAK II 130
51 THE GREAT OX 131
52 THE GREAT PIG 132
53 THE ELK I 133
54 THE ELK II 134
55 ELK AND SNAKE 136
56 THE FISHING 137
57 LEAVETAKING I 138
58 LEAVETAKING II 139
59 THE MESSIAH I 140
60 THE MESSIAH II 145
61 THE MESSIAH III 148
62 THE MESSIAH IV 151
63 ST STEPHEN 155
64 ST CATHERINE I 157
65 ST CATHERINE II 158
66 ST HENRY I 159
67 ST HENRY II 162
68 THE TREE 164
69 THE FOREST 165
70 THE FOUNDLING I 166
71 THE FOUNDLING II 167
72 THE MAID AND THE DRAGON I 169
73 THE MAID AND THE DRAGON II 170
74 THE MAID AND THE DRAGON III 171
75 MAGDALEN I 172
76 MAGDALEN II 174
77 SERF AND MASTER I 176
78 SERF AND MASTER II 178
79 SERF AND MASTER III 179
80 DEATH ON THE PROWL I 182
81 DEATH ON THE PROWL II ... 183
82 THE WIDOW I 184
83 THE WIDOW II 185
84 THE DEATH OF ELINA 186
85 THE FAITHFUL BRIDE I 190
86 THE FAITHFUL BRIDE II 191
87 DEATH OF THE BRIDE I 192
88 DEATH OF THE BRIDE II 193
89 THE PRIEST-KILLER 195
90 THE INTRUDER-KILLER 197
91 THE HUSBAND-KILLER 198
92 THE FORSAKEN MAID I 199
93 THE FORSAKEN MAID II 200
94 THE FORSAKEN MAID III 201
95 THE WIFE-KILLER I 203

96 THE WIFE-KILLER II 204
97 THE DAUGHTER-KILLER I . 206
98 THE DAUGHTER-KILLER II 208
99 THE DAUGHTER 210
100 THE SON 211
101 THE MOTHER 213
102 THE DYING MAID I 215
103 THE DYING MAID II 216
104 THE HANGED MAID I 218
105 THE HANGED MAID II 220
106 THE LOSS I 221
107 THE LOSS II 222
108 THE LOSS III 223
109 THE LOSS IV 224
110 THE DANCE 225
111 THE SUITORS FROM
THE SEA I 227
112 THE SUITORS FROM
THE SEA II 228
113 THE SUITORS FROM AFAR 230
114 THE FOUL MAID 231
115 THE THIEF AS SUITOR 232
116 THE USELESS BRIDEGROOM 234
117 THE CRANE I 235
118 THE CRANE II 236
119 THE EARLY RISER 237
120 FINDING A HUSBAND 239
121 THE UNWELCOME VISITOR 241
122 THE UNHAPPY BRIDE I 243
123 THE UNHAPPY BRIDE II 245
124 THE WATER-CARRIER I 246
125 THE WATER-CARRIER II 249
126 THE MAID AND
THE BOAT I 251
127 THE MAID AND
THE BOAT II 252
128 THE MAID AND
THE BOAT III 254
129 BOY AND CLOUD I 256
130 BOY AND CLOUD II 257
131 MAID AND CLOUD 258
132 THE LOST BRUSH 259
133 THE LOST GOOSE I 260
134 THE LOST GOOSE II 261
135 THE LOST BROTHER I 262
136 THE LOST BROTHER II 263
137 THE WARRIOR'S
DEPARTURE I 264
138 THE WARRIOR'S
DEPARTURE II 265
139 THE WARRIOR'S
DEPARTURE III 266
140 NEWS OF DEATH I 267
141 NEWS OF DEATH II 269
142 THE WARRIOR 270
143 DUKE CHARLES 272
144 JACOB PONTUS 274
145 IVAN 275

146 CHARLES XII 276
147 THE CONSCRIPT 277
148 EPILOGUE 280
NAME INDEX 281
MOTIF INDEX 293
KALEVALA AND KANTELETAR
CONCORDANCE 298
SOURCE INDEX 299
COLLECTION LOCALITY
INDEX 301
COLLECTOR INDEX 303
SELECT BIBLIOGRAPHY 306

TO THE READER

Finland's share in world chronicles begins with a description written by the Roman Cornelius Tacitus in the year 98:

'The Fenni are astonishingly savage and disgustingly poor. they have no proper weapons, no horses, no homes. They eat wild herbs, dress in skins, and sleep on the ground. Their only hope of getting better fare lies in their arrows, which, for lack of iron, they tip with bone. The women support themselves by hunting, exactly like the men; they accompany them everywhere and insist on taking their share in bringing down the game. The only way they have of protecting their infants against wild beasts or bad weather is to hide them under a makeshift covering of interlaced branches. Such is the shelter to which the young folk come back and in which the old must lie. Yet they count their lot happier than that of others who groan over field labour, sweat over house-building, or hazard their own and other men's fortunes in the hope of profit and the fear of loss. Unafraid of anything that man or god can do to them, they have reached a state that few human beings can attain: for these men are so well content that they do not even need to pray for anything.'

'Fennis mira feritas, foeda paupertas' probably refers to the Lapps rather than the Finnish settlers, who were moving from north-western Estonia to the river valleys of western Finland as Tacitus was writing. These, too, were poor barbarians: it was to be 1,444 years before the first book that has survived for posterity was written in their tongue. Where the Icelanders have their *Edda*, the Germans their Merseburg spell-book, the Russians the chronicle of Nestor and the bark-writings of Novgorod, and the Hungarians, the Poles, and even the Komi their own solid base of early literature in their own languages, in Finland only names of persons and places in the foreign-language documents of the mediaeval period demonstrate that the Finnish language was already then in existence. Not a single stone-hewn runic inscription exists to tell us – as they do for the Norwegians, the Swedes and the Danes – the nature of the poetry of the fifth century, or even of the time of the Vikings.

The most fateful unifying and insulating factor in Finnish literature has been language. Like strange ancient relics, the Basques, the Hungarians and the Baltic Finns survive in a Europe dominated by the Indo-European languages. From the dim Finno-Ugrian past, the assimilative, destructive, fruitful pressure of the Indo-European peoples has shaped our culture. In the area once defined by the comb-ceramic culture that stretched from Finnmark to the Vistula and from the Gulf of Bothnia to western Siberia, the Finnic peoples are now an ever-decreasing minority. It is worth nothing that the most viable of them wandered down from the forest of north-eastern Europe farthest west to become those who dared settle the plains or the sea-shores: the Hungarians, the Estonians, the Finns. Their non Indo-European mother tongue has, in their cultural histories, often meant contempt, sometimes a defensive wall for their own individuality, always an additional threshold, an extra test of strength, in the import and export of international influences. The literature of Rome was able, in its early stages, to base itself on Greek, the literary language of France and Italy on Latin; Germany and England, in turn, on French; Denmark, Sweden and Norway on the continental tradition and each other. Some impression of the initial difficulties of Finnish literature may be gained by imagining how, for example, the literature of Denmark might have developed had Chinese been spoken at its southern border and had the language of the opposite northern shore been Japanese, or by considering the attempts to establish the Celtic tongues as literary languages.

Two factors that explain why the Finns (and their closest relatives, the Estonians) were able, unlike all the other tribes of northern Europe that spoke non Indo-European languages, to achieve, in the 20th century, a place among the independent cultural peoples.

1. During its short period as a great power in the 17th century, Sweden put Martin Luther's radical cultural policies into practice in its eastern provinces: each people had the right to read the Bible and receive instruction in Christianity in its own language. In 1632 and 1640, respectively, the universities of Tartu and Turku began their slow development toward high culture.

2. In 1630 the Swedish king, Gustaf II Adolf, required his subordinates to gather evidence of the ancient greatness of the great power: both ancient material goods and old heroic poems, stories and charms. The great power crumbled, but the collection and theoretisation of 'antiquities' on their basis continued.

Suprising in this process, and far-reaching in its consequences, was the discovery of the poetry of the 'unlearned people' of Finland, the international interest it attracted, the slow, thoroughgoing rise in self-awareness it engendered.

As early as the first half of the 18th century, university men in Finland, as elsewhere, had dared to print the poem-texts they had recorded from the mouths of common people in distant parishes. 'I do not consider it a matter for shame only that a born Finn does not know the poetry of our people, but also that he does not admire it,' wrote Professor Henrik Gabriel Porthan, professor of rhetoric, in the foreword to his work *De Poësi Fennica* in 1766. At the beginning of the subsequent century, a Finnish love-poem published by Porthan in *De Poësi Fennica*, carried by travellers, spread to the wider the world; it provided the inspiration for Goethe's 'Finnisches Lied', and references to it recur many times in the writings of men of letters.

Between 1700 and 1809, four wars had been waged in northern Europe, as a result of which the Finns, the Karelians and the Estonians ceased to be part of the sphere of influence of the Swedish king and entered that of the Russian tsar. Contrary to expectations, the tsarist authorities permitted the cultivation of Finnish-language culture. Finnish-language schools and libraries were established, and the Finnish-speaking peasant estate was strong both at the Diet and in society as a whole. This cultural and political development led to the declaration of independence in 1917.

The *Kalevala* marked a decisive turn on the road to independence. The educated son of a poor village tailor, later the district physician of Kajaani, a small town in northern Finland, Elias Lönnrot (1802-1884) travelled by foot, skis, boat, sleigh and ship, visiting previously unknown areas and covering an estimated total of 14,000, and recording in his note-book previously unknown epic and lyric poetry, charms, laments, proverbs. On the basis of these and poem-texts that had been gathered in the 18th century, he published first, between 1829 and 1831, four collections of verse under the title *Kantele*, then, in 1835 to 1836, a unified epic of 32 poems and 12,078 lines, entitled *Kalevala, taikka Vanhoja Karjalan runoja Suomen kansan muinosista ajoista* ('Kalevala, or poems of Old Karelia from the ancient times of the Finnish people'), and finally, in 1849, an extended work based on the preceding one, the *Uusi Kalevala* ('New Kalevala'), consisting of 50 poems and 22,795 lines. This last has assumed the mantle of national epic in Finland; it has, so far, been translated into 44 different languages.

In Estonia, F.R. Kreutzwald composed a corresponding epic called *Kalevipoeg*; it was printed in Estonian and German in 1857-1861.

Scholars realised as early as the end of the 19th century that the original poems gathered in different provinces were not the raw material only of Lönnrot's *Kalevala* and its lyric companion work the *Kanteletar* (1840). Each original poem brought shadowy messages, open to interpretation, from the past, distant or close. Between 1910 and 1950 a 33-volume monument, *Suomen Kansan Vanhat Runot* ('Ancient poems of the Finnish peoples'), consisting of some 85,000 folk-poem texts, was published. Like the Edda, the Nibelungenlied, the Song of Roland or the Russian bylinos, these ancient Finnish-Karelian and Estonian poems and their traditional background have given rise to an entire tradition of learning. Various methods have been applied to determine the poems' probable 'original form', their deepest message or, at least, the direction of development of possible interpretations.

The selection published here consists of some 148 relatively clear and conservatively authentic examples of folk epic. Gathered in Finland, Karelia and Ingria between 1670 and 1930, these poem texts do not, as a whole, follow the plot of the 1849 *Kalevala* so much as the concept of the general developmental history of ancient epic that has become established during the 20th century. The selected poems follow a certain chronology of subject-matter and stylistic periods.

Like the performances of the poem-singers of old, the selection begins and ends with brief words of greeting and farewell. Readers must imagine the accompaniment of the *kantele* and the black log walls of the chimneyless cabin for themselves.

Examples 2-56 are, in all probability, the most archaic layer represented in the anthology. At the beginning, the story of the birth of the world and its basic elements is told, and of the *heros* figures who participated in its creation. Correlations have been found on the one hand with palaeoarctic cultures, and on the other in the direction of India–Indonesia–Polynesia. The Sampo poems (numbers 12-15) mark a shift to culture myths, fairy-tale like sea journeys and courtship trips. Narrative realistic and psychological adventure epic telling of Kaukamieli, Ahti and the maidens of the Island beyond the sea (37-40), which have been dated to the Viking period, have survived only in rare examples. The same ethos of violence may also appear in a couple of ballad-like descriptions of neighbourly strife, incest and springtime rituals (41-47). From a fairy-tale like gallery of animals and trees (48-56), we move on to early Christian poetic subjects, culminating in a great Karelian-Byzantine messiad (59-62) and in the 'death-hymn' of Bishop Henry, killed in Finland on 20 January 1156. Relatively strong in the legends is the pauperist antipathy of the mendicant Dominican monks toward rich braggarts and 'great landlords' who do wrong to their subordinates (75-79, 82-84). Pan-European themes appear in poems dealing with love and death, particularly favoured among them ballads of women who reject, curse or kill their seducers (89-94). Melancholy songs of fate continue to poem 109, after which we move on to lyric epic poems generally expressing women's joys, fears and disappointments (110-136) and, finally, to the panorama of wartime tribulation that lasted from the mediaeval period to the 19th century (137-147).

More detailed background information and explanation can be found in *Finnish Folk Poetry. Epic* (607p., Finnish Literature Society, Helsinki 1977), in which original texts and English translations are published in parallel; their numbering corresponds to that of this book, and also relates to numerous appendix indexes.

MATTI KUUSI
Translated by Hildi Hawkins

TRANSLATOR'S NOTE

Epic poetry is about heroes making history, or what is perceived as history. Its language combines the elevated with the matter-of-fact, that 'perfect plainness of speech... allied with perfect nobleness' which Matthew Arnold found only in the *Iliad* and the Bible. These qualities, plus a transeendence of the personal, became the basis of Classical taste. But oral tradition can only be impersonal: when he or she performs, a bard draws on a common fund, sometimes adding to it, but more often reshaping it or – as a tradition dacliness – merely repeating it. When a bard speaks in the first person, it is usually a professional 'I', as in the first poem in this book: 'Shall I start to sing / shall I begin to recite...' So we can imagine an audience's delight on hearing in an epic context what sounds like a personal aside, as in poem 21: 'The maid might be good-looking / but I do not know her ways.'

To must Westerners today, all this most sound very remote; and that is the translator's problem. His closest mode is the ballad tradition of northern and central Europe; but this is not epic poetry, nor is it our 'great' tradition as their oral poetry is for Finns. The translator can only listen and bring to life as best he can, knowing that whatever he writes is bound to sound odd sometimes. After much trial and error I felt the need to use another metre: there being none suitable, I had to invent one, which continues to stand me in good stead twenty years later. I still believe that to translate Finnish oral poetry into Hiawatha metre (a crude derivative) is to do it no favour. I also abandoned any thought of reproducing its alliteration: in five lines of poem 104 there are ten words beginning with *k*, and the standard modern Finnish dictionary lists 618 pages – in double columns – of such words. Another feature of Finnish oral poetry is its parallelism that demands a steady supply of synonyms. If a translator is committed to reproducing at least this, he must match 'strike' with 'smite', 'turf' with 'sward' and so on, inviting charges of archaism – especially when he discovers that many Finnish words have exact English equivalents forgotten by town-dwellers, such as 'glade' and 'grove'.

The guiding spirit of this book in its original form (1977) was Michael Branch, now Professor of Finnish at and Director of the School of Slavonic and East European Studies in the University of London: he steered Matti Kuusi towards a worldwide audience, recruited me, and wrote an extensive commentary.

Two final thoughts about the original title of this book, *Finnish Folk poetry: Epic.* The term oral poetry is now generally preferred for the material in hand, since folk poetry can also refer to poetry written by literate peasants; Finnish literature has plenty of such, outside the scope – alas – of this book. Also outside its scope is the great wealth of material to which we originally planned (and some of us still hope) to devote a companion volume, to be called *Finnish Folk Poetry: Lyric.*

KEITH BOSLEY

FENNO-SCANDINAVIA AND NORTH-WEST RUSSIA

showing where the poems in the present work were collected and other places mentioned in the book. The inset map shows the traditional provinces of Finland and Karelia, the larger map the Baltic-Finnish area. In the latter, the villages which were especially rich sources of folk poetry, and towns, are marked in small letters; small capitals are used to show administrative districts, the geographical areas by which poems are generally identified.

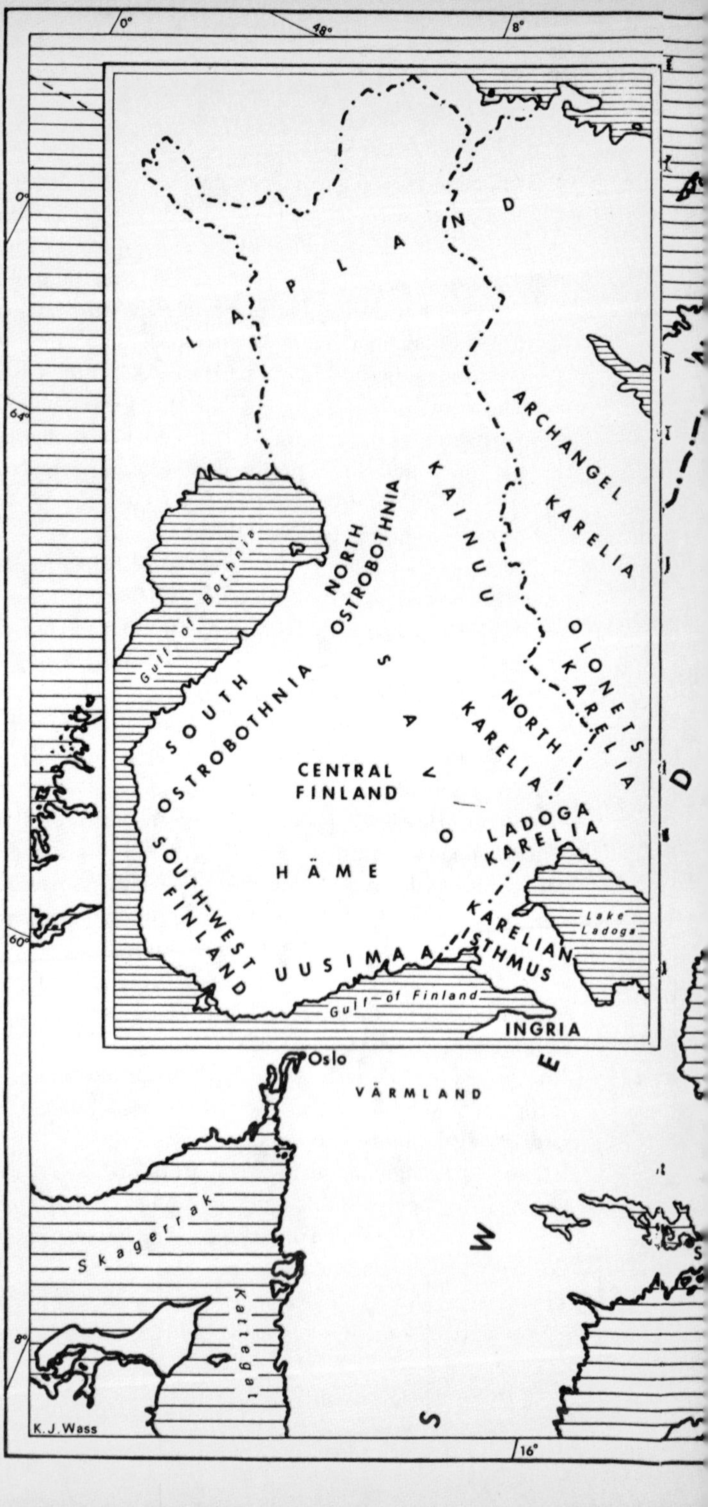

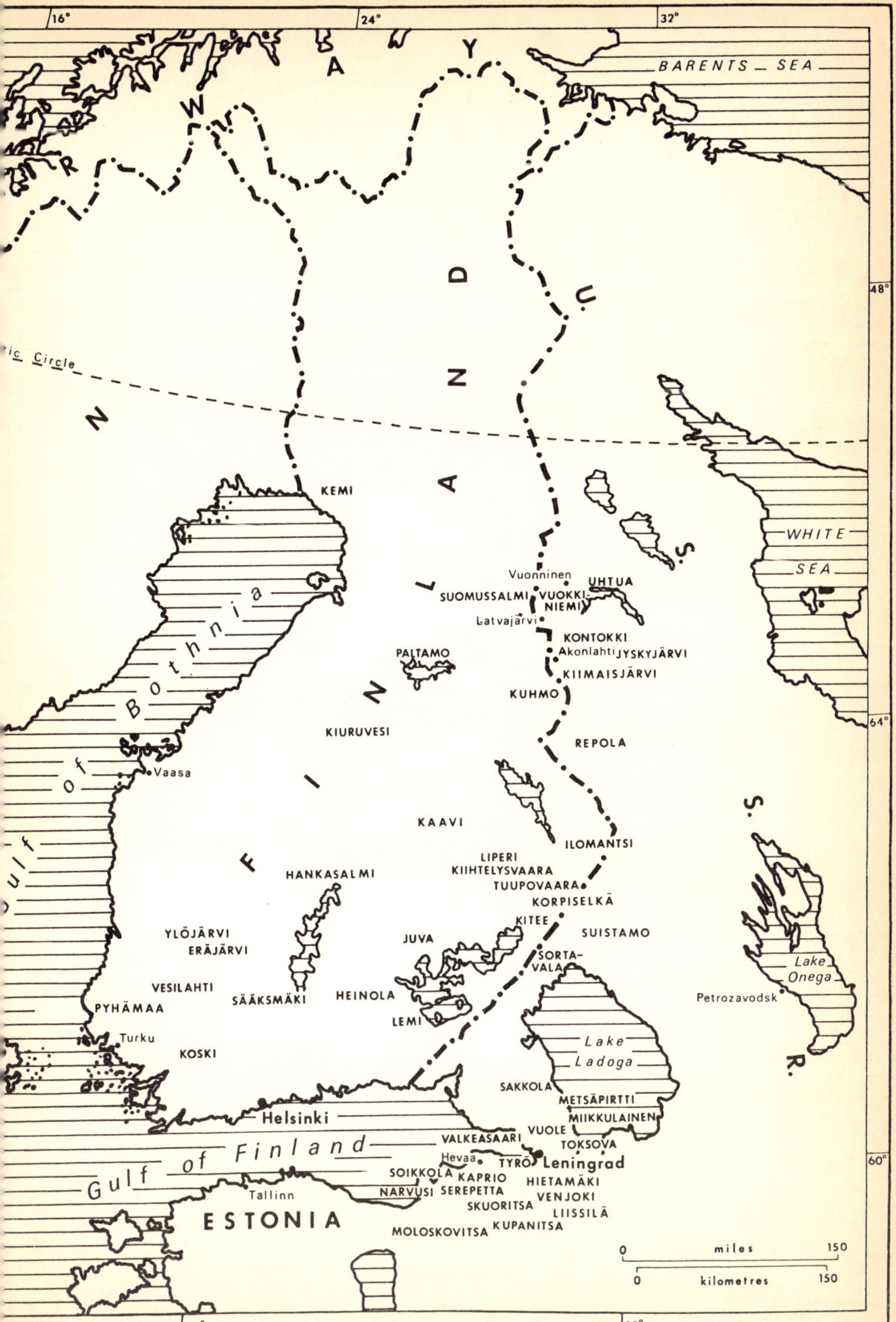

16°
24°
32°
N O R W A Y
BARENTS SEA
Arctic Circle
U. S. S. R.
F I N L A N D
KEMI
WHITE SEA
Gulf of Bothnia
Vuonninen
UHTUA
SUOMUSSALMI
VUOKKINIEMI
Latvajärvi
KONTOKKI
PALTAMO
Akonlahti
JYSKYJÄRVI
KIIMAISJÄRVI
KUHMO
48°
64°
KIURUVESI
REPOLA
Vaasa
Gulf of
KAAVI
ILOMANTSI
LIPERI
KIIHTELYSVAARA
HANKASALMI
TUUPOVAARA
KORPISELKÄ
KITEE
SUISTAMO
YLÖJÄRVI
ERÄJÄRVI
JUVA
SORTAVALA
Lake Onega
VESILAHTI
SÄÄKSMÄKI
HEINOLA
Petrozavodsk
PYHÄMAA
LEMI
Turku
Lake Ladoga
KOSKI
SAKKOLA
METSÄPIRTTI
Helsinki
MIIKKULAINEN
VUOLE
VALKEASAARI
TOKSOVA
Gulf of Finland
Hevaa
TYRÖ
Leningrad
60°
SOIKKOLA
KAPRIO
HIETAMÄKI
NARVUSI
SEREPETTA
Tallinn
VENJOKI
SKUORITSA
LIISSILÄ
ESTONIA
MOLOSKOVITSA
KUPANITSA
0 miles 150
0 kilometres 150
24°
32°

PRONUNCIATION

The orthography used in this book is phonetic. Each letter represents a single sound. If it is written twice, it indicates, in the case of vowels, that the sound is double the length of the single sound; where consonants are written twice, they are at syllable junctures and should be pronounced twice. Native English-speakers should take special care not to lengthen short consonants between two vowels, for this can sometimes change the meaning of a word. In normal spoken Finnish, the main stress always falls on the first syllable of a word, with decreasing secondary stress on the third and fifth syllables (provided they are not in the final syllable of the word); the requirements of the Kalevala metre, however, can alter this stress patter.

CONSONANTS **f**, **l**, **m**, **n**, **r** are similar to the corresponding sounds of English; **b**, **d**, **k**, **p**, **t**, as in English but without aspiration; **g** occurs in loanwords when it is pronounced as in *goat*; in the cluster **ng**, the combined sound as in *singer*; **h** as in *hat* at the beginning of a syllable and *loch* at the end of a syllable; **j** as **y** in *yoke*; **s** is always voiceless; **š** as in *shoe*; **tš** as **ch** in *church*; **ž** as **j** in French *jour*.

VOWELS **a** as in *father*; **e** as in *pet*; **i** as in *hit*; **o** as in *hot*; **u** as in *pull*; **y** as in French *tu*, German *über*; **ä** as in bad; **ö** like its German counterpart, or as in French *peu*.

1

Prologue

Shall I start to sing
shall I begin to recite
with a good man as partner
two who grew up together?
Come, let us put hand in hand
and finger in finger-gap
each grip in the other's grip.
One word from you, one from me
splendid speech from both:
we will shape our mouths
we will pitch our tunes
like two kanteles
like five or six gates
three doors of a hut.

*

Even the Lapp children sing
after draining water-mugs
in their nests of pine
in their rooms of fir:
why don't I sing too
with my well-fed mouth
full of barley beer
of meal made from rye?

*

I myself sing when I hear
and what I hear I carol –
words I found before
charms I have been taught:
my own finding are my words
my own snatching from the road
my grinding from the grass tops
my snapping from the heather.

When small I was a herdsman
as a child minding cattle
I went then to a hummock
to the side of a bright rock
the edge of a thick boulder:
I found words by the hundred
put them up in the shed loft
in a purse of gold
in a copper box.

When the time is truly come
I'll open the chest of words
the bright lid slam back
right across my knees.
There's no lack of sampo-words
Lemminkäinen-charms:
he will rot upon the charms
grow old upon the verses.

*

I'll ski a trail for singers
for the skilled set out a road:
from here to here the road goes
the road goes and the land crawls
a new track leads off.

1–14 *Miihkali Perttunen*
Latvajärvi, Vuokkiniemi, Archangel Karelia
A. A. Borenius, 1877

15–22 *Singer unknown*
Suomussalmi, Kainuu
K. Saxa, recorded before 1823

23–47 *Arhippa Perttunen*
Latvajärvi, Vuokkiniemi, Archangel Karelia
E. Lönnrot, 1834

48–52 *Mishi Sissonen*
Ilomantsi, North Karelia
D. E. D. Europaeus, 1845

2

The Creation I

A summer bird, a song-bird
a sun-bird, a swallow-bird
fluttered on a summer day
a dark autumn night
searching for land to lie on
a grove to rest in
for some brushwood to lay eggs:
it found no land to lie on
no grove to rest in
nor yet brushwood to lay eggs.

It flew to shores, flew to seas
to shores by water
beside white water:
it found three hummocks
and it laid three eggs
on the three hummocks.
One hummock was blue
the second was red
the third was yellow:
which hummock was blue
on it a blue egg
which hummock was red
on it a red egg
which one was yellow
there a yellow egg.

Ukko's great cloud came
the sea's angry howl
the sea's right fierce wave
rolled the eggs in the water
dropped the nest into the waves.
The swallow-bird, the sun-bird
flew straight to the smith's dwelling
flew to the smithy:
"O my smith, my clever man
careful craftsman of old times
you hammered once, yesterday,
hammer too today
hammer a rake of iron
cast the prongs out of copper
fashion the shaft from maple!"

He hammered an iron rake
fashioned the shaft from maple
out of copper cast the prongs.

The swallow-bird, the sun-bird
raked up all the sea
all the reeds out of the sea
all the rushes from their bed.
It found a part from the yolk
another part from the white
and a third from the yellow:
which part was the yolk
became the moon for gleaming
which part was the white
became the sun for shining
which was the yellow
became scudding clouds.

Paroi, Saku's wife
Hevaa, Kaprio, Ingria
V. Porkka, 1883

3

The Creation II

A swallow-bird, a sun-bird
a night bird, bat of a bird
fluttered on a summer day
    a dark autumn night
searching for land to lie on
    a grove to rest in:
found no land for bird to lie
no grove for a bird to rest.
Now, it flew to a great hill
    flew to a high peak:
it saw a ship on the sea
    a red-mast sailing
it flew on to the ship's deck
on the ship's prow alighted
it cast a nest of copper
    laid an egg of gold.

    God brought a great wind
sent from the western corner:
the ship went into a list
heeled over on to its side.
The egg rolled in the water
the nest trundled after it
down into the sea's black mud
down among the heavy clay.

There a blessed island sprang
on the island lovely grass
upon the grass a young maid.
    All went to woo her:
masters went, pastors went, slim
gentlemen-in-waiting went
rural deans from Sweden went
and Naari's haberdashers.
The maid would not go to them.

Finally Turf Thomas came
put the maiden in his sledge
struck the stallion with the reins
the horse with the beaded whip:
the horse ran, the road rang out
the sledge of iron rumbled
the golden heathland echoed
the rowan collar-bow squeaked.

Loviisa Karvanen
Valkeasaari, Ingria
A. A. Borenius, 1877

4

The Creation III

The Laplander, the lean boy
    for ages harboured hatred
against old Väinämöinen
    for long bore ill-will.
He cut a pile of arrows
of three-edged arrows he cut
a whole lot, for three whole years.

The cripple took an arrow
the lame one flexed the bow taut
    and the blind man shot
shot a day at Pohjola
another at great Savo
he shot upon the third day
he shot towards the north-east.
Now he shot Väinämöinen
    in the right shoulder
    under the left arm
    through the bones, through the
    flesh, through the warm flesh.

Then on his face in the snow
he fell, headlong in the flakes
his palms turned towards the sea.
Here he bubbled for six years
he bobbed for seven summers
he roused six seas to fury
and he softened a seventh:
that Imandra Island grew
on the knee of old Väinö.

A scaup-duck, straight-flying bird
    flew, glided about
it searched for a nesting-place:
now it found a nesting-place
there on Imandra Island
on the knee of old Väinö.
It cast a nest of copper
and it laid an egg of gold
on the knee of old Väinö.

    He shifted his knee
    he jolted his limb:
the copper was smashed to bits
the golden egg to pieces.

What was the egg's upper shell
became the heavens above
what was the egg's lower shell
became mother earth below
what was the white of the egg
became the moon in the sky
what was the yolk of the egg
became the sun in the sky
what on the egg was mottled
became the stars of heaven
what on the egg was blackish
became the clouds in the sky.

Iivana Shemeikka
Suistamo, Ladoga Karelia
O. A. Hainari, 1893

5

The Creation IV

Sturdy old Väinämöini
built a boat on a mountain
beat it upon a boulder:
the axe did not touch the rock
nor the blade strike the boulder.
At last it slipped into flesh
in the holy hero's knee
the nail of Kaleva's son.

  There was no hummock
  that was not flooded
  and no high mountain
  that was not flooded
from the toe of old Väinö
from the holy hero's knee.

A golden sleigh was prepared
  a silver wheel whirled
the track of iron clattered:
now, that old Väinämöini
raised himself into his sleigh
flung himself into his sledge
  drove rumbling away.
He drove through ten villages:
  half way through a tenth
he asked across the threshold
inquired under the window:
"Is there any in this house
who can know a hero's pain
who can partake of troubles
who can close a vein's rapids
who can speak of a tree's birth
who knows the birth of iron?"

An old crone indeed answered:
"There is no one in this house
who can know a hero's pain
who can partake of troubles
who can close a vein's rapids
who can speak of a tree's birth
who knows the birth of iron."

Well, that old Väinämöini
himself put this into words:
"Be that as it may, now comes
old Väinämöini's downfall
the everlasting singer."

He raised him into his sleigh
flung himself into his sledge
drove through marshes, drove through lands
drove on the clear stretch of sea
through clearings seen long ago.
He drove through ten villages:
  half-way through a tenth
he asked across the threshold
inquired under the window:
"Is there any in this house
who can know a hero's pain
who can close a vein's rapids
who can partake of troubles
who can speak of a tree's birth
who knows the birth of iron?"

An old man built a net of iron
  of steel he made it.
Now, he put this into words:

"Still bigger things have been closed –
rivers from mouths, lakes from ends
and from narrow necks of land."

The slit-eyed crone of Pohjo
for ages harboured hatred
anger all the time.
She struck the man by the heart
through the warm flesh, from
under the left arm
to the right shoulder.

He sank, fingers to the waves
he turned, palms seaward
he sank, fingers to the waves:
"Wander that way for six years
drift there for seven summers
and throughout nine years –
or even for twelve.
Which way you roll to stretch out
there a bluish hole shall be
which way you rise to sit up
the top of a shoal shall form
the top of a reef shall grow."

Now, that old Väinämöini
sank, fingers seaward
he turned, palms seaward
he sank, fingers to the waves.

A poor eagle, wretched bird
wretched bird in Turja Land
glided and hovered
it looked for a nesting-place
spied a black speck on the sea
a bluish speck on the wave:
it looked for a nesting-place
scratched at the dry grass
and it laid three eggs
laid three golden eggs.
It rubbed them, it sat on them.
Now, the old Väinämöini
felt his knee burning:
as he shook his knee
the eggs rolled in the water.

A pike came prowling
a water-dog lumbering:
it swallowed up the three eggs
gulped down the three golden eggs.
The poor eagle, wretched bird
wretched bird in Turja Land
the first time it lunged –
the bird of the air glided –
it no more than brushed the scales
the next time it lunged
it only tore the belly
when the third time came
it split the pike's guts.

It looked, it turned it over:
"What have my eggs changed into
what has become of my catch!
What was the white of the egg
is now the sun for shining
what was the yolk of the egg
is now the moon for gleaming
is now the stars of heaven
what was the egg's upper half
is now the copper heavens
what was the egg's lower half
is now iron mother earth."

Ohvo Harmonen
Vuokkiniemi, Archangel Karelia
A. A. Borenius, 1871

6

The Wound

Tuulikki, maid of Tapio
Honkela's slim daughter-in-law
Salakaarto's lovely wife
sat on the air's collar-bow
glimmered upon the sky's arch.

The old Väinämöinen said:
"Will you come to me, maiden?"
The maid knowingly answered:
"I'd speak of you as a man
think of you as a hero
    if you split a hair
with a knife that had no edge
with a blade that had no point
pulled an egg into a knot
so the knot could not be felt."

Sturdy old Väinämöinen
    split a hair in two
with a knife that had no edge
with a blade that had no point
pulled an egg into a knot
so the knot could not be felt.

The old Väinämöinen said:
"Will you come to me, maiden?"
The maid knowingly answered:
"No, I will not come to you
before you have carved a boat
from bits of my spinning-shaft
pieces of my carding-knife
with your axe not on the rock
your blade-tip making no noise."

Sturdy old Väinämöinen
carved a boat on the mountain
pounded away on the crag:
his axe did not touch the rock
    beat upon the crag.
At last it slipped into flesh
into Väinämöinen's toe
in the holy hero's knee.

The blood came forth like a flood
the gore ran like a river:
    there was no hummock
    and no high mountain
    that was not flooded
all from Väinämöinen's toe
from the holy hero's knee.

Sturdy old Väinämöinen
into his sledge dragged himself
rolled himself into his sleigh
drove off to another house
away to a cold village.
Across the threshold he asked:
"Would there be within this house
anyone to stem this flood
someone to check this deluge?"
A child spoke up from the floor
a baby from the hearth-bench:
"There is not within this house
anyone to stem this flood
to subdue a vein's rapids:
go off to another house!"

Sturdy old Väinämöinen
drove off to another house.
Across the threshold he asked:
"Would there be within this house
anyone to stem this flood
someone to check this deluge?"

An old man from the table-head
spoke, a beard sang, a head wagged:
"Still bigger things have been closed
still greater things been achieved –
rivers from mouths, straits from ends
open waters from capes, necks
of land at their narrowest."

Singer unknown
Kemi, North Ostrobothnia
Z. Topelius, 1803 or 1804

7

The Tasks

That smith, God's creature
the everlasting craftsman
was hammering, was tapping
upon the clear stretch of sea.
He used his shirt for bellows
his breeches for puffing air
he set serfs to blow
hirelings to work the bellows
and himself looked on.
They blew a day, another
soon they started on a third:
the smith looked – a handsome room.

The smith squeezed into the house
in the space between two pots
where three hooks turned to and fro.

"Come, O little girl, to me!"
"No, I will not come to you.
Fashion a vault for the sky
on which is no hammer-mark
nor trace of where tongs have held."

He forged a vault for the sky
and there was no hammer-mark
nor trace of where tongs had held.

"Come, O little girl, to me!"
"No, I will not come to you.
Shoot a star down from the sky
without using your right hand
without using your left thumb!"

The smith, God's creature
shot a star down from the sky
without using his right hand
without using his left thumb.

"Come, O little girl, to me!"
"No, I will not come to you.
Kill the wife you have wedded
the mistress you have brought home
kill the children you have had!"

The smith, God's creature
killed the wife he had wedded
the mistress he had brought home
killed the children he had had.

"Come, O little girl, to me!"
"No, I will not come to you:
you have killed your wedded wife
the mistress you had brought home
and you will want to kill me."

The smith wrung his hands: "Poor me
I have done an evil thing
I have fallen for a whore
for an evil woman's whim:
I have killed my wedded wife!"

Singer unknown
Korpiselkä, Ladoga Karelia
D. E. D. Europaeus, 1846

8

The Smith

By night born, Ilmollini
by day went to the smithy
forged a hundred locks
and a thousand keys.
No smith is better than he
and no craftsman more careful
though born on a charcoal hill
brought up on a coal-black heath.
That smith is a god:
he has forged the sky
beaten out the air's arches
and there is no hammer-mark
nor trace of where tongs have held
of forked iron's rule.

Miihkali Perttunen
Latvajärvi, Vuokkiniemi, Archangel Karelia
A. A. Borenius, 1877

9

Fire

Ilmarinen struck
fire, Väinämöinen
flashed above eight heavens, in
the ninth sky: a spark
dropped down through the earth
through Manala, and
through the smoke-hole caked with soot
the children's cradle
it broke maidens' breasts
and burned the mother's bosom.
The mother knew more of it:
she shoved it into the sea
lest the maid go to Mana
lest the fire should burn her up
lest the flame roast her.

That gloomy Lake Alue
three times on a summer night
foamed as high as the spruces
in the torment of the fire
the flame's overwhelmingness.

A smooth whitefish swam
and swallowed the spark:
torment to the swallower
came, hardship to the gulper.
A grey pike swam up
swallowed the whitefish
a light lake-trout swam
swallowed the grey pike
a red salmon swam
and swallowed the light lake-trout:
it swam, it darted about
in between the salmon-crags
in the torment of the fire.

It said in these words
it uttered along these lines:
"Fire once burned much land
one evil summer of fire
one year of flame without help.
A small piece was left unburned
at the turn of Ahti's fence
at the rear of Hirska's bank."
It was hoed and dug
and Tuoni's maggot was found
and Tuoni's maggot was burned
in a copper boat
in an iron-bottomed punt.
Its ashes were sown upon
the shore of Lake Alimo:
flax without like grew
peerless linen rose
in a single summer night.
It was quickly stripped
now taken to the water
now the linen put in soak.
The sisters spun it
the brothers wove cloth
and fashioned a net.

Sturdy old Väinämöinen
put the young ones on the net.
They drew across the water:
that fish did not come
for which the net was fashioned.

They drew along the water:
    that fish did not come
for which the net was fashioned.
They drew against the water:
the salmon splashed in the sea.

Sturdy old Väinämöinen
could not bear to put his hand
without mittens of iron:
took his mittens of iron
split open the red salmon –
    the light lake-trout came
from the red salmon's belly
split open the light lake-trout –
    the grey pike came out
he split open the grey pike –
    the smooth whitefish came
split open the smooth whitefish –
    and the spark came out.

There the fire was lulled
and the flame was rocked
at a misty headland's tip
there the fire was lulled
in a silver sling:
the golden cradle jingled
the copper mantle trembled
as the fire was lulled.

Singer unknown
Akonlahti, Kontokki, Archangel Karelia
M. A. Castrén, 1839

10

The Singing Match I

First was young Joukavainen
then was old Väinämöinen
driving together head on:
traces were jammed with traces
collar-bow with collar-bow.
There and then they stopped.
The collar-bow sprang a shoot
and the shafts sprouted aspens
the traces a willow-clump.

The young Joukavainen said:
"He whose knowledge is the worse
must move aside from the road."

The old Väinämöinen said:
"Say some things exactly true
tell some lies of long ago."

The young Joukahainen said:
"And yet I know a little
I understand more:
I know the tit is a bird
the ruff is a water-fish
the willow the oldest tree
I know the hollows were scooped
the mountains heaped together
I know the fish-holes were dug
the troughs of the sea deepened."

At that Väinämöinen said:
"A child's mind, a woman's lore
is not a bearded hero's.
The hollows were my scooping
the mountains were my heaping
the fish-holes were my digging:
I was man among men there
the third hero there
the seventh among heroes
bearing the arch of heaven
pushing up the sky's pillar
spangling the heavens with stars
straightening out the Great Bear."

Väinämöinen grew angry
towards young Joukahainen:
he sang young Joukahainen
in a marsh up to his belt
in a meadow to his waist
in a heath to his armpit
he sang Joukahainen's dog
with its claws in a cold rock
with its teeth in a wet log
he sang Joukahainen's bow
to an arch on the water
sang Joukavainen's arrow
to a hawk streaking
high in the heavens.
Having done so he felt shame.

At that Joukahainen said:
"Make your holy words harmless
turn your sentences backwards:
I'll fill a helmet with gold
for the release of my head
for the ransom of myself."

The old Väinämöinen said:
"I don't care for your silver:
I have gold coins of my own
    twice, three times better."

At that Joukahainen said:
"Make your holy words harmless
turn your sentences backwards:
I'll give my only stallion
for the release of my head
for the ransom of myself."

"I do not care for your horse
    mean man, your stallion:
I've a stallion of my own
    twice, three times better
    five, six times brisker
six, seven times more bonny."

The young Joukahaine said:
"Make your holy words harmless
turn your sentences backwards:
I'll give my only sister
for the release of my head
for the ransom of myself."

At that old Väinämöinen
made his holy words harmless
turned his sentences backwards.

Then Joukahaine was free:
    he went weeping home
    wailing to the farm.

Father was at the window
mother towards the storehouse.
Mother hastened to inquire:
"Why do you weep, my offspring?
You have nothing to weep for."

The young Joukahainen said:
"I have something to weep for
I have trouble to lament:
I gave my only sister
for the release of my head
for the ransom of myself."

The mother indeed answered:
"For this I hoped all my life –
Väinö for my son-in-law
the great man for my kinsman
the singer my relative."

Ontrei Malinen
Vuonninen, Vuokkiniemi, Archangel Karelia
A. J. Sjögren, 1825

11

The Singing Match II

Against each other they drove
against each other they raced:
first old Väinämöin
then young Joukamoin
on a one-night-old stallion
along the one-night-old ice
and no trace was on the ice
no hoof-blow on the hard lake
no hoof-mark upon the heath.
They collided on the road
collar-bow caught collar-bow
shaft against shaft did violence
blood boiled from the collar-bow
and fat from the traces-tip
and redness fell from the shaft.

Old Väinämöin said
to young Joukamoin:
"Hey, young Joukamoin!
Do you remember the time
when a stump grew in the sea
water sprang up in the flood
apples rolled in the water
apples were on every bough
and nuts were on every tree?"

Against each other they drove
against each other they raced:
first old Väinämöin
then young Joukamoin
on a one-night-old stallion
along the one-night-old ice
and no trace was on the ice
no hoof-blow on the hard lake
no hoof-mark upon the heath.
They collided on the road
collar-bow caught collar-bow
shaft against shaft did violence
blood boiled from the collar-bow
and redness fell from the shaft
and fat from the traces-tip.

Old Väinämöin said
to young Joukamoin:
"Hey, young Joukamoin!
Do you remember the time
when the seas were ploughed
were ploughed up, were sown
when the rocks beat together
when the cairns were first piled up
when the waves gave way to land?
The seas were of my scooping
the stump-roots of my digging
the rocks of my gathering
and the cairns of my piling."

Against each other they raced
against each other they drove:
first old Väinämöin
then young Joukamoin
on a one-night-old stallion
along the one-night-old ice
and no trace was on the ice
no hoof-blow on the hard lake
no hoof-mark upon the heath.
They collided on the road

collar-bow caught collar-bow
shaft against shaft did violence
blood boiled from the collar-bow
and fat from the traces-tip
and redness fell from the shaft.

Old Väinämöin said
to young Joukamoin:
"Let us have a singing-match
and a reciting-contest:
let him who recalls the more
remain on the open road
let him who recalls the less
from the road remove himself."

Now, that old Väinämöinen
he sang Joukamo's saddle
to a duck in gravel-sea
he sang Joukamo's stallion
into scudding clouds
into running wisps of cloud
he sang Joukamoinen's cloak
into a birch-whisk slashing
he sang Joukamo's helmet
to a seal leaping
he sang Joukamoinen's whip
into bulrushes whipping.
Now, that young Joukamoinen
himself could not help weeping.

The old Väinämöinen said:
"So: I have done reciting."
Now, that young Joukamoinen
formed in words, declared by mouth
to old Väinämöi:
"Withdraw now your wicked words
your utterly evil deeds.
I'll give my only sister
I'll leave the well-fed dainty
every Sunday fed on grouse
and every weekday on perch:
when she could not eat
butter, she'd eat pork
on weekdays plates of black grouse."

Now, that old Väinämöinen
turned his wicked words backwards
his utterly evil deeds:
called Joukamo's stallion
back from scudding clouds
back from running wisps of cloud
called Joukamoi's cloak
back from a birch-whisk slashing
called Joukamoinen's saddle
from a duck in gravel-sea
called Joukamoinen's helmet
from a seal leaping
he called Joukamoinen's whip
back from bulrushes whipping.

Now, that young Joukamoinen
went weeping homeward
wailing to the farm.
Mother was going towards the shed.
"O my generous mother
O dear one who carried me
old woman who cared for me:
I have done what I should not
I gave my only sister
I left the well-fed dainty
for old Väinämöi."

The mother answering said
answering declared:
"For this I hoped all my life
longed throughout my days –
Väinö for my son-in-law
the great man for my kinsman."

Olgoi
Hevaa, Kaprio, Ingria
V. Porkka, 1883

12

The Sampo I

The Laplander, the slit-eyed
for ages harboured hatred
    for long bore ill-will
against old Väinämöinen:
he waited evenings, mornings
for Väinämöinen to come
for the man from Umento.
Then the old Väinämöinen
into his sledge flung himself
in his sleigh hoisted himself
with the straw-coloured stallion
with the pea-stalk-coloured horse
    drove rumbling away
upon the clear stretch of sea
    the open water.

The Laplander, the slit-eyed
on a day among others
one morning among many
spied a black speck on the sea
a bluish speck on the wave:
he took up his fiery bow
    from the fiery hut
    he flexed the bow taut
laid an arrow on the stock
    and chose the best shaft.
So then he uttered a word:
    "If my hand comes down
    let the arrow rise:
    if my hand comes up
    let the arrow fall."
He shot the straw-hued stallion
from under Väinämöinen
and the pea-stalk-coloured horse
    through the collar-bone
    through the right shoulder
    under the left arm.

Then the old Väinämöinen
sank with fingers to the waves
turned with palms to the water:
there he wandered for six years
stopped there for seven summers
    wandered as a spruce
as a log from a pine-tree
    in tears he drizzled
    he prayed to Ukko
and worshipped Pavannainen:
"Raise up, Ukko, a great wind
let the weather know no bounds
    raise lumps of black slime
to fall on the clear waters!"

Ukko raised up a great wind
let the weather know no bounds
    raised lumps of black slime
to fall on the clear waters.
He bore old Väinämöinen
    to dark Pohjola
to the side of a bright rock
the edge of a thick boulder.
    In tears he drizzled.

The gap-toothed crone of Pohjo
rose when it was quite early
quite early in the morning:

quickly warmed her room
cleaned all through the rooms
taking a broom to the floor
then she took the dust outside
to the farthest field
and stopped at the rubbish-tip.
There she listened from six sides
attended from eight:
she could hear a man weeping
could hear a hero wailing.
The sobs were no woman's sobs
nor were the sobs a child's sobs:
these were Väinämöinen's sobs
the wails of Untamoinen.

There, then the crone of Pohjo
dressed herself and decked herself
adorned her head prettily
splendidly adorned her head.
She went to Väinämöinen
she uttered a word, spoke thus:
"Why are you weeping, Väinö
why, Untamo, do you wail?"

The old Väinämöinen said:
"For this I weep all my life
grieve throughout my days:
I've swum to strange lands
to quite unknown doors."

So the crone of Pohjo said:
"So what will you give me, if
I take you to your own lands
there to hear your own cockcrow
far from these strange lands
these quite unknown doors?"

The old Väinämöinen said:
"Well, what do you ask of me?"

So the crone of Pohjo said:
"If you shaped a new sampo
worked a brightly-worked cover
from one feather of a swan
from one piece of a distaff
one snippet of wool
the milk of a barren cow
from one barley-grain."
The old Väinämöinen said:
"I myself cannot hammer
nor can I work a cover.
I'll get smith Ilmorinen:
he is the most skilled craftsman
he knows how to work covers."

At that the crone of Pohjo
delivered the man from death
took up old Väinämöinen
brought him to her home:
gave the man food, gave him drink
nursed him back from death
she set a stallion running
a flaxen-maned one moving
from dark Pohjola
from the gloomy arctic sea
from the man-eating village
the village that drowns heroes.

When he got back home
he went to the smith.
He uttered a word, spoke thus:
"Smith Ilmorinen
my kinsman, my mother's child!
Set out to bring back a maid
to look for a plaited head
from dark Pohjola:
now a maiden has been wooed
a plaited head bargained for."

Then the smith Ilmorinen
washed, cleaned himself up

from the autumn-hued charcoal
from the winter-hued forge-grime
he drew broadcloth about him
buckled on his armoured belt
into his sledge flung himself
into his sleigh stirred himself
brought the lash down on his horse
clouted with the beaded whip:
the stallion ran, the road sped
    to dark Pohjola
to the gloomy arctic sea
to the man-eating village
the village that drowns heroes.

When he got to Pohjola
the gap-toothed crone of Pohjo
set him to shape the sampo
to work the bright-worked cover
from one feather of a swan
    from one barley-grain
    one snippet of wool
the milk of a barren cow
from one piece of a distaff.

Then the smith Ilmorinen
by day he built the sampo
and by night courted the maid:
then the smith Ilmorinen
    fashioned the sampo
brightly worked the bright-covered
but the maid was not courted.

The new sampo was grinding
the bright-covered was rocking:
it ground a binful at dusk
ground a binful for eating
ground a binful for selling
a third for storing away.

The crone of Pohjo was charmed
and she gave her own daughter
to the smith Ilmorinen
to be his wife for ever
be a hen under his arm
    to place his pillow
to be always on her feet.

Then the smith Ilmorinen
as he came towards his home
    cuckoos were calling
on the prow of the bright sleigh
    squirrels ran about
    on the maple shafts
    black grouse were cooing
on the collar-bow of elm.
The smith Ilmorinen's hand
was in a bright-worked mitten
the other on the maid's breasts
his foot in a German boot
the other between her thighs
as he came from Pohjola.

    When he arrived home
the old Väinämöinen went
to the smith Ilmorinen
    and asked him, spoke up:
"Brother, smith Ilmorinen
my kinsman, my mother's child!
Have you made the new sampo
brightly worked the bright-covered?"

The smith Ilmorinen said:
"I have shaped the new sampo
from milk of a barren cow
    one snippet of wool
from one piece of a distaff
    from one barley-grain."
The old Väinämöinen said:
"Has it ground, the new sampo
the bright-covered been rocking?"

The smith Ilmorinen said:
"It has ground, the new sampo
the bright-covered been rocking:
it ground a binful at dusk
ground a binful for eating
ground a binful for selling
a third for storing away."

Then the old Väinämöinen
when he understood this news
set about building his ship
launched his ship out on the sea
uttered a word, speaking thus:
"Who is there among these men
with the old Väinämöinen? –
Iku Tiera, Niera's son
    foremost of my friends."

    He hoisted his masts
like a pine-clump on a hill
he sailed out on the blue sea
leaning on his curved paddle
he sailed a day, another:
Pohjola's gates were in sight
the evil hinges shining
the evil doorways squealing.

He fumbled in his pocket
then Väinämöinen groped
    about in his purse
    took out sleeping-darts
sent the wicked folk to sleep
oppressed the pagan people.
He sailed out on the blue sea
    to dark Pohjola.

He uttered a word, spoke thus:
"Iku Tiera, Niera's son
    foremost of my friends
go and seize the sampo, you,
carry off the bright-covered!"

Iku Tiera, Niera's son
    quick to take orders
    easy to persuade
went off to seize the sampo
carry off the bright-covered
but the sampo would not move
the bright-covered would not shift:
its roots were rooted in earth.
The old Väinämöinen went
himself to seize the sampo
carry off the bright-covered
but the sampo would not move:
its roots were rooted in earth.
Then the old Väinämöinen
ploughed the roots of the sampo
with a hundred-horned ox
a thousand-headed sea-worm
bore the sampo to his boat
and placed it in his vessel.
    He hoisted his mast
he sailed out on the blue sea
he sailed a day, another
    so on the third day
an ant, a ballocking boy
pissed on the leg of a crane
    in dark Pohjola.
The crane let out a great squawk
screeched out in an evil tone:
the whole of Pohjola woke
the evil realm was awake.

The gap-toothed crone of Pohjo
groped about for her sampo:
"The sampo has been removed
the bright-covered carried off!"
She built the craft of Pohjo –
a hundred men to punt it
a hundred fellows to oars
a hundred men armed with swords
a hundred men for shooting:
she sailed out on the blue sea.

Iku Tiera, Niera's son
uttered a word, speaking thus:
"O you old Väinämöinen
    sing, you well-born man
now you've got the good sampo
now you've trodden the good road!"

The old Väinämöinen said:
"It is too early to cheer
    still too soon to sing:
Pohjola's gates are in sight
the evil hinges glitter
and the evil portals squeal.
If our own doors were in sight
our own portals were squealing
then it would be right to sing
and fitting to make merry."

    He said in these words
did the old Väinämöinen:
    "Foremost of my friends
climb up now to the mast-tip
    clamber up the mast
look eastward, look to the west
look along Pohjo's coastline!"

Iku Tiera, Niera's son
    quick to take orders
    easy to persuade
climbed up then to the mast-tip
    clambered up the mast
looked eastward, looked to the west
looked along Pohjo's coastline
    and said in these words:
"Now Pohjo's craft is coming
a hundred rowlocks chopping –
a hundred men punting it
a hundred fellows at oars
a hundred men armed with swords
a hundred more for shooting."

Then the old Väinämöinen
    saw his doom coming
his day of distress dawning:
he fumbled in his pocket
he groped about in his purse
found a tiny piece of flint
a little scrap of tinder
pitched them right into the sea
cast them in the arctic sea
straight over his right shoulder
    under his left arm.
He himself uttered these words:
"A crag was formed in the sea
a hidden isle spirited
stretching eastward for ever
    westward without end
on and on to Pohjola
upon which craft would be jammed
    and boats would be caught!"
And so Pohjo's craft was jammed
the strong-rowlocked boat was split.

The gap-toothed crone of Pohjo
rose on a skylark's pinions
on a bunting's wings went up
she beat bath-whisks into wings
upon an eagle's wing-bones:
    she flew, she fluttered
upon the clear stretch of sea
    the open water.
    She glided, hovered
to Väinämöinen's mast-head:
the craft's bow began to sink
the ship to smash to pieces.
So old Väinämöinen said:
"Iku Tiera, Niera's son
    foremost of my friends
    take up your own sword
    now in your right hand
from its scabbard on your left:

smite the eagle on the claws
the wyvern upon the toes!"

Iku Tiera, Niera's son
        took up his own sword
        took in his right hand
from its scabbard on his left
smote the eagle on the claws
the wyvern upon the toes
but he did not cut the hide
nor take off the outer skin.
He struck once, he struck again
soon a third time he laid waste:
he left no mark on the hide
he took off no outer skin.

Old Väinämöinen himself
raised a paddle from the sea
        his oar from the waves
smote the eagle on the claws
the wyvern upon the toes.
One nameless finger was left
        to seize the sampo
carry off the bright-covered.
Then the old Väinämöinen
        took up his own sword
        took in his right hand
from its scabbard on his left.
Then he shattered the sampo
the bright-covered brightly flashed
upon the clear stretch of sea
        the open water.
        And the wind lulled them
and the soft breeze shifted them
        about the blue sea:
washed all the other pieces
        up on the seashore
        up on the sea-slush.
The gap-toothed crone of Pohjo
carried the cover home, the
handle to the cold village
bore with her nameless finger
        bore with her left toe.

Arhippa Perttunen
Latvajärvi, Vuokkiniemi, Archangel Karelia
E. Lönnrot, 1834

13

The Sampo II

Old Väinämöinen and young Jompainen went off to the land of Pohja to fetch the sammas. And they got the sammas too. They Sailed away. Young Jompainen said to old Väinämöinen: "Now begin your song."

"It is still too soon to sing:
Pohjola's gates are in sight
and the house-stoves dimly glow."

Now, the sammas flew into a cloud. Young Jompainen with his sword struck two toes off the sammas: one flew into the sea, the other was brought to the land. The one that flew into the sea, from it salt came to the sea: the one that was brought to the land, from it grass came to the land. Had several got there, corn would have come up without sowing.

Maija Turpoinen
Säfsen, Dalecarlia
C. A. Gottlund, 1817

14

The Sampo III

First the old Väinämöinen
then the smith Ilmarinen
third the young Joukamoinen
went on the clear stretch of sea
    on the boundless waves
right into far Pohjola
to the man-eating village
the village that drowns heroes.

The ancient Väinämöinen
went into the threshing house
for spoils, oiled the doors with beer
with ale moistened the hinges
that Pohja's doors might not squeal
nor Hiitola's hinges whine.
He loaded the ship up full
he got the great sampo full
launched his ship upon the sea
got the sampo on the waves:
he went off in good spirits
rejoicing to his own lands.

That old Väinämöinen sailed
on the water of the sea
    on the boundless waves
    sailed for the first day.
Young Joukamoinen uttered:
"Sing now, old Väinämöinen
hum now, man of good family
now you've been to Pohjola
now you've got the good sturgeon!"

Old Väinämöinen uttered:
"It is too early to cheer
    still too soon to sing:
Pohjola's gates are in sight
the evil gateways glitter
the bright covers are glowing
of the man-eating village
the village that drowns heroes."

Well, then on the second day
young Joukamoinen uttered:
"Sing now, old Väinämöinen
hum now, man of good family
now you've been to Pohjola
now you've got the good sturgeon!"

Old Väinämöinen uttered:
"It is too early to cheer
it is still too soon to sing:
Pohjola's gates are in sight
the evil gateways glitter
the bright covers are glowing
of the man-eating village
the village that drowns heroes."

Smith Ilmarinen uttered:
"If it was me at the stern
well, I'd sing, I'd know how to."

Just then Väinämöinen sang
and the hero's voice thundered
over the waves as it sang
on the water as it shrilled:
it jarred mountains, jolted hills

it set all the cliffs trembling.
        But jaws did not move
at Väinämöinen's singing
Ilmarinen's rejoicing.

A pismire, wretched fellow
pissed on the legs of a crane:
the crane let out a great squawk
the strong bird made a large sound
screeched out in an evil tone.

At that Pohjola woke up
the dame of Pohja rose up
Pohjola's mistress ran out
to the threshing-house for spoils
ran to look over her farm:
all the spoils had disappeared.
She saw her cattle failing
saw her riches declining:
she got a band with their bows
got men ready with their swords
a hundred men for rowing
a thousand sitting idle
went after Väinämöinen.

Now on the third day
smith Ilmarinen uttered:
"Take care, old Väinämöinen:
        there's clear sky in front
        but behind it's dim."

Now Pohja's craft was coming
the hundred-rowlocked cleaving –
a hundred men rowing it
a thousand sitting idle.
The smith Ilmarinen said:
"Look out, old Väinämöinen!
Take a tiny piece of flint
quite a small bit of tinder:
we'll form a crag in the sea
a hidden isle we'll spirit
a crag stretching to the north
even further to the south
stretching eastward for ever
        without end westward
on which Pohja's craft will jam
Hiitola's boat will be caught."

It was old Väinämöinen
took a tiny piece of flint
quite a small bit of tinder:
on it Pohja's craft was jammed
the hundred-rowlocked stuck fast.

That dame of Pohja herself
stepped feet first in the water
set about raising the craft
        lifting up the ship
but the craft was not moving.
Then she changed to a black bird
she turned into an eagle
put a hundred men upon her wing
a thousand on her wing-tips
ten upon her feather-ends
went after Väinämöinen.

Smith Ilmarinen uttered
at the end of the third day:
"Take care, old Väinämöinen:
        there's clear sky in front
        but behind it's dim.
Now Pohja's dame is coming
a hundred men on her wing
a thousand on her wing-tips
ten upon her feather-ends."

        She glided, hovered
over Väinämöinen's craft:
soon she settled on the prow.
Smith Ilmarinen uttered:
"Hey there, old Väinämöinen:
raise a paddle from the sea

your spade from the waves
hit the woman on the nails."

Then the old Väinämöinen
raised a paddle from the sea
his spade from the waves
struck the woman on the nails.
Other nails went to pieces:
the one on the small finger
was left for raising the craft
for lifting the boat.

Old Väinämöinen uttered:
"Were you, craft, the Creator's,
boat, of God's shaping
you'd plunge sideways in the sea
run broadside into the waves!"

Now it went into the sea
the ship fell into the waves.
Old Väinämöinen himself
plunged sideways in the water
fell, ship and all, in the waves
went into the sea's inside.

Pohjola's mistress herself
raised a mist into the sky
lifted fog into the air.

And old Väinämöinen sang
in the open sea's inside
in the boundless waves:
"Not even a worse
man is drowned by haze
overcome by spray."

Pohjola's mistress herself
went weeping homeward
wailing to the town.

Väinämöinen rose again
having rested for three nights
in the open sea's inside
in the boundless waves
took a grass-hued whip
struck the water with the lash
smote the sea with the whiplash:
honey swished from the whip's path
haze from where the lash whistled
the mist rose into the sky
the haze lifted in the air
the haze cleared up from the sea.

Simana Sissonen and Simana Huohvanainen
Ilomantsi, North Karelia
D. E. D. Europaeus, 1845

15

The Sampo IV

Old Väinämöine went off
he went off to woo the maid
to angle for the sea-trout
in dark Pohjola
in careful Tapivola.

The girl Anni, matchless maid
was washing her little things
bleaching what she'd rinsed
at the end of the long quay
when she saw a shoal of fish.

"If you are a shoal of fish
then away with you, swim off!
If you are a flock of birds
then begone with you, fly off!
If you are a water-rock
then roll off in the water!
If you're old Väinämöine
bring yourself here for a talk
come here for a word!"

The old Väinämöine came
took himself there for a talk
went there for a word.

And she put this into words:
"Where are you off to, Väinö?"

"I am off on a swan-hunt
down at Tuoni's black river."

"Now I know a liar
see a speaker of false words!
Otherwise was my father
my noble parent
when he went on a swan-hunt
down at Tuoni's black river:
he had a big dog in chains
he had a big bow drawn taut.
Where are you off to, Väinö?"

"I am off salmon-fishing
down at Tuoni's black river."

Now I've known a liar
see a speaker of false words!
Otherwise was my father
my noble parent
when he went salmon-fishing:
he had a boatful of nets
a shipful of fishing-gear.
Where are you off to, Väinö?"

"I am off to woo a maid
in dark Pohjola
in careful Tapivola."

The girl Anni, matchless maid
in her fists gathered her skirt
in her hands bundled her dress
squeezed into the smith's workshop.

"O you smith Ilmolline
you everlasting craftsman!
Hammer me five chains

three pairs of earrings
I will tell good news
I will speak good things."

The smith, that Ilmolline
hammered a day, another
hammered a third day
hammered her five chains
three pairs of earrings
and she told good news:
"Your loved one has been taken
the one you wooed three years long
you bargained for two years long."

He got into a horse-sledge
hit the courser with a lash
clouted with the beaded tip:
courser ran, the way was quick
the sledge flew, the road grew short.
He drove steadily
to dark Pohjola
to careful Tapivola.

There the watchdog was barking
the island's dog made a din.

The mistress of Pohjola
told the servant-girl to see
why the watchdog was barking
the island's dog made a din:
no watchdog barks for nothing
no island's dog makes a din.

The servant answering said:
"I've no time to look!
There's a big stone for grinding –
the stone big and the flour fine."

Still the watchdog was barking
the island's dog made a din.

The mistress of Pohjola
ordered the hired man to look:
"Go, hired man, and see
why the watchdog was barking
the island's dog made a din:
no watchdog barks for nothing
no island's dog makes a din."
The hired man indeed answered:
"I've no time to look!
There's a big pile to be made –
the pile big and the sticks fine."

It was old Väinämöine
arrived in dark Pohjola
in careful Tapivola:
there the maid was wooed
the sea-trout was angled for.

The old crone indeed answered:
"For this I'll give my daughter:
if you fashion the sampo.

It was smith Ilmolline
hammered a day, another
hammered a third day:
now he fashioned the sampo.

It was old Väinämöine
lulled to sleep Pohja's old man
to sleep Pohja's old woman
all the rest of Pohjoinen:
and then I took your daughter
took your sampo off with me
put the sampo in my ship
sailed away upon the sea.

I sailed a day, another
I sailed a third day.
Pohjola's mistress woke up:
"My daughter's been carried off!"

She sailed away in pursuit
on wings she was borne along:
she flew a day, another
and she flew for a third day
till she came to the boat's mast
glided on to that boat's mast.

It was old Väinämöine
reached for his touchwood
he turned to his tinder-box.

Old Man of the Air struck fire
Väinämöine made a flash
made with three eagle-feathers
with five tail feathers.

From the place a spark shot out
through the earth, through Manula
through the smoke-hole caked with soot
through a child's little cradle
burnt the breasts of the mother
the firm nipples of the maids.

And there his ship was ablaze:
then he went into the sea.

Then he drifted for three years:
where his finger touched
there an island came
and where his knee touched
there a boulder came.

A little duck built a nest
there upon the very knee
of that old Väinämöine.

Even there it laid an egg.
The egg broke into pieces;
he used it for salve.

Then he came to life
then went off on his journey.

He met Joukone
then he put this into words:
"Whichever of us can sing
need not leave the road."
"Sing, Joukone, first."

Joukone put this into words:
he sang the stars in the sky.

It was old Väinämöine
put this into words:
"Mine the spangling of the sky."

He sang him into a marsh
belt-high, in the ground hip-deep.

It was old Väinämöine
put this into words:
"If you give your one sister
I'll get you out of the marsh."

He pledged his sister.

Joukone went home
was plunged into bad spirits
his mouth down, in bad spirits
and his helmet all askew.

'Twas his mother who bore him
put this into words:
"Why, my son, are you in bad spirits
and your helmet all askew?"

"For this I'm in bad spirits
and my helmet's all askew:
I've given my one sister
to look after that old man

to cheer the ancient
to get me out of the marsh."

'Twas his mother who bore him
put this into words:

"My only offspring!
Do not be in bad spirits:
for this I yearned all my life
longed throughout my days –
Väinö for my son-in-law!"

Miihkali Senkkanen
Kiimaisjärvi, Archangel Karelia
A. A. Borenius, 1872

16

The Courtship I

Annikki the island maid
smith Ilmorini's sister
went off to do her washing
on the shore of the blue sea
at the end of Laisa Quay.

She spied a black speck on the sea
something bluish on the waves
herself put this into words:
"If you are my father's boat
turn homeward, turn to your house
away from other havens!
Or else if my brother's craft
away from other havens!
Or yet Väinämöini's boat
bring yourself here for a talk!
If a darling flock of ducks
    spread out into flight!
Or again a water-stone
draw the water over you!"

It was Väinämöini's boat
took itself there for a talk.

Annikki the island maid
talked away, prattled away:
"Where are you off to, Väinö
where, bridegroom of Umanto?"

The old Väinämöini said:
"I'm off to catch a salmon
down in Tuoni's black river
in the pit of Manala."

Annikki the island maid
    put this into words:
    "Now I know a liar
sense a speaker of false words!
Otherwise was my father
when he went to catch salmon:
he had a boatful of nets
fishing-spears under the thwarts.
Hoho, old Väinämöini –
just tell the truth carefully!"

    "I'm off after geese
to look out for slobber-mouths."

Annikki the island maid
    put this into words:
    "Now I know a liar
sense a speaker of false words!
Otherwise was my father
when he went off after geese
to look out for slobber-mouths:
he had a big bow drawn taut
    dogs bowling like balls
and pups straying on the shores."

    Still Annikki asked
and the tin-breasted inquired:
"Tell me, old Väinämöini
and tell the truth carefully:
where are you off to, Väinö?"

The old Väinämöini said:
"There's a maid in Pohjonen

a girl in the cold village:
through her flesh you see the bones
  through bone the marrow
half Pohja's land praises her.
I am off to woo the maid
  in dark Pohjonen."

Annikki the island maid
in her fists gathered her hem
in her hands bundled her dress
quickly ran on long journeys
  short distances fast.
She went to the smith's workshop:
"O smith, my little brother
she you bought is being taken
she you redeemed carried off
she who cost a hundred marks!"

The hammer dropped from his hand
the tongs slipped out of his palm.
"Anni, my little sister
warm the bath-house secretly
quickly stoke up the bathroom
with some finely-cut firewood!
  Prepare some thick lye
  some bone-marrow soap
with which the chaffinch may wash
the autumn-hued charcoal off
the winter-hued forge-grime off!
Open the furthest storehouse
fling wide the one next the shore:
take some coats of foreign wool!"

He dressed himself, decked himself.
"Anni, my little sister
put the colt into harness
at the front of the brown sledge
in the farmyard at the back
  at the oaken post!"

Then the smith Ilmorini
  drove rumbling away
by the sea's sandy ridges
  with an elk-hued horse
  with pike-coloured hair
  a black salmon's shape
  to dark Pohjola.

And that old Väinämöini
  sailed on the red sea
  in a red-sailed boat.
Pohjo's watchdog barked at them
  the castle's dog howled.

And Pohjola's master said:
  "Go, crone, and see why
  Pohjo's watchdog barked
  the castle's dog howled!"

And Pohjola's mistress said:
"I won't go out, I don't care.
  Go yourself and look."

And so Pohjola's master
  went himself and looked:
and that smith Ilmorini
was driving rumbling along
  with an elk-hued horse
  with pike-coloured hair
  a black salmon's shape
and old Väinämöini too
was sailing on the red sea
  in a red-sailed boat.

And Pohjola's master said:
  "He shall have the maid
who on his decks brings money
who in his ships brings treasure."

And Pohjola's mistress said:
  "He shall have the maid

the pledged gift will be given
to whom the maid is promised –
smith Ilmorini."

Then the old Väinämöini
grew very angry and wild
thrust gold pieces in the fire
a felt hat full of silver.

Vassilei Malinen
Vuonninen, Vuokkiniemi, Archangel Karelia
A. A. Borenius, 1872

17

The Courtship II

The girl of night, maid of dusk
was rinsing clothes she had washed
what she had bleached was bleaching
at the end of the long quay
a bright-carved bat in her hand.

A red boat went by:
one side of the boat was red.

The girl of night, maid of dusk
spoke out to that boat
and talked from her boat:
"Where are you bound, Swede to feed?"

And the Swede indeed answered
and talked from his boat:
"I am bound for the fish-spawn
the splashing of the spine-tail."

The girl of night, maid of dusk
now indeed answered:
"Don't tell lies to me!
Just tell me the truth this time.
I know about fish-spawn too:
one man for'ard, one astern
the nets amidships
the long rods for'ard
longer ones astern."

The girl of night, maid of dusk,
spoke out to that boat:
"Where are you bound, Swede to feed?"

And the Swede indeed answered
and talked from his boat:
"I am going off to war."

The girl of night, maid of dusk
now indeed answered:
"Don't tell lies to me!
Just tell me the truth this time.
I know about warriors too:
a hundred men at the oars
a thousand sitting idle
the guns upright at the prows
swordblades ready for action."

The girl of night, maid of dusk
spoke out to that boat
now indeed answered:
"Where are you bound, Swede to feed?"

And the Swede indeed answered
and talked from his boat:
"I'm off to be a suitor
to the old demon's daughter
to the white one men yearn for."

The girl of night, maid of dusk
now changed into a black speck
turned herself into a snake
flew as a golden cuckoo
in a silver pigeon's form
flew, viper, to the threshold
as beast to the smithy door:
"Hullo, smith Ilmarinen

hammer a cross for my breasts
then touch up my metal brooch
    forge earrings for me!
Then I will tell you good news."

Smith Ilmarinen uttered:
"If you tell me good news, I'll
hammer crosses for your breasts
then touch up your metal brooch
    forge earrings for you:
but if you tell me bad news
I'll thrust your head in the fire
yourself in the endless space
under Ilmarinen's forge."

The girl of night, maid of dusk
    put this into words:
"A Swede to feed has just come
just come to be a suitor
to the old demon's daughter
to the white one men yearn for."

The smith Ilmarinen heard:
the tongs slipped out of his hand.
The smith Ilmarinen sang:
"When next will the tongs be held
    the hammer wielded?"

Smith Ilmarinen uttered:
"Hullo, mother who bore me
    lay provisions in a bag
put flour in a linen sack!
I'm going as a suitor
to the old demon's daughter
to the white one men yearn for."

    Loud the big dog barked
the cruel pup leapt about
in the demon's great castle
    in the dreadful town.

Slowly the castle's demon
uttered, in slow words grunted:
    "Just go, serf, and see
    why the big dog barks
the cruel pup leaps about!"

The serf knowingly answered:
    I've no time to look:
there's a large pile to be made –
the pile large and the stick fine
the small chip must be gathered."

Slowly the castle's demon
uttered, in slow words grunted:
"Just go, servant-girl, and see
    why the big dog barked
the cruel pup leapt about
yonder by the fertile field
twirling its tail round and round:
no dog barks without reason
no pup slavers without cause."

The servant indeed answered:
    I've no time to look:
there's a big stone for grinding –
the stone big and the slab thick."

Slowly the castle's demon
uttered, in slow words grunted:
    "Just go, maid, and see
    why the big dog barked
the savage pup leapt about
yonder by the fertile field
twirling its tail round and round:
no dog barks without reason
no pup slavers without cause."

The maid, a meek underling
    the maid went to look.
The maid came back from looking
said as soon as she arrived:

"A red boat's coming
a red craft's lapping
on this side of Lempi Bay:
a red stallion is trotting
a bright sleigh is drawing close
on that side of Siimet Isle."

Slowly the castle's demon
uttered, in slow words grunted:
"In the boat he brings money
in the ship he brings treasure
the bright sleigh brings spells."

Slowly the castle's demon
uttered, in slow words grunted:
"Put the rowan in the fire!
If blood oozes out
then war is coming
but if water drips
suitors are coming."

Now the Swede to feed arrived
at the demon's great castle
in the dreadful town.
The smith Ilmarinen came
he asked as soon as he came
spoke up at once from the floor:
"Is a wife to be given –
she, the old demon's daughter
she, the white one men yearn for?"

Slowly the castle's demon
uttered, in slow words grunted:
"Hey there, smith Ilmarinen:
a wife is to be given
if you plough the viper-field
turn the field of snakes over."

Smith Ilmarinen uttered:
"O girl of night, maid of dusk
do you recall your old vow
the eternal vow you took
before the god of copper
facing the virgin of gold
when you promised you would come?"

The bride gave her help.
Now, that smith Ilmarinen
ploughed the viper-field
turned the field of snakes over.
He asked at once when he came
spoke up at once from the floor:
"Is a wife to be given –
she, the old demon's daughter
she, the white one men yearn for?"

Slowly the castle's demon
uttered, in slow words grunted:
"Hullo, smith Ilmarinen:
a wife is to be given
if you bring back Tuoni's bear
from within the blue backwoods
from the gates of Pohjola."

Smith Ilmarinen uttered:
"O girl of night, maid of dusk
do you recall your old vow
the eternal vow you took
before the god of copper
facing the virgin of gold
when you promised you would come?"

The bride gave her help.
Now, the smith Ilmarinen
brought back Tuoni's bear
from within the blue backwoods
from the gates of Pohjola.
He asked as soon as he came
spoke up at once from the floor:
"Is a wife to be given –
she, the old demon's daughter
she, the white one men yearn for?"

Slowly the castle's demon
uttered, in slow words grunted:
"Hullo, smith Ilmarinen:
a wife is to be given
if you bring back Tuoni's pike
out of Tuoni's black river
from the pit of Manala."

Smith Ilmarinen uttered:
"O girl of night, maid of dusk
do you recall your old vow
the eternal vow you took
before the god of copper
facing the virgin of gold
when you promised you would come?"

The bride gave her help.
The smith Ilmarinen went
brought back Tuoni's pike:
the bride turned to an eagle
put herself on guard.
Then the smith Ilmarinen
raked up the pike of Tuoni
out of Tuoni's black river
from the pit of Manala.
Now, that smith Ilmarinen
was seized by a water-sprite:
the eagle pounced on its neck
twisted the water-sprite's head.

Water was not like water
for the great pike's scales
air did not feel like air for
the great eagle's down.

Then the smith Ilmarinen
brought back Tuoni's pike
out of Tuoni's black river
from the pit of Manala.
He asked as soon as he came
spoke up at once from the floor:
"Is a wife to be given –
she, the old demon's daughter
she, the white one men yearn for?"

Slowly the castle's demon
uttered, in slow words grunted:
"A wife is to be given –
she, the old demon's daughter
she, the white one men yearn for."

Slowly the castle's demon
uttered, in slow words grunted:
"Let her sprawl as a seagull
let her call as a seamew
let her drag the nets of men
let her fasten stones to them!"

Simana Sissonen
Ilomantsi, North Karelia
D. E. D. Europaeus, 1845

18

The Courtship III

The squat smith of the mainland
tall bridegroom of Koivisto
    shod his lively feet
handsomely tied on ribbons
    bound his legs in silk
drew on bordered cloth
    jerked up leather boots
    and went for Tuoni's daughter
the bride from the underworld.

Tuoni sat on the road-ridge
underworldling at world's edge:
    "Give, Tuoni, your girl,
underworldling, your berry!"

And Tuoni indeed answered:
"Anni will be given up
the precious head yielded up
the curly head bundled up
if you perform our command
if you walk in our footsteps
hammer a steed of money
a money-cross on the steed."

The squat smith of the mainland
undertook even that task
rather than be on his own
than live without a woman:
hammered a steed of money
a money-cross on the steed.
He went for Tuoni's daughter
the bride from the underworld.
Tuoni sat on the road-ridge
underworldling at world's edge:
"Give, Tuoni, your girl,
underworldling, your berry!"

And Tuoni indeed answered:
"Anni will be given up
the precious head yielded up
the curly head bundled up
if you perform our command
if you walk in our footsteps
and hammer a church of stone
a stone cross upon the church."

The squat smith of the mainland
undertook even that task
rather than be on his own:
he hammered a church of stone
a stone cross upon the church.
He went for Tuoni's daughter
the bride from the underworld.
Tuoni sat on the road-ridge
underworldling at world's edge:
    "Give, Tuoni, your girl,
underworldling, your berry!"

    They indeed answered:
"If you perform our command
if you walk in our footsteps
and hammer a horse of beads
a sledge of beads behind it
a man of beads on the sledge
a whip of beads in his hand."

The squat smith of the mainland
undertook even that task
rather than be on his own
than live without a woman:
he hammered a horse of beads
a sledge of beads behind it
a man of beads on the sledge
a whip of beads in his hand.

He went for Tuoni's daughter
the bride from the underworld.
Tuoni sat on the road-ridge
underworldling at world's edge:
    "Give, Tuoni, your girl,
underworldling, your berry!"

They indeed answered:
"Anni will be given up
the precious head yielded up
the curly head bundled up
if you perform our command
if you walk in our footsteps
build a bridge on open sea
out of saplings one year old
    treestumps two years old
    birches three years old."

The squat smith of the mainland
built a bridge on open sea
out of saplings one year old
    treestumps two years old
    birches three years old
took a stallion one night old
    rode over the bridge
on the one-night-old stallion.
He went for Tuoni's daughter
the bride from the underworld.

Only then was Anni given
the curly head bundled up
the precious head yielded up.

Kati
Soikkola, Ingria
V. Porkka, 1883

19

The Gift I

"Useless born, useless I grew
useless I rose in the world.
If I went to Joukoni
Jouko would keep me useless
without work, belt, clothes
on my foot no sock
on my hand no glove:
he'd give me river-water
to drink, and buck-beans to eat."

Kojo happened to hear this
to be standing by the wall.
He asked for Kommi's daughter:
"Give, Kommi, your only one
give your lively little one!"

"I'll not give my only one
nor my lively little one.
Fetch a star down from the sky
a blaze from between the clouds:
then I'll give my only one
give my lively little one."

He went to the smith's workshop:
"Smith, my dear brother
you everlasting craftsman!
Hammer me five chains
six rings of iron
to fetch a star from the sky
a blaze from between the clouds!"

Now, that smith Ilmorini
the everlasting craftsman
he hammered five chains
six rings of iron:
fetched stars from the sky
blazes from between the clouds.
He brought them to Kommi's hand.

He asked for Kommi's daughter:
"Give, Kommi, your only one
give your lively little one!"

"I'll not give my only one
nor my lively little one.
Now, if you swim the sealed pool
and catch the great pike in it
the golden-scaled, golden-streaked
bring it into Kommi's hand:
then I'll give my only one
give my lively little one."

He went to the smith's workshop:
"O smith, O Ilmorini
you everlasting craftsman!
Hammer for me iron clothes
in which I'll swim the sealed pool
and catch the great pike in it
the golden-scaled, golden-streaked!"

Now, that smith Ilmorini
the everlasting craftsman
hammered iron clothes:
he swam the sealed pool
and caught the great pike in it
the golden-scaled, golden-streaked
brought it into Kommi's hand.

He asked for Kommi's daughter:
"Give, Kommi your only one
give your lively little one!"

"I'll not give my only one
nor my lively little one.
Tread for a whole day on needle-points:
then I'll give my only one
give my lively little one."

He went to the smith's workshop:
"O smith, O Ilmorini
hammer for me iron shoes!"

Now, that smith Ilmorini
the everlasting craftsman
    hammered iron shoes:
he trod a whole day on needle-points.
He asked for Kommi's daughter:
"Give, Kommi, your only one
give your lively little one!"

Then he gave his only one:
there he wooed, there was betrothed
snatched the maid into his sleigh
got the maid in his saddle
he struck the horse with the lash
clouted with the beaded tip.

"Courser, run, be quick, journey,
sledge, glide onward, road, grow short."
The birchwood sledge bumped along
the curly-birch runners slammed
    the twig thongs whistled.
"We shall go to Kojo's house
on the high hill of Kojo!"

The maiden said from the sleigh
under the rug found her voice:
"What just went across the road?"
"A wolf went across the road."
"Better it were for poor me
in the running wolf's footsteps
the tracks of the wanderer."

"Never mind, whore of Hiisi!
We're going to Kojo's house
on the high hill of Kojo
hard upon Kojo's rapids
to carve meat without a knife
to pour blood with no ladle."

He struck the horse with the lash
clouted with the beaded tip.
"Courser, run, be quick, journey,
sledge, glide onward, road, grow short."
The birchwood sledge bumped along
the curly-birch runners slammed
    the twig thongs whistled.
    "We'll reach Kojo's house
on the high hill of Kojo!"

The maiden said from the sleigh
under the rug found her voice:
"What just went across the road?"
"A fox went across the road."
"Better it were for poor me
in the wretched fox's steps
the tracks of the wanderer."

"Never mind, whore of Hiisi!
We're going to Kojo's house
on the high hill of Kojo
hard upon Kojo's rapids
to carve meat without a knife
to pour blood with no ladle."

He struck the horse with the lash
clouted with the beaded tip.
"Courser, run, be quick, journey,
sledge, glide onward, road, grow short."
The birchwood sledge bumped along

the curly-birch runners slammed
    the twig thongs whistled.
    "We'll reach Kojo's house
on the high hill of Kojo!"

The maiden said from the sleigh
under the rug found her voice:
"What just went across the road?"
"A hare went across the road."
"Better it were for poor me
in the running hare's footsteps
the paths of the crooked-kneed."

"Never mind, whore of Hiisi!
We're going to Kojo's house
on the high hill of Kojo
hard upon Kojo's rapids
to carve meat without a knife
to pour blood with no ladle."

Now they went to Kojo's house
hard upon Kojo's rapids
on the high hill of Kojo:
meat was carved without a knife
blood was poured with no ladle.
Now he made a little pie
pressed the gift upon Kommi
pressed it into Kommi's hand.

He started the vile supper
set out places for a meal.
A serf said from a beam-end
a herdsman behind a post:
"Now, if you knew what it is
    you would not eat it!"
"Tell me, tell me, poor herdsman:
I will give you a day's rest!"
"I will not tell yet for that."

He started the vile supper
set out places for a meal.
A serf said from a beam-end
a herdsman behind a post:
"Now, if you knew what it is
    you would not eat it!"
"Tell me, tell me, poor herdsman:
I will give you a month's rest!"
"I will not tell yet for that."

He started the vile supper
set out places for a meal.
A serf said from a beam-end
a herdsman behind a post:
"Now, if you knew what it is
    you would not eat it!"

"Tell me, tell me, poor herdsman:
I will give you a year's rest!"

"Shoulders of your Oljona
bits of your Palaka's head."

Hoto Lesonen
Vuokkiniemi, Archangel Karelia
K. Karjalainen, 1894

20

The Gift II

Iivana, Kojonen's son
the titchy son of woman
harnessed up a horse of fire
in a fiery field:
fire shot from the gelding's mouth
blood dripped from the collar-bow
and fat from the traces-tip.
He went wooing to Kontu
into Narentka to wive.

He asked the maids of Kontu:
"Well, is there a man's woman
among you, a young squire's bride?"

The maids of Kontu answered:
"There is not a man's woman
among us, a young squire's bride:
among girls who have nothing
one to be a grown man's wife
a young squire's bride, there is not."

Iivana, Kojonen's son
the titchy son of woman
he went wooing to Oapsu
drove to Oapsu's farm. Oapsu
was going to his storehouse
a copper box in his hand
a copper key in the box.

Iivana, Kojonen's son
the titchy son of woman
he began to ask Oapsu:
"Give, Oapsu, your girl
to me who am a good man
me, a man made of honey
one begotten of sugar."

Oapsu answering replied:
"At market is a horse-deal
a mare-deal in a farmyard
a maid is sold in a house
a deal done under a roof."

Iivana, Kojonen's son
the titchy son of woman
began to squeeze in the house
to push in under the beam.

He began to ask Oapsu:
"You'll give, Oapsu, your daughter?"

Oapsu answering replied:
"Yes, I will give my daughter
if you set the house on fire
yourself sitting in the eaves."

"I'll take on even that task
rather than be on my own."

Iivana, Kojonen's son
kept asking Oapsu:
"You'll give, Oapsu, your daughter?"

Oapsu answering replied:
"Yes, I will give my daughter:
twine a rope of chaff
begin it with husks."

Iivana, Kojonen's son
the titchy son of woman:
"I'll take on even that task
rather than be on my own:
long the night lying wifeless
long the day without dinner!"

Iivana, Kojonen's son
the titchy son of woman
got the maid into his sledge
struck the stallion with the reins
the horse with the beaded whip.

He began to ask the maid:
"Will you make me a long shirt
from a single strand of flax?"

The maiden pondered:
"What will come out of nothing
and what will a lie produce?"

Iivana, Kojonen's son
kept asking the maid:
"Will you make me a long cloak
from a single tuft of wool?"

The maiden pondered:
"What will come out of nothing
from a single tuft of wool?"

Iivana, Kojonen's son
took the maid to a hummock
cut the breasts off his maiden
put them in a pie, made them
gifts to his mother-in-law.

Mother-in-law ate and praised:
"Now I have eaten something:
I've not eaten such till now –
brought by my new son-in-law
sent by my daughter.
I've had salmon from a spring
I've had whitefish from the sea
but I have not eaten such –
brought by my new son-in-law
sent by my daughter."

A serf sat on the beam-end
a hireling upon the bench:
"If you knew but a little
understood a bit
you'd not be eating, praising
what your new son-in-law brought
what your daughter sent."

"Tell me, tell me what, poor serf!
I'll give Whiteback from tether."
"I will not tell, poor mistress."
"Tell me what, poor serf! I'll give
a fine one from the manger:
tell me, tell me what, poor serf!"
"I will not tell, poor mistress."

"I will give my only son."
"Now I will tell, poor mistress:
you were eating your bird's flesh
eating your pretty fledgeling."

Anni Vasilova
Vuole, Ingria
F. Pajula, 1894

21

The Golden Bride I

'Twas the smith Ilmollini
his head down, in bad spirits
helmet all askew
went to the forge of the smiths
took a little gold
a felt hatful of silver.

He set the young men blowing
the hirelings pressing
but the serfs did not blow well
neither did the hirelings press.

He himself took to blowing:
he blew once, flapped the bellows
he blew twice, flapped the bellows
now at the third time
a sword squeezed out of the fire
a gold-bladed from the heat.
The sword might be good-looking
but evil ways came of it:
every day it killed a man
even two on many days.

He added more gold
a felt hatful of silver.
He set the old men blowing
but the old did not blow well
neither did the hirelings press.

He himself took to blowing:
he blew once, flapped the bellows
he blew twice, flapped the bellows
now at the third time
a stallion squeezed from the fire
a golden-maned from the heat.
The stallion might have good looks
but evil ways came of it:
every day it killed a mare
even two on many days.

He added more gold
a felt hatful of silver
and he set the serfs blowing
and set the hirelings pressing
but the serfs did not blow well
neither did the hirelings press.

He himself took to blowing:
he blew once, flapped the bellows
he blew twice, flapped the bellows
now at the third time
a maid squeezed out of the fire
a golden-locks from the heat.
The maid might be good-looking
but I do not know her ways.

And so during the first night
he kept himself in his cloak
he held tight in his fur coat:
that side certainly was warm
which was next to the wool cloak
that side was freezing
which was next to the maid's side
icy as ice on the sea
and as hard as rock.

So during the second night
he held tight in his fur coat
he kept himself in his cloak:
that side certainly was warm
which was next to the wool cloak
    that side was freezing
which was next to the maid's side.

And so during the third night
he kept himself in his cloak
he held tight in his fur coat:
that side certainly was warm
which was next to the wool cloak
    that side was freezing
which was next to the maid's side.

Let not those who come before
and let not those after them
make a maid's likeness in gold
finish her off in silver:
the breath of silver is chill
and the glow of gold is cold.

Miihkali Perttunen
Latvajärvi, Vuokkiniemi, Archangel Karelia
A. A. Borenius, 1871

22

The Golden Bride II

The Island is staked in strips
Estonia criss-crossed:
the fields are measured with rods
the clearings reckoned with spans.
There was one strip left unstaked
one field was not rod-measured
one clearing not span-reckoned
for one fence's bounds lots were not cast:
    there the smith settled
there the craftsman put his forge.
He made a very small forge
a low hut sunk in the ground
    with room for one man
with swinging-room for one arm
with headroom for one hammer:
he used his shirt as a forge
and his trousers for bellows.

The smith hammered and clattered
the serfs were busy blowing:
he hammered this, hammered that
hammered pegs for the estate
and sickles for the parish
and knife-blades for the province
he hammered beads for Hekkoi
and coins for Maie's daughter.
Hekkoi did not praise her beads
nor Maie's daughter her coins
nor did the estate its pegs
nor the parish its sickles
nor the province its knife-blades:
the smith grew angry and wild
he stuck his tongs in the eaves
dropped his hammers on the ground
    set his forge on fire
left his bellows in the blaze.

So he rose as a sledge-smith
set up as a sleigh-builder:
one month long he made a sledge
for two months put it on sale
for a year fitted wicker
adorned it with a cat's bones
    and with a pike's teeth.

The sleigh was finished
and the smith went visiting
his grannies and his grandads
his nimble brothers-in-law.

He set his brothers guessing
his sisters calling to mind:
    "Guess now, my brothers
call to mind now, my sisters:
what is the sleigh adorned with
    the sledge-back decorated?"

The brothers answering said:
"It's adorned with a cat's bones
    and with a pike's teeth."

They vied, answering the smith
vied, unharnessing the grey
vied in taking him indoors
vied in giving the smith food
vied in giving the smith drink

vied in giving the smith blame:
"Trees wear out and lands wear out
trees wear out by being felled
lands wear out by being ploughed:
a smith will wear out wifeless
grow old without a mistress."

The smith grew angry and wild
the smith drove home like the wind
the smith hammered and clattered
the serfs were busy blowing
the smith flung gold in the fire
silver into the furnace
as much as an autumn ewe
as much as a winter lamb:
a horse squeezed out of the fire
a golden-hoof from the heat.
All the other kin were charmed:
Ismaro himself was scared.

The smith flung gold in the fire
silver into the furnace
the smith hammered and clattered
the serfs were busy blowing:
a cow squeezed out of the fire
a golden-horn from the heat.
All the other kin were charmed:
Ismaro himself was scared.

The smith flung gold in the fire
silver into the furnace
as much as an autumn ewe
as much as a winter lamb
the smith hammered and clattered
the serfs were busy blowing:
a pig squeezed out of the fire
a gold-bristle from the heat.
All the other kin were charmed:
Ismaro himself was scared.

The smith flung gold in the fire
silver into the furnace
as much as an autumn ewe
as much as a winter lamb
the smith hammered and clattered
the serfs were busy blowing:
a girl squeezed out of the fire
a golden-locks from the heat.
All the other kin were scared:
Ismaro himself was charmed.

Now there's sure to be trouble:
an enemy has moved in! –
The girl was led to lie down
    taken for a rest:
which side was next to the gold
that side was the chilly side
which was not next to the gold
that side was the thawing side.

Singer unknown
Soikkola, Ingria
J. Länkelä, 1858

23

The Kantele I

Old Väinämöinen himself
was out searching for his horse
looking for the bridled one
at his belt the yearling's reins
shouldering the colt's harness
when he found a boat weeping
    a vessel wailing:
"Why do you weep, wooden boat
strong-rowlocked vessel, why yearn?
Do you weep for your wood's sake
for your rowlocks do you yearn?"

"I don't weep for my wood's sake
for my rowlocks I don't yearn:
other boats go off to wars
they are filled up with money
their sterns are weighed down with coins
while I rot on my shavings
I stretch out upon my stocks
and the earth's most evil worms
are living beneath my ribs
and the air's most loathsome birds
are nesting upon my side."

    And he launched the craft
pushed the boat into the waves:
    he stowed on one side
    brush-headed bridegrooms
noble ones, spurs on their feet
he stowed on the other side
maidens with tin on their heads
tin-headed, copper-belted
copper-belted . . .

And he launched the craft
pushed the boat into the waves:
he himself sat in the stern
like a sack of Finnish salt
sailed a day through land-waters
another through marsh-waters
a third day through sea-waters.
    Now on the third day
    the boat was jammed hard.
Old Väinämöinen himself
    pondered with his brain:
on a rock? or on a log?
or else on a pike's shoulder
on a water-dog's hooked bones?
Old Väinämöinen himself
pulled the head into his craft
dropped the tail on the planking.
He looked, he turned it over:
"What could a smith do with this
what might a mighty man do?"
He made a harp of pike-bones
a kantele of fish-fins
put strings on the kantele
of hair from a demon's maid
of hairs from a stud-stallion
put pegs in the kantele
of shoots from Tuoni's barley
of the teeth of Tuoni's pike.

The young played and the old played
and the married fellows played
and the unmarried men played:
joy had not the feel of joy

music was unmusical.
Let the joy be borne that way
the kantele be carried
to the hands of its maker
    its tuner's fingers.
Väinämöinen made music
with small hands, slender fingers
his thumb rose, lightly touching:
the young wept and the old wept
and the married fellows wept
and the unmarried men wept
even old Väinämöinen
had water roll from his eyes
rounder than a grouse's eggs
larger than an oxeye's flowers.
There was none in the forest
    running on four feet
    whirring on two wings
that did not come to listen
to the Father making joy:
even the forest's mistress
leaned her breasts upon the fence.
There was none in the water
    moving with six fins
that did not come to listen:
even the water's mistress
drew herself up on a rock
clambered up on her belly.

Singer unknown
Ostrobothnia
Copied from the manuscript of an
unknown collector by K. Ganander, ca 1760

24

The Kantele II

Kauko shaped a kantele
Estonia's smith a curved thing
neither of wood nor of bone
but of a blue elk's shoulder
  a reindeer's knee-bones.

What the kantele's sound-board? –
made from a red salmon's tail.
And what the kantele's pegs? –
from the teeth of a great pike.
And what, I say, the kantele's strings? –
the hair of a demon's dame
from the mane of a stud-horse.

The kantele was finished.
The lasses played, the lads played
and the unmarried men played
and the married fellows played:
joy had not the feel of joy
nor had song the sense of song.
There was a search for players
for players and for singers
among high-born and low-born
among gods, through all the earth.

It was old Väinämöinen
gave a greeting on the road
said good morning in the lane:
"Give, Kauko, your kantele
Estonia's smith, your curved thing
into the blind boy's fingers
to the dim-sighted one's hands."

He struck it once, struck it twice
soon struck it a third time too:
now joy had the feel of joy
and song had the sense of song.
His fingers began to work
his arms to move back and forth.

There was none in the forest
  running on four feet
that did not come to listen
to Väinämöinen's playing.
There was nothing in the air
  flying on two wings
that did not come to listen
  as Väinämöinen
played, as he plucked the loud strings
as the salmon-tail rejoiced,
to the fish-bone kantele.
There was nothing in the sea
  moving with six fins
  darting with a tail
that did not come to listen –
  as Väinämöinen
played, as he plucked the loud strings –
to the fish-bone kantele
  the red salmon-tail.
The demon's dame herself gave
her purse with the golden mouth
her knife with the silver haft
the one whose haft cost hundreds –
no one knew how much the blade.

Ontrei Vanninen
Sortavala, Ladoga Karelia
K. Killinen, 1882

25

The Kantele III

I was a serf in Estonia
a herdsman in the bad land.
What was I made to do there? –
I was made to go herding.
What was I made to eat there? –
bones from meat and heads from fish
and the middle parts of soups.
What was I given for pay? –
brought a gallon of barley.
I took the grains in my palm
sowed the grains in Swedish soil
threw them on German tillage
flung them on Estonia's strips.

I went straight to look
at the end of two, three nights:
a ram was in my barley
a blue-horn on my tillage.
I took the ram, brought it home
led it into the farmyard
took the horns off the ram's head
brought the horns to the smith's forge.

"O my smith, my splendid man
you hammered yesterday, once
hammer still today as well!
Hammer me a kantele
to play when I am at war
below the castle to pluck."

The kantele lacked something
the kantele lacked two strings:
I went off in search of them.

I saw a maid on the road
a lass on the sandy path.
I began to ask the maid:
"Will you give, maid, of your hair
lass, some of your locks?"
The maid gave me of her hair
the lass of her locks:
I got the kantele strings.

I took it in to the men.
The young played and the old played –
with no joy at all.
A blind man called from a nook
dim-sighted from a corner:
"Put it on a blind boy's knees
let a poor boy have a strum!"

And when the blind boy played it
when the poor boy had a strum
only then it shone with joy.
What old men were in the house
were leaning forward
listening to the kantele
admiring the joy.
What old crones were in the house
had hands on cheekbones
listening to the kantele.
What girls there were in the house
all had water in their eyes
listening to the kantele.
What boys there were in the house
lay with bellies on the floor
listening to the kantele

admiring the joy
the blind boy's music.

A wolf ran through the great woods
a bear over the wide heath
ran to hear the kantele
and the wolf broke its great head
and the bear its rigid neck.

Singer unknown
Vuole, Ingria
F. A. Saxbäck, 1859

26

The Voyage I

I went to the forest in summer
at midsummer, at hay-time
near the feast of Peterkin
the warm time of great Mary.
I walked on a cone-strewn heath
through honeysuckle backwoods:
    I met an aspen.

The aspen indeed answered:
"What, man, do you seek of me?"
    I answering said:
"I seek boats for my brother
where my only one may step."
The aspen answering said:
"No boats will be had from me
not from me hard-wearing hulls."

I walked on the cone-strewn heath
through honeysuckle backwoods:
    I met a birch-tree.

The birch-tree indeed answered:
"What, man, do you seek from me?"
    I answering said:
"I seek boats for my brother
where my only one may step."
The birch-tree answering said:
"No boats will be had from me
    but clear wood for wheels
    or tarry rollers
    or laths better still."

I walked on the cone-strewn heath
through the honeysuckle backwoods:
    I met an oak-tree.
I struck it once with an axe
struck it twice with a hatchet
a third time with a whole blade:
I struck once, one side was born
I struck twice, the other side
a third time and the whole boat.
    That boat was finished.

What would the ribs be formed of? –
the boat's ribs of a bear's ribs.
What would the pegs be made of? –
    a fine wolf's back-bones.
    That boat was soon built
the hundred-sided was hewn:
the boat was borne to water
the hundred-boarded to waves
the thousand-boarded windward.
Many folk were in the ship
    most were fully fledged
they did not know about wind
did not understand the gale.

An old crone lives on the shore
stays on the water's surface:
the crone had an only son
one who was called Antero.
She gave him to help Ahti
gave him to be an oar-hand
gave him to know the wind's ways
put his mind to the sea air:
in his hair he knew the wind
evil weather in his shirt
and the sea air in his mind.

Untamo, Ylermö's son
hoisted a sail, a red one
up among the shrouds
another sail, a blue one
and a third all of linen
bringing it against the mast:
the ship ran, the voyage sped
over frost and under ice
hard by a fishing-island.
God the merciful
turned the wind round against him:
he rode steady at anchor.
The wind flared, the storm started
and the waves moved heavily.

Untamo, Ylermö's son
set the old rowing
the young looking on:
the old rowed, their heads trembled.
The old were praying:
"O merciful God
turn the wind to the north-west
give the oars some help!"
God the merciful
turned no wind to the north-west
gave the oars no help.

Untamo, Ylermö's son
took the old ones off rowing
set the young rowing
the old looking on:
the young rowed and their oars swung
the grey foam was foaming up
the yellow spray was seething
from within the sea's water.
So the young ones were praying:
"O merciful God
turn the wind to the north-west
give the oars some help!"
God the merciful
swung the wind northward
gave the oars no help.
The wind flared, the storm started
and the waves moved heavily
from within the sea's water:
the ship was driven
driven fast on to a rock –
the folk were quite tired –
driven fast on to a rock
by Little Pentti's castle
whose lord was Little Pentti.

Untamo, Ylermö's son
asked, made inquiries:
"Are there loaves in the castle
without baking any bread
for the weary folk?"

The boy–lord answered:
"No loaves are in the castle
for the weary folk."

Untamo, Ylermö's son
answering replied:
"Is there meat in the castle?"

"No meat is in the castle
without slaughtering the ox
without slaying the bullock."

For a month a squirrel ran
along the ox's backbone
a summer day a swallow
flew between the ox's horns.
Now, who would slaughter the ox
and who would slay the bullock?
A man squeezed in from market:
came, a bone axe in his hand
a bone axe, copper-hafted.
When he struck with the bone axe

beat with the copper-hafted
it bellowed, rolling its eyes
    and its hoofs clattered.
The man fled up a pine-tree
other gods up other trees.

Of what use are we singers
what good we cuckoo-callers
if no fire spurts from our mouths
no brand from beneath our tongues
and no smoke after our words!

Singer unknown
Soikkola, Ingria
J. Länkelä, 1858

27

The Voyage II

Sampsa the Pellervo boy
went off in search of timber
to try and find oak
find a mast for God
a keel for the Creator.

He met an oak-tree.
He asked it, he spoke to it:
"Will there come from you, oak-tree
a keel for the Creator?"

The oak-tree answered:
"One would never come from me:
three times this summer
the worms have crawled at my roots
three times this summer
the devil twisted my heart
the ravens croaked in my crown."

He kept advancing onward:
he met an oak-tree.
He asked it, he spoke to it:
"Will there come from you, oak-tree
come a mast for God
a keel for the Creator?"

The oak knowingly answered:
"One would never come from me:
three times this summer
the worms have lain at my roots
the devil twisted my heart
the ravens croaked in my crown."

And so he advanced onward:
so on the third day
he met an oak-tree.
He asked it, he spoke to it:
"Will there come from you, oak-tree
come a mast for God
a keel for the Creator?"

The oak knowingly answered:
"Yes, timber will come from me
and a mast for God
a keel for the Creator:
three times this summer
honey has dripped from my leaves
the sun has gone round my heart
three times this summer
the cuckoo called in my crown."

Then he could fell the oak-tree
overthrow the handsome tree
and he built a boat ready
from the fragments of the oak
from bits of the broken tree.

The boat was finished:
and he launched the boat
upon rollers stripped of bark
upon thick pine-logs.
He himself put this in words:
"Boat, be bubbles on water
water-lilies on the waves."

He sat himself in the stern –
Sampsa the Pellervo boy
and Saint Ann was at the oars
    and Saint Peter said
    Saint Ann considered:
"Come into the boat, O God
come aboard, merciful one
to the pillows fit for you
curl up under the blankets."
And God came into the boat
the merciful one aboard
to the pillows fit for him
curled up under the blankets
and Saint Peter after him.

They sailed a day, another
    so on the third day
the sea swelled till it was big
the world filled till it was large
the surge rose till it was high
the waves till they were heavy.
    And Saint Peter said
    Saint Ann considered:
    "Famous Son of God
    uncurl your blankets
away from your lovely face:
the sea swelled till it was big
the world filled till it was large
the surge rose till it was high
the waves till they were heavy."

So the famous Son of God
into his blankets curled up
    uncurled his blankets
away from his lovely face
from the pillows fit for him.

Iku Turso, Äijö's son
raised his head out of the sea
    his poll from the waves
    beside the red boat.

So the famous Son of God
lifted him straight by the ears
and pulled him into his boat.
He asked him, he spoke to him:
"Iku Turso, Äijö's son
why did you rise from the sea
wherefore come up from the waves
in front of the sons of men
let alone the Son of God?"

Iki Turso, Äijö's son
neither was he very charmed
nor was he greatly frightened.
So the famous Son of God
    questioned thoroughly
asked him three times straight away:
"Why did you rise from the sea
wherefore come up from the waves
in front of the sons of men
let alone the Son of God?"

    And so the third time
    Turso, Äijö's son
uttered a word finally
    like this the third time:
"I thought of overturning
dropping the boat in the waves."

So the famous Son of God
lifted him straight by the ears
threw him into the clear sea
    the open water.
He himself put into words:
"Iki Turso, Äijö's son
do not rise out of the sea
do not come up from the waves
in front of the sons of men
let alone the Son of God
while the moon lasts, and the sun
    the lovely daylight!"

Since that day Turso
has not risen from the sea
neither come up from the waves
in front of the sons of men.

From there to there the road goes
a new path leads off.

Arhippa Perttunen
Latvajärvi, Vuokkiniemi, Archangel Karelia
J. F. Cajan, 1836

28

The Spell I

Sturdy old Väinämöinen
made a boat with his knowledge
built a craft with his singing:
three words were lacking
as he reached the ship's gunwales
as he was hewing rowlocks
as he was making thwart-planks.

So he said these words:
"There might be a hundred words
on a flock of swallows' heads
there might be a hundred words
on a skein of geese' shoulders
where a line of swans ended
within a white squirrel's mouth
beneath a summer-deer's tongue."

He killed a flock of swallows
he scattered a skein of geese
he killed off a line of swans
he killed a roost of squirrels
he laid low a field of deer:
he got not a single word
no, not half a word.

"There might be a hundred words
a thousand songs in the mouth
of Antervo Vipunen
who has lain ages in earth
who has rested long at rest:
on his chin is a wide grove
a willow-clump on his beard
boat-aspen on his shoulders
but then, travelling is bad
upon men's sword-blades
women's needle-points."

An hour came to leave
another was ripe to go
as of old for the hired man
or for the serf, the hireling.

He trod for a day clinking
upon men's sword-blades
he trod a day, another
upon women's needle-points
so on the third day
one of his feet tripped
his left slipped into the mouth
of Antervo Vipunen
who had lain ages in earth
who had rested long in soil.

Then the old Väinämöinen
felt his knee burning
his limb warming in the mouth
of Antervo Vipunen.
From his shirt he made a forge
from his fur coat made bellows
a hammer from his elbow
from his little fingers tongs:
he hammered, he tapped
hammered an iron cowlstaff.

He plunged it into the mouth
of Antervo Vipunen.

Then Antervo Vipunen
bit in two the soft iron:
he could not bite through the steel
eat the iron's heart.

Then Antervo Vipunen
uttered a word, speaking thus:
"Go, villain, out of my lung
earth's elect, from my liver:
charcoal comes into my mouth
iron dross into my throat."

And so Väinämöinen said:
"I, villain, will leave your throat
earth's elect, leave your liver
if you say a hundred words
the tips of a thousand songs."

Then Antervo Vipunen
who had lain ages in earth
who had rested long in soil
said a hundred words
the tips of a thousand songs:
then the old Väinämöinen
finished off his boat.

Arhippa Perttunen
Latvajärvi, Vuokkiniemi, Archangel Karelia
E. Lönnrot, 1834

29

The Spell II

Old Väinämöine himself
made a boat with his knowledge
built a craft with his singing:
    three words were lacking
    as he reached the stern
    at the midship point.

Old Väinämöine himself
went off for words from Tuoni
    songs from Manala.
Tuoni's daughters scolded him
and Manala's children said:
"Now, who comes down to Tuoni
who arrives in Manala?"

Old Väinämöine himself
rolled in the sea as a stone
plopped in the water as smoke
    but found no words there.

Virone had long been dead
Anderus was long perished:
alders had sprung from his jaws
from his brows squirrel-spruces
tall aspens from his shoulders
out of his feet splendid pines
junipers out of his heels
strong birches out of his toes.

Old Väinämöine himself
felled the spruces by their roots
the pines by their foundations:
there he found a pair of words –
even as many as three.
So now he finished his boat
    on the copper stocks
    on the steel rollers.

Old Väinämöine himself
uttered with outspoken mouth
    with a shining tooth:
"Is there one of these young folk
one of the rising people
    to push out this craft
to point the boat the right way?"

Young Jougamoine uttered:
"Yes, there's one of these young folk
one of the rising people!"
The young Jougamoine tried:
the boat did not reach water.

Old Väinämöine himself
uttered with outspoken mouth
    with a shining tooth:
"All sorts are made to be man
appointed to wear a beard."
The old Väinämöine tried:
now the boat reached the water.

Once I rowed in marsh-waters
another time land-waters
and a third time sea-waters:
Väinämöine's craft was jammed

the boat of Tabie stuck fast
not on a rock, not a log
but on a great pike's shoulders.

Old Väinämöine uttered
uttered with outspoken mouth
    with a shining tooth:
"Is there one of these young folk
one of the rising people
    to release this craft
to point the boat the right way?"

Young Jougamoine uttered:
"Yes, there's one of these young folk
one of the rising people!"
He struck the sea with his sword
thrashed about below the side
but the pike took no notice:
the sword broke in three pieces.

Old Väinämöine himself
uttered with outspoken mouth
    with a shining tooth:
"All sorts are made to be man
appointed to wear a beard."

Old Väinämöine himself
took the sword he was wearing
    drew from his left flank:
he struck the sea with his sword
thrashed about below the side
and the pike in three pieces.
The tail-piece floundered about
the middle bit tumbled down
in the black mud of the sea
into the depths of the sea:
there the head came to his hand.

"Where shall we take this?
We'll take it to the smithy:
O smith, make music for us!"

Old Väinämöine himself
uttered with outspoken mouth
    with a shining tooth:
"Is there one of these young folk
one of these rising people
    to play this instrument
someone to enjoy this joy?"

Young Jougamoine uttered:
"Yes, there's one of these young folk
one of these rising people!"
Took music in his fingers
the fair thing in his two hands:
music was unmusical
joy had not the feel of joy.

Old Väinämöine himself
took music in his fingers
the fair thing in his two hands
    started to play it:
now music was musical
now joy had the feel of joy.
What forest-beasts there might be
    running on four feet
what water-fishes there were
    bubbling with six fins
    all came to listen:
the water's mistress herself
splashed with her breasts on the grass
swirled upon a clump of sedge.

Old Väinämöine himself
uttered with outspoken mouth
    with a shining tooth:
"Is there one of these young folk
one of the rising people
    someone to shoot her?"

The young Jougamoine shot:
she jerked down into the mud
she swirled into the water.

Old Väinämöine himself
grew angry, grew furious then
twisted his mouth, tore his head
tugged at his black hair
sang him into a fishless
pond, one quite empty of perch
with his nails on a cold rock
with his teeth on water-logs.

"What will you take in return?
I've two little boats:
one is light to row
one carries a lot of folk."

"I have something much better
five times swifter than that one."

"I have two horses:
one is strongly built
one is light to drive."

"I have something much better
five times swifter than that one.
If you give Anni, your one sister
you will be freed from the fishless pond
the one quite empty of perch
with your nails off the cold rock
your teeth off the water-logs."

O that young Jougamoine
went running homeward:
"O my mother who bore me
I gave Anni, my only sister."

His mother replied:
"For this I longed all my life
throughout half my days –
Väinö for my son-in-law
the young man for my kinsman
the singer my relative."

Simana Höttönen
Repola, Olonets Karelia
A. A. Borenius, 1872

30

The Visit to Tuonela

Now, that old Väinämöini
set out for church, resplendent
above the other proud folk:
his springy sledge-runner split
his curly sledge-runner bumped
on the rocky road to church.

The old Väinämöini said:
"Is there one of the old folk
to go for spikes from Tuoni
a crowbar from Manala?"

And all the people answered:
"There is none of the old folk
to go for spikes from Tuoni
a crowbar from Manala."

The old Väinämöini said:
"Is there one of the young folk
the rising generation
to go for spikes from Tuoni
the crowbar from Manala?"

And all the people answered:
"There is none of the young folk
to go for spikes from Tuoni
the crowbar from Manala."

Then the old Väinämöini
went off for spikes from Tuoni
a crowbar from Manala.
Went to Tuonela's river:
there the daughters of Tuoni
iron-clawed, iron-fingered
spinners of an iron thread
were busy with their washing.

Then the old Väinämöini
called out, shouted out:
"Bring a boat, girl of Tuoni
child of the grave, a vessel!"

The daughters of Tuoni said
the children of the grave clanked:
"When your business is stated
a boat will be brought to you."

The old Väinämöini said:
"Iron brought me to Mana
and iron to Tuonela."

The daughters of Tuoni said
the children of the grave clanked:
"If iron brought you to Mana
and iron to Tuonela
your garments would drip with gore
your clothes would be oozing blood."

Then again he called out, shouted out:
"Bring a boat, girl of Tuoni
child of the grave, a vessel!"

The daughters of Tuoni said
the children of the grave clanked:
"When your business is stated
a boat will be brought to you."

The old Väinämöini said:
"Fire has brought me to Mana
    fire to Tuonela."

The daughters of Tuoni said
the children of the grave clanked:
"If fire brought you to Mana
    fire to Tuonela
your garments would be on fire
your clothes would be spitting sparks."

Then the old Väinämöini
    called out, shouted out:
"Bring a boat, girl of Tuoni
child of the grave, a vessel!"

The daughters of Tuoni said
the children of the grave clanked:
"When your business is stated
a boat will be brought to you."

The old Väinämöini said
"I came for spikes from Tuoni
a crowbar from Manala."

Then the daughters of Tuoni
iron-clawed, iron-fingered
spinners of the iron thread
    brought a little boat.
They treated the man as man
the hero like a hero:
they gave him food, gave him drink –
    some serpent-venom
    and some lizard-heads.
They even laid him to rest
    on a bed of silk
which was of serpent-venom.

Then the old Väinämöini
    felt his doom coming
his day of distress dawning:
changed himself to a brown worm
slithered into a lizard
swam across Tuoni's river.

Then he went to his people
himself put this into words:
    "Do not, young men, go
to Mana unless you're killed
to Tuonela unless dead."

Then the old Väinämöini
drove off to church, resplendent
above the other proud folk.

Jyrki Malinen
Vuonninen, Vuokkiniemi, Archangel Karelia
A. A. Borenius, 1871

31

Sun and Moon I

Where, tell me, has our sun gone
whither has our moon vanished?
The sun's gone into a rock.

By night born, Väinämöinen
by night born, by night brought up
went by day to the smithy
hammered some tools for the lord.
A snake flew to the threshold
as Väinämöinen hammered.
Old Väinämöinen himself
uttered a word, speaking thus:
"Why are you on the threshold?"

The snake knowingly answered:
"For this I'm on the threshold –
I bring a message:
the moon's risen from the stone
the sun's come out of the rock
as Väinämöinen hammered."

He uttered this word, spoke thus:
"I'll go now to Pohjola
among the sons of Pohjo
to the Lapp children's paddocks
since from the stone I have freed
the moon, from the rock the sun."

He trod a day, another
now on the third day
Pohjola's gates were in sight
the bad place's gateways shone
and the doors of Hiisi creaked.

"Come with fingers not rowing
and without using your hands
and not holding with your thumb
without wielding your paddle
across Pohjola's river."

Old Väinämöinen himself
when he called out, shouted out
when he shrilled out, whistled out
a wind came and wafted him
across Pohjola's river.
"Come now to Pohjola's yards!"
He went to Pohjola's yards.

Singer unknown
Paltamo, Kainuu
Collector unknown, recorded before 1825

32

Sun and Moon II

There was a time when we lived
at the far end of the ditch
burned wood from the ditch
ate fish from the ditch
without the moon, without sun
without the Creator's light.
With our hands we searched the ground
with our fingers the marshes
with our thumbs for where to tread.
We planted by candlelight
sowed with the help of torches.

The smith's girl, the skilful girl
careful maid of the craftsman
got up to search for the sun
and to look out for the moon
put a whetstone on her breast
took a brush on her shoulder
took a jug under her arm
and took a bundle of dreams.
She went a verst, another
went a little of a third:
Iittova village loomed up
Hiitoi's houses gleamed.
She tossed the bundle of dreams
she lulled Hiitoi's men to sleep
she weighed Hiitoi's women down:
no bark of a dog was heard
nor the neighing of a horse
nor the weeping of a child.

She took the moon on her brow
put the sun upon her head:
she came a verst, another
came a little of a third.
She looked behind her:
Iittova's men were coming
they were about to catch her
about to lay hands on her.

She flung the whetstone from her back
and said as she was flinging:
"Let a thick slab grow
which Iitto's men cannot pass
neither over nor under
cannot pass whichever way!"

She came a verst, another
came a little of a third.
She looked behind her:
they were about to catch her
about to lay hands on her.

She flung the brush from her shoulder
and said as she flung:
"Let a thick wood grow
let splendid backwoods be born
which Iitto's men cannot pass
neither over nor under
cannot pass whichever way!"

She went a verst, another
went a little of a third.
She looked behind her:
they were about to catch her
about to lay hands on her.

She flung the jug from her arm
    and said as she flung:
"Let a great river be born
a great river, a great hill
which Iitto's men cannot pass
neither over nor under
nor can come in boats either
    nor can sail in ships!"

Smith's woman, skilful woman
    thus reached her own lands.
There at her father's window
a golden birch had sprung up
a silver pine had sprung up:
    there she placed the sun
    placed the moon to gleam.

    The sun rose to shine
and the moon came out to gleam
on the rich, on the cherished
not on the poor, the beggars.
The poor people were praying
the beggars were bowing down:
"Smith's woman, skilful woman
place the sun that it may shine
    that God's moon may dawn
on the rich, on the cherished
and on the poor, the beggars!"

    She could not be stern,
smith's woman, skilful woman:
placed the sun that it might shine
that its riches might bring joy
to the poor, to the beggars.

Natelia
Soikkola, Ingria
V. Porkka, 1883

33

Sun and Moon III

Once we lived without the sun
groped about without the moon
 but folk nowadays
cannot live without the sun
grope about without the moon.

Who would search for the sun, would
look carefully for the moon?
 The one Son of God
the prompt servant of Jesus
he would search for the sun, would
look carefully for the moon:
in a jug he put some beer
in another jug some mead
in a third angry liquor.

To the stable on the hill
 he went: seven cobs
and eight good pacers were there
and he took from his stallions
he chose from among his colts
which had a pool on its loins
a ditch on the stallion's flank
a cold well under its hoofs
had a spring in its withers.
He leapt on the good one's back
jumped on the handsome one's loins
struck the stallion with a whip
 whacked it with a rod:
the stallion squirmed like a snake
 wriggled like a worm
the stallion ran, the way shrank
the distance grew swiftly short.

He went on a little way
 went a short distance
 and he met a log:
he could not get past the log
neither over nor under
nor round it to run away.

 The one Son of God
the prompt servant of Jesus
flung down some of his liquor
some of his beer splashed on it
some of his mead sprayed on it
and the log was split in two:
an everlasting road came
a crack aged as the shore
where Unto, where Vento, where
the Creator with his kin
 God with his family
a weak lord with his household
a priest with his flock could walk.

He went on a little way
 went a short distance
 and he met a rock:
he could not get past the rock
neither over nor under
nor round it to run away.

 The one Son of God
the prompt servant of Jesus
flung down some of his liquor
some of his beer splashed on it
some of his mead sprayed on it

and the rock was split in two:
an everlasting road came
a crack aged as the shore
where Unto, where Vento, where
the Creator with his kin
      God with his family
a weak lord with his household
a priest with his flock could walk
and a king with his castle.

He leapt on the good one's back
jumped on the handsome one's loins
he went on a little way
      went a short distance
      and he met a ditch:
he could not get past the ditch
neither over nor under
nor round it to run away.

      The one Son of God
threw an apple in the ditch
lobbed a leek into the pool
and the ditch was split in two:
an everlasting road came
a crack aged as the shore
where Unto, where Vento, where
the Creator with his kin
      God with his family
a weak lord with his household
a priest with his flock could walk
and a king with his castle.

      The one Son of God
he went on a little way
      went a short distance:
      he met a village.

All other villagers slept:
a crone was at the window.
"Hullo, crone, my old mother!
Where are you keeping the moon
where are you hoarding the sun?"

The crone answering replied:
"There we are keeping the moon
there we are hoarding the sun –
inside a thick willow-bush
in a dense birdcherry wood."

      The one Son of God
      went, looked for the sun:
the sun was still lying down
      the moon still resting.

And a little time went by
an hour went by, another.
He went and looked for the sun:
now the sun's head could be seen
plenty of feet in the bed
hands enough under the quilt.

      The one Son of God
took the sun on his shoulder
folded it over his arm
brought the sun to his own lands
      from other strange lands.

      The one Son of God
now set his sun in its place
upon the highest branches.
The sun did not shine justly:
the sun shone upon the rich
the moon gleamed upon the poor.

The poor people were praying
with knees on the ground begging:
"Wherefore has our Creator
      and why has our God
      not done this justly
that no sun should shine on us?"

The one Son of God
gave ear to the prayer:
he set his sun in its place
upon the lower branches.
The sun did not shine justly:
the sun shone upon the poor
the moon gleamed upon the rich.

The rich people were praying
with knees on the ground begging:
"Wherefore has our Creator
and why has our God
cast the sun down from shining?
What have we done that is wrong
that no sun should shine on us?"

The one Son of God
gave ear to the prayer:
he set his sun in its place
upon the middle branches
and then the sun shone justly
on the rich, on the cherished
on the poor, on the beggars.

Paroi, Saku's wife
Hevaa, Kaprio, Ingria
V. Porkka, 1883

34

Lemminkäinen I

Smoke flared on the island, fire
at a point on the headland:
it would be small for war-smoke
too big for a herdsman's fire.
Osmotar was brewing beer
the woman was mixing ale
a forest of trees was burnt
a forest on the island.

A day there was, another:
the beer did not start to turn
the golden ale to ferment.

The mistress was well-behaved
rubbed her two palms together
she made friction with them both:
she rubbed a stoat from her palms
pushed a squirrel from her mouth.
    She put this in words:
"Hear how I advise my maid
    instruct my squirrel.
Go the way I command you:
make your way over nine seas
    over half a tenth.
There are three slender spruces:
two are covered with a cloak
the third has no covering.
    Bring cones from a spruce
    some shoots from a pine."

She brought some cones from a spruce
    some shoots from a pine
put them in the woman's hand
who put them into the ale
Osmotar into the beer.

A day there was, another
    now on the third day
the beer was starting to turn
the golden ale to ferment:
now the beer had turned ready
the mead to be drunk by men.

The mistress was well-behaved
    put this into words:
"Hear how I advise my maid
    instruct my squirrel.
Go the way I command you:
ask the crippled, ask the lame
    ask the blind from birth
drag the crippled in sledges
drive the lame here on horseback
row the blind from birth in boats.
Ask Ahti and ask Kaugo
ask ruddy-cheeked Veitikki."

"I do not know Ahti's house
    neither Kaugo's farm
nor Veitikki's dwelling-place."

"Ahti lives on the island
Kaugo in the headland's crook
Veitikki upon its tip.
Do not ask Lemmingäine:
Lemmingäine's a wanton
he is always quarrelsome."

Lemmingäine the wanton
hurtled out into the yard
through the doorway to the yard
past the place where the splint burns:
thudding rang from the village
thumping from beyond the lakes
stamping from the frozen ground.

He rushed into his small room
put this into words:
"O mother who carried me
bring here my war-gear
carry here my battledress
for me to wear at the feast
to display at the wedding:
I'm off to Päivölä's feast
to the island folk's revels."

The mother forbade her son
the woman told her man no:
"Don't go to Päivölä's feast
to the island folk's revels!
There are three deaths on the way."

"O mother who carried me
say what the foremost death is."

"My only offspring
you will go a little way
quite a short distance
you'll meet a fiery river
amid it fiery rapids
amid them a fiery crag
on the crag a fiery birch
on the birch fiery branches
in them a fiery eagle:
the eagle is sharpening
its claws, is grinding its teeth
to eat Lemmingäine with.
It's eaten a hundred men
destroyed a thousand heroes
a hundred under its wing
a thousand beneath its tail."

"O mother who carried me
there is no death for men there
there is no doom for heroes –
Lemmingäine above all!
He'd snatch a grouse from a grove
or a black grouse from the woods
a meal for the eater's mouth
a bit for the biter's beard
for the chewer's jaws.
Eagle, God's creature
clap your eyelids together
let your ear-flaps flop over
let a travelling man go –
Lemmingäine above all!
O mother who carried me
say what the middle death is."

"My only offspring
you will go a little way
quite a short distance
a worm lies across the road
longer than the room's timbers
thicker than the room's pillars:
it's eaten a hundred men
destroyed a thousand heroes."

"O mother who carried me
there is no death for men there
nor is there doom for heroes –
Lemmingäine above all!
O black worm from underground
crawler among withered grass
get into a berry clump
let a travelling man go –
Lemmingäine above all!
O mother who carried me
say what the hindmost death is."

"My only offspring
you will go a little way
quite a short distance
you'll enter Päivölä's lane:
an iron fence has been built
with lizards bound together
with snakes it is wound around
from the earth up to the sky
with their bulbous heads hissing
with their mouths sizzling
with their tongues seething
wolves with bridle-chains
bears with fetters of iron.
They are in Päivölä's lane."

"There is no death for men there
nor doom for heroes –
Lemmingäine above all!
I shall melt them with my mouth
stop them with my words."

Now he went to Ahti's house
to the island folk's revels
and he stopped in the doorway
by the door beneath the beam
in the space between two pots
where three hooks turned to and fro.

'Twas Ahti the islander:
"Why come unasked to the feast
unannounced to the revels?"

"A stranger bidden is fine:
one not bidden is finer.
A fine one waits to be asked:
a good one thrusts in without."

'Twas Ahti the islander
he sang a white hare
upon Lemmingäine's head
to drop soot on him
scatter grime on him.

Lemmingäine the wanton
he sang a brown fox:
it ate the white hare
upon Lemmingäine's head.

'Twas Ahti the islander
sang a brown squirrel
upon Lemmingäine's head
to drop soot on him
scatter grime on him.

Lemmingäine the wanton
sang a gold-breasted marten
and it ate the brown squirrel
upon Lemmingäine's head:
it did not drop soot
did not scatter grime.

'Twas Ahti the islander
sang a pond upon the floor
there under Lemmingäine.

Lemmingäine the wanton
sang a gold-horned ox:
its tail waved in Tornivo
head swung in Kemi River.
A month, a day, a squirrel
ran down the ox's tail-bone:
still it did not reach the end.
For a day a swallow flew
between the horns of the ox:
still it did not reach the end.
It drank the pond off the floor
from under Lemmingäine.

'Twas Ahti the islander
brought some beer in a flagon

bore in a two-handled one:
maggots squirmed in the bottom
worms were wriggling down the sides.
He took the knife from his flank
an iron hook from his bag
and he put this into words:
"Cast the serpent to the ground
    feed food to the mouth:
to Tuoni with the flagon-bringer
to Mana with him who bears the jug!"

He drank the beer for good cheer
the black mead for good spirits
hurtled out into the yard
    upon men's sword-points
on the hatchet's fiery blade
himself put this into words:

"O Ahti, you islander
come outside into the yard:
in the yard blood is better
    on horse-dung fairer.
    Let us size up swords
    let us look at blades
to see whose sword is to be
preferred, whose blade is fairer."

Ahti went into the yard
    and they sized up swords
    and they looked at blades.

Ahti slashed Lemmingäine:
Lemmingäine did not mind.
Lemmingäine slashed Ahti
slashed like cropping a turnip.

Nasto, Huotari's wife
Kiimaisjärvi, Archangel Karelia
A. A. Borenius, 1872

35

Lemminkäinen II

Now, Väinölä held a feast
and Sinivermo revels:
masters, pastors were bidden
the crippled, the lame were asked
the crippled were rowed in boats
the lame driven on horseback
all Christian people were asked
but Lemminkäinen was not.
Lemminkäin, he the blackguard
enjoyed his only sister
and ruined his mother's child.

Wanton Lemminkäinen said
said to his only father
said to his darling mother:
"I'm off to Väinölä's feast."

Father banned, mother said no:
"Don't go, my offspring
to that feast at Väinölä!
There are three harsh deaths:
a pond lies across the road
brimming over with hot rocks
with boulders on fire."

Wanton Lemminkäinen said:
"A father's knowledge is good:
my own knowledge is better.
Yes, I shall find a way out:
I'm off as I intended
to that feast at Väinölä
to Sinivermo's revels."

Father banned, mother said no:
"Don't go, my offspring!
A worm lies across the road
longer than the standing trees
thicker than the lane's pillar."

Wanton Lemminkäinen said:
"A father's knowledge is good:
my own knowledge is better.
Yes, I shall find a way out:
I shall sing the worm aside.
That's how I'll deal with that one."

Wanton Lemminkäinen said:
"Dear father, my only one
quickly bring my war-stallion!
I'm off as I intended
to that feast at Väinölä
to Sinivermo's revels."

Father banned, mother said no:
"Don't go, my offspring!
There is a third, harsher death:
a wolf is bridled ready
and bears in iron fetters
stand across the steps."

Wanton Lemminkäinen said:
"A father's knowledge is good:
my own knowledge is better.
Yes, I shall find a way out:
I shall sing a flock of sheep
a cluster of curly-wools

into the iron wolves' mouths
in the iron bear's fetters.
That's how I'll deal with that one."

Wanton Lemminkäinen said:
"Dear father, my only one
dear mother, my darling one!
I'm off as I intended
dear mother, my darling one:
    bring my battledress!"
She quickly brought his war-gear.

Wanton Lemminkäinen said:
"Quickly bring me, my father
that old war-stallion of mine
get my battle-colt ready!"

His father, his only one
quickly brought his war-stallion
got his battle-colt ready
for his son, his only one
leaving for Väinölä's feast.

Wanton Lemminkäinen left
for that feast at Väinölä:
'twas wanton Lemminkäinen
flung his brush against the wall.
Wanton Lemminkäinen said:
"When the brush is oozing blood
then Lemminkäinen is lost
things look black for the bad boy
at that feast at Väinölä
at Sinivermo's revels."

And still his mother said no:
    "Don't go, my offspring!
Over there you will be sung
you'll be sung, you'll be sentenced
into Tuoni's black river
Manala's eternal stream
with your nails on a cold rock
with your teeth in a wet log
to weep everlastingly
    and wail for ever."

Wanton Lemminkäinen left
and he drove a little way
he made tracks a short distance.
A pond lay across the road
brimming over with hot rocks
    with boulders on fire:
'twas wanton Lemminkäinen
    cooled the pond to ice
and froze the water to frost.
That's how he dealt with that one.

And he drove a little way.
A worm lay across the road
longer than the standing trees
thicker than the lane's pillar:
'twas wanton Lemminkäinen
    sang the worm aside
whose throat was boiling with fire.
That's how he dealt with that one.

'Twas wanton Lemminkäinen
drove into Väinölä's yards
    to those sloping yards
into the level paddocks.
There were wolves bridled ready
and bears in iron fetters
    stood across the steps
and they went to attack him:
'twas wanton Lemminkäinen
    sang a flock of sheep
a cluster of curly-wools
into the iron wolves' mouths
in the iron bear's fetters.
That's how he dealt with that one.

He uttered the moment he
    came to that great house

he arrived at Väinölä:
"Greetings, for I have come here!"

Old Väinämöinen uttered:
"Greetings to who shouts greetings!
Hail, wanton Lemminkäinen:
you have not been invited."

Wanton Lemminkäinen said:
"A wretch comes at a summons:
a good man leaps up without."

Wanton Lemminkäinen said:
"Is there room in a corner
for the guest who is coming
for the one on his way in?
Are there nails for bright mittens
a stall where a horse may stay
barley for a horse to munch
beer for a hero to drink?"

Old Väinämöinen uttered:
"There is no room for you here
for the guest who is coming
and there are no nails for bright mittens
there is no stall where a horse may stay
and no barley for a horse to munch
and no beer for a hero to drink:
by the door, beneath the beam
in the space between two pots
where three hooks turn to and fro
if you will behave inside."

Wanton Lemminkäinen said:
"In the old days my father
was not by the door, beneath the beam
nor was my noble parent
in the space between two pots
where three hooks turn to and fro:
there was room in a corner
there were nails for bright mittens
there were walls to size up swords
a stall where a horse might stay
barley for a horse to munch
beer for a hero to drink –
so why is there not for me
as there was for my father?"

Old Väinämöinen uttered:
"You're wanton Lemminkäinen
you are the worst of blackguards
you ruined your mother's child
enjoyed your only sister:
    go, scoundrel, to hell
bad boy, flee to your country
away from all Christian folk!"

Old Väinämöinen uttered:
"If you don't do as you're told . . ."
Lemminkäinen paid no heed.

The ancient Väinämöinen
the everlasting wise man
son of doughty days, it was
he who sang Lemminkäinen
damned the son of Kaleva
into Tuoni's black river
Manala's eternal stream
where trees topple uprooted
    grasses fall headlong
with his nails on a cold rock
with his teeth in a wet log
to weep everlastingly
    and wail for ever.
Then Lemminkäinen was lost
things looked black for the bad boy.

The brush started oozing blood.
Lemminkäinen's mother said:
"Now Lemminkäinen is lost
things look black for the bad boy
when the brush is oozing blood."

Lemminkäinen's mother went
away in search of her son
to that feast at Väinölä
to Sinivermo's revels:
where logs were across the road
    she turned them aside
where there were rocks on the road
moved them all to the roadside.

Lemminkäinen's mother said
    asked questions, spoke up:
"Hail, old Väinämöinen: where
have you sung Lemminkäinen
damned the son of Kaleva?"

Old Väinämöinen uttered:
"I don't know your son, harlot
nor, bitch, do I know your fruit."

Lemminkäinen's mother said:
"Hullo, old Väinämöinen:
if you don't tell of my son
where you've sung, where sentenced him
damned the son of Kaleva
if you don't tell of my son
the new threshing-house doors I'll
break down, smash the sky's hinges."

Väinämöinen grew worried
the bearded hero was pained.
Old Väinämöinen uttered:
"I have sung Lemminkäinen
into Tuoni's black river
damned the son of Kaleva
where trees topple uprooted
    grasses fall headlong
with his nails on a cold rock
with his teeth in a wet log
to weep everlastingly
    and wail for ever."

'Twas Lemminkäinen's mother
flew to Tuonela's river
Manala's eternal stream:
    gliding, hovering
    she searched for her son
down in Tuoni's black river
but she did not find her son.

'Twas Lemminkäinen's mother
made a rake out of iron
fitted it with copper teeth
and raked with it for her son
along Tuonela's river:
now Lemminkäinen was caught
upon the copper rake's teeth
caught by his nameless finger.

'Twas Lemminkäinen's mother
    asked questions, spoke up:
"Will a man still come of you
a new hero be active?"

"There's no man in the one gone
no hero in the one drowned:
down there is this heart of mine
beside a blue rock, within
the liver-coloured belly.
Bitter now are my shoulders
rotten is my mound of flesh
down in Tuoni's black river
Manala's eternal stream
for I have been long in the grim place
ages in the chill water
with my nails on a cold rock
with my teeth in a wet log:
bitter there are my shoulders
rotten is my mound of flesh."

Wanton Lemminkäinen said:
"Never may my kinsmen put
the blame on who is blameless

the guilt on who is guiltless:
the wages are badly paid
down in Tuoni's black river
Manala's eternal stream
where trees topple uprooted
    grasses fall headlong."

Wanton Lemminkäinen said:
"Never may earthly people
nor ever may my kinsmen
my excellent tribesmen put
the blame on who is blameless
the guilt on who is guiltless:
here is surely room for you
down in Tuoni's black river
Manala's eternal stream.

Room is sure, bed is ready
    a bed of hot rocks
    of boulders on fire
a cover laid on the bed
    of the earth's black worms
    and of stabbing snakes."

And still Lemminkäinen said:
"Room is sure, the place is bad
in the hands of death the harsh.
My mother, my only one
not of me will a man come
of father's son no hero:
there's no man in the one gone
nor in one who is quite lost."

Simana Sissonen
Ilomantsi, North Karelia
D. E. D. Europaeus, 1845

36

Lemminkäinen III

Kalervikko the young lad
knocked upon the cottage door
rattled where the eaves stuck out:
there a little maid jumped up.

"Where do you go, little boy?
Take me as your companion
as a buckle on your cap
as a ring on your finger!"

"Where shall I take you?
In Estonia it rains
in Alje snow is sent down."

And I shook my cap
against a tree, on the ground
and against a hard rock too:
the ring fell from my finger
and the buckle from my cap.

I went to my stern sister
to my brother-in-law Lemmasterva.

Lehenlemmykkäine the sister
knew her brother was coming
and she had tarry gates made
and fences of snakes put up.

Kalervikko the young lad
went over the tarry gate
without catching on the tar
went under the fence of snakes
without a snake tasting him.

Lehenlemmykkäine the sister
let the dogs out of fetters
the hounds out of their muzzles.

Kalervikko the young lad
snatched his sword out of its sheath
struck the dogs down dead
and the hounds lifeless.

Lehenlemmykkäine the sister
sat her brother down
sat him down on the threshold.

The sword spoke out from its sheath:
"Kalervikko my brother
Kalervikko my bearer
do not sit on the threshold:
in it are the village tongues!"

Lehenlemmykkäine the sister
sat her brother down
sat him down in the mortar.

The sword again spoke out from its sheat
"Kalervikko my brother
Kalervikko my bearer
do not sit in the mortar:
in it are the manor's cares!"

Lehenlemmykkäine the sister
sat her brother down
sat him down on the hearthstone:
brother sat on the hearthstone.

Lehenlemmykkäine the sister
brought some beer in a flagon
bore in a two-handed one.

The sword spoke out from its sheath:
"Look there inside the flagon
look underneath the two lids!"

Kalervikko the young lad
looked there into the flagon
looked underneath the two lids:
there was a toads' spawning-ground
there snakes' assizes.

Kalervikko the young lad
snatched his sword out of its sheath
struck a blow at his sister
then slashed his brother-in-law:
sister fell to the ground dead
brother-in-law fell lifeless.

Varpu Luukka
Narvusi, Ingria
V. Alava, 1892

37

Kaukamoinen I

Päivölä set out a feast
the canny folk held revels
the crippled, the lame were asked
the blind were rowed there in boats
the crippled dragged in sledges.
That handsome Kaukamieli
was left unbidden.

Then handsome Kaukamieli
uttered a word, speaking thus:
"O my mother who bore me
bring here my war-gear
carry here my battledress:
I'm off to Päivölä's feast
off to Sariola's revels."

Father ordered, mother banned
a pair of witches said no
three nature-spirits forbade:
"Do not go, Kaukamieli:
many freaks are on your way
many marvels on your road!"

"What is the first freak?"

"There's a hill bristling with poles
they are bristling with men's heads:
one pole has been left empty
kept for Kaukamieli's head."

Handsome Kaukamieli said:
"Yes, I shall find a way out:
I shall take a dead man's skull
I'll strike the head off one gone
and set it upon the pole."

He himself put this in words:
"O my mother who bore me
bring me my war-gear
carry here my battledress:
I'm off to Päivölä's feast
off to Sariola's revels."

Father ordered, mother banned
a pair of witches said no
three nature-spirits forbade:
"Don't you go, Kaukamieli:
many freaks are on your way
many marvels on your road!"

"Well, what is the second freak?"

"On your way fiery rapids
in them a fiery birch-tree
on top a fiery eagle:
by night it sharpens its teeth
and by day it whets its claws
kept for Kaukamieli's neck."

"Yes, I shall find a way out
find a way out, know a road:
I'll sing a man of alder
for the eagle's grasping claws
for the toes of the wyvern.
So I'll get by that hardship
I'll manage the day's journey.

O my mother who bore me
bring here my war-gear
carry here my battledress!"

Father ordered, mother banned
a pair of witches said no
three nature-spirits forbade:
"Do not go, Kaukamieli:
many freaks are on your way
many marvels on your road!"

"What is the third freak?"

"The wolves are bridled ready
the bears in iron fetters
to meet you at the gateways
kept for Kaukamieli's head."

"Yes, I shall find a way out:
I shall sing a flock of sheep
a cluster of curly-wools
into Untamo's wolves' mouths
to the jaws of the bewitched.
So I'll get by that hardship.
Bring now my war-gear
carry here my battledress!"

She brought his war-gear
carried there his battledress.

Then Kaukamieli went off
and he took a dead man's skull
he struck the head off one gone
where a pole was left empty
kept for Kaukamieli's head
he sang a man of alder
to wander in front of him
for the eagle's grasping claws
and he sang a flock of sheep
a cluster of curly-wools
into Untamo's wolves' mouths
to the jaws of the bewitched.
So he got by that hardship
he managed the day's journey.

Now he squeezed into the house
and he drove under the roofs
to where caps were taken off
to where mittens were slipped off.

Ugly Herod in shirtsleeves
ate, drank at the table-head
at table in his shirtsleeves
wearing only his linen.

Handsome Kaukamieli said:
"You asked the crippled, the lame
you rowed the blind here in boats
drove the lame here on horseback
some carried gifts in ladles
some meanly measured with bowls
to this feast at Päivölä
to the Sariola revels
so why did you not ask me?
I did not bother
to measure out mere binfuls
for this feast at Päivölä
for the Sariola revels."

Ugly Herod in shirtsleeves
quickly grew angry and wild.
He uttered a word, spoke thus:
"Let us size up swords
let us look at blades to see
which one has the longer sword
whose blade is fairer:
he shall be the first to strike!"

Handsome Kaukamieli said:
"Let's go out into the yard:
in the yard blood is better
on grass readier

on heather fairer.
We would spoil the scrubbed benches
we would ruin the new house."

They went out into the yard
and they sized up swords
and they looked at blades.

Handsome Kaukamieli said:
"Your sword is longer
and your blade fairer:
my sword has been chipped by bones
and broken by skulls.
You shall be the first to strike."

Ugly Herod in shirtsleeves
struck at the man with his sword
but he did not cut the hide
nor take off the outer skin.
He struck once, he struck again
soon he hit him a third time:
this was no better than that.

Handsome Kaukamieli said:
"Let me try with my sword too
though it has been chipped by bones
and broken by skulls!"

He took the head off the shoulder
like the top off a turnip
or a fin off a whole fish.

Then handsome Kaukamieli
his head down, in bad spirits
and his helmet still askew
made his way homeward.
He met his mother:
"My offspring, my younger one
my child, my support
why are you in bad spirits
and your helmet still askew
as you make your way homeward:
has your cup been insulted
at that feast at Päivölä?"

"O my mother who bore me
had my cup been insulted
I'd insult a hundred men
take on a thousand others."

So his mother said:
"Have the women abused you?"

"O my mother who bore me
had women abused me, I'd
abuse a hundred women
take on a thousand others."

So his mother said:
"Have you been shamed with horses
at that feast at Päivölä?
Then buy a better stallion
with your father's harvest, with
what your parent has laid in."

"O my mother who bore me
had I been shamed with horses
I'd shame a hundred horses
take on a thousand others.
O my mother who bore me
for this I'll weep all my life:
I killed a man, a fellow
at that feast at Päivölä
at the Sariola revels
I killed a man, a fellow
and I don't know any place
where a blackguard may be hid
and an evil one may flee."

Mother knowingly answered:
"Out there once your father hid
upon the blue stretch of sea

in the great summers of war
in the weary battle-year."

Then handsome Kaukamieli
then went down into a ship
    stepped into a craft:
    he hoisted the masts
    as pines on a hill
launched out upon the blue sea
to the Island out at sea
    the land without trees.

And so he said in these words:
"Has the Island any place
is there land on the Island
where a blackguard may be hid
where an evil one may flee?"

    Both the youngest said
    and the oldest said:
"Yes, the Island has a place
there is land on the Island
where a blackguard may be hid
where an evil one may flee."

And they fussed over the craft
hauling the boat up on land
turning it over to dry.
Then handsome Kaukamieli
on the Island out at sea
in a single summer night
    laid a hundred maids
    knew a thousand brides.
Then handsome Kaukamieli
on a day among others
one morning among many
visited ten villages –
    well, half of a tenth:
    and he saw no house
where three men were not at home
    and there was no home
where there were not three fellows
    there was no fellow
who was not whetting his sword
kept for Kaukamieli's neck.
Then handsome Kaukamieli
    saw his doom coming
his day of distress dawning.

So one day among others
    he rose quite early
quite early in the morning.
He uttered a word, spoke thus:
"Ah, the day's sun has risen
the darling sun has come up:
I heard no cock, could not rise
heard no hen's chick, could not stir.
Ah, the day's sun has risen
the darling sun has come up:
the maids are left unembraced
    those embraced unlaid."

He launched his boat on the sea
    he hoisted the masts
he launched out on the blue sea
leaning on the hooked paddle.

Then the Island's young girls wept
the brides of the Island wept
till the mast was out of sight
and the iron rowlock dim.
    They put this in words:
"I do not weep for the masts
yearn for the iron rowlocks
but for him below the mast
guarding the iron rowlock."

And then Kaukamieli wept
till the Isle was out of sight
and the church roof-ridges dim.
    He himself put this in words:
"I do not weep for the Isle

yearn for the church roof-ridges
but for the Island's young girls
the maids of the headland's tip."

From there to there the road goes.

Arhippa Perttunen
Latvajärvi, Vuokkiniemi, Archangel Karelia
E. Lönnrot, 1834

38

Kaukamoinen II

A tomtit was brewing beer
a wagtail carried water
a bullfinch was chopping wood.

Who'd be the brewer of beer?
The curly lad Kalervo
he was a brewer of beer.
They got a barrel of beer
poured it into two basins:
the beer did not start to work
the man's mead did not rumble
nor did the man's vatful move.

A bee carried some honey
put it in the brewer's hands
gave it to the boiler's thumb:
the beer did not start to work
the man's mead did not rumble
nor did the man's vatful move.

The curly lad Kalervo's
      pair of pigs in heat
tumbled below a mountain
twisted about on a crag:
they were foaming at the mouth
were slobbering at the snout.
The curly lad Kalervo
carried it to the mixture
      brought it to the vat:
then the beer started to work
and the man's mead to rumble
and the man's vatful to move.

Unto drank and Vento drank
many a man, a young squire
many a splendid fellow
that way drove, smoothly gliding
that way Veitikkä made tracks
that way Kaukamoinen came
down to the famous man's home
      to the famed man's vat.

The curly lad Kalervo
drank a gallon, another
drank a third to go with them:
tipped a gallon, another
tipped a third to go with them
over Kaukamoinen's cloak.

Kaukoi grew angry and wild:
"A cloak is not for wetting
a coat is not for soiling:
this coat was obtained with blood
this cloak by twisting a heel.
Let us go out to the yard
out to the stockyard to fight!
This is narrow for swinging
for the uproar of man–play:
      let's go to the yard –
there is space to turn about."

      Kaukoi boy, sly man
drew the dagger from his thigh
tugged the grim one from its sheath
thought he'd strike him with the tip
      rip him with the edge

but he slashed with the whole blade
lashed out with all the iron.

As he was running homeward:
"O my mother, my father!
I have done a dreadful deed
done what I should not have done –
killed a man, brought down a head
brought a fine on my father
injury on my parent
on my brother a levy."

And his mother asked:
"O my Kaukoi, my offspring!
Was it a great iron wound
and a great steel wound?"

"A magpie flew right through it
a fox escaped from the hole
so great was the iron wound
so great the steel wound.

O my mother, my father!
Put provisions in a bag
put meal in a cloth
and put a day's food on top:
I shall run away
go into hiding!"

"O my Kaukoi boy!
He who leaves has far to go
he who flees into willows."

He went on a little way
went a short distance:
he met a forest.
"O forest, take wretched me!
Old man, woman of the woods
ancient mistress of the woods
take in wretched me!"

Old man, woman of the woods
answering replied:
"And where to put wretched you?
Trees before you will be felled
your hiding-place will be found
with the load brought home."

Kaukoi boy, sly man
went a little way further
went a short distance:
he met a meadow.
"O meadow, take wretched me!
Old man, woman of the fields
take in wretched me!"

"And where to put wretched you?
The grass will be mowed
by steel you will be torn up
with the load brought home."

He went on a little way
went a short distance:
now he met the sea.
"Sea, take wretched me!
Old man, woman of the sea
ancient mistress of the sea
take in wretched me!"

They answering said:
"And where to put wretched you?
In seines you will be lifted
in fish-nets carried
in knapsacks brought home."

Kaukoi boy, sly man
stepped into a boat that leaked
started rowing out to sea
rowed to Finland's shore:
the Finnish maids were washing
the blond-headed were bleaching.

Kaukoi boy, sly man
made to speak, his mouth spelt out:
"Is there some room in Finland
where a blackguard may be hid
an evildoer may flee?"

The Finnish maids gave answer:
"There is no room in Finland
where a blackguard may be hid
an evildoer may flee."

Kaukamo lay with them all
in a single summer night.
Kaukoi boy, sly man
himself sat down in the boat
started rowing out to sea
rowed out to the Island's shore.
The Finnish maids wept as long
as the sail-mast was in sight
long as the ship's frame was glimpsed
not weeping for the sail-mast
not shrieking for the ship's frame:
wept for him below the mast
shrieked for him beside the frame.
Kaukamoinen shrieked as long
as he heard the bats pounding.

Kaukoi boy, sly man
went on to the Island's shore:
the Island's maids were washing
the blond-headed were bleaching.

He asked the Island's maidens:
"Is there room on the Island
where a blackguard may be hid
an evildoer may flee?"

The Island's maids gave answer:
"There's no room on the Island
where a blackguard may be hid
an evildoer may flee."

Kaukoi boy, sly man
Kaukamo lay with them all
in a single summer night:
uncountable the widows
innumerable the wives.

The Island's eldest spoke out:
"There's no room on the Island
where a blackguard may be hid
an evildoer may flee."

Kaukoi boy, sly man
went to the shores of the sea
himself sat down in the boat
started rowing out to sea.
The Island's maids wept as long
as the sail-mast was in sight
long as the ship's frame was glimpsed
not weeping for the sail-mast
not shrieking for the ship's frame:
wept for him below the mast
shrieked for him beside the frame.
Kaukamoinen shrieked as long
as he heard the bats pounding.
Then he rowed out on the sea:
he found no land to lie on
no grove to rest in.

Singer unknown
Moloskovitsa – Tyrö, Ingria
A. Törneroos, T. Tallqvist, 1859

39

The Bond I

'Twas Ahti the Islander
wore out boots, a hundred pairs
getting the Island's maiden
courting Kyllikki.
An eternal bond was formed
an eternal vow was taken
before a copper icon:
Ahti would not go to war
Kyllikki would not go out.

Anni was Ahti's sister:
"Darling Ahti my brother
Kyllikki's in the village
now, at the gates of strangers."

Ahti the Islander said:
"Bring me my war-gear
carry here my battledress!"

Kyllikki for certain said:
"Dear Ahti the Islander
don't go off to war.
I had a dream as I slept
as I rested in slumber:
fire like a forge was burning
underneath Ahti's window."

"I don't believe woman's dreams
nor the lie of wives either:
I'm off, I won't heed."

Kyllikki for certain said
the housewife answered:
"We have some beer in the house
in a barrel of alder
behind an oak bung."

"I don't care for home-brewed beer:
I'd sooner drink seawater
off a tarry paddle-blade –
that is sweeter for my drink."

Kyllikki for certain said
the housewife answered:
"Don't go off to war:
we have money in the house!
The serf ploughed a viper-field
turned one full of snakes over:
the plough lifted a chest-lid
the sole raised a coin –
there are many hundreds there."

"I do not care for home-goods:
if I get one mark in war
I'll deem it better."

He slid his left ski in the snow
his right ski on to the road:
the left ski went sliding off
the heel of the right kicking.
He himself uttered, chattered:
"Where shall I rest for the night?"

Simana Kyöttinen
Repola, Olonets Karelia
D. E. D. Europaeus, 1845

40

The Bond II

Ahti boy, the darling boy
he took an eternal vow:
Ahti would not go to war
    for sixty summers
whether for want of silver
or yet for need of gold, nor
    Kyllikki go out
for need of another man.
Already on the first night
Kyllikki had had enough
had enough of the elbow
her fill of the angry hand.

Now the boat of Ahti wept
the hundred-rowlocked one yearned:
    "I stretch on my stocks
and I rot on my shavings
while the air's most loathsome birds
are shitting on my red side
and the earth's lowliest worms
are living beneath my ribs."

He himself put this in words:
    "Teuri whom I know
    Kuuro who is near
shall be war-mate to Ahti
shall follow the mighty one!"

Ahti put this into words:
"Let Teuri prepare for war
to be war-mate to Ahti
to follow the mighty one!"

Father was at the window
was whittling an axe-handle:
"Teuri has no time for war:
he has married a young wife
has taken his own mistress.
The nipple's still unfingered
    the buttocks unwhipped
    the loins untickled."

Teuri was beside the stove
shod one foot upon the stove
shod the other on the floor
at the gates girded himself
outside he strutted about.

His was not a great big spear
nor a little tiny spear:
it was a middle-sized spear.
    He put in his spear
    with the other spears.

Ahti's boat put out to sea
uncared for by any arms
unhelped by any shoulders
off the rollers made of steel
    the copper lining.
The old rowed, their heads trembled:
the young rowed and their oars swung
the shafts squeaked like hazel-grouse
    the thwarts cooed like grouse
the prow chanted like a swan
the stern croaked like a raven.

Then it chilled with a great cold
    frost was freezing hard
when it chilled Ahti at sea
chilled with ice a cubit thick
snow fell deep as a ski-stick
deep as a spear-haft it swirled
on a single autumn night.

He made a ski for a year
he steamed his ski for a spring
slid his left ski in the snow
    just like a brown fox
    or else a white hare.
The left ski bent at the hole
the stick snapped at the ferrule.

Lari Bogdanov
Uhtua, Archangel Karelia
A. A. Borenius, 1872

41

The Orphan I

A poor, feeble man
a plodder, a weak workman
scratched ten furrows round
and round one tree-stump
and he sowed ten seeds
between ten furrows.
The stump split in two
and two boys were born:
one of them rose in Untoi
and one grew in Kaarasa.
He who rose up in Untoi
rose up to be Untamoi
he who grew in Kaarasa
grew to be Kalervikkoi.

Kalervikko sowed his oats
in front of Untamoi's door.
Untamoi had a black ewe
it ate all Kalervoi's oats:
Kalervoi had a fierce dog
and it slew Untamoi's ewe.

Untoi grew angry and wild
raised a war from his fingers
a host from his toes
a nation from his heel-veins.

Kalervoi's woman looked out
from the window by the door:
"The sky has a glint of blue
and the cloud is glowing red."

Kalervoi himself
looked from the corner window:
"The cloud is not glowing red
nor is the sky glinting blue:
it is a shirt glowing red
trousers glinting blue.
Untamoi's war is coming
to cut Kalervoi to shreds."

It cut the great, cut the small
cut down children in cradles
the unknowing in their shawls
and the infants in their clothes.

And Untoi said to his serfs:
"O my serfs, my own
my nimble servant-children
go from here and see
whether anyone is left
from the wreck of the great war
in the train of the great host
in the field where it passed by:
leap with the leap of a wolf
walk with the toes of a stoat!"

The serfs went to see.
Yes, someone was left
from the wreck of the great war
in the field where it passed by:
a boy rocked in a cradle
the hair on his head was fluff
the shirt on him was linen
the strings of silk were humming
the lime cradle was rattling
the maple beam was creaking.

The serfs showed their swords to him
but the boy only chuckled
so the serfs chattered:
"Now there's sure to be trouble:
an enemy has moved in."

The serfs said to Untamoi:
"Yes, someone is left
from the wreck of the great war
in the train of the great host
in the field where it passed by."

And Untoi said to his serfs:
"Make a fire in the market
a bonfire beneath the walls
of hard-wearing birch
thirty sledges full
of ash a hundred
of supple maple
fifty sledges full:
put the boy into the fire
and push him into the flames!"

The boy was put in the fire
pushed into the flames.
He did not burn in the fire
nor blaze in the flames:
the boy sat upon the fire
a golden hook in his hand
poking the embers
spreading the cinders.

Oute
Soikkola, Ingria
V. Porkka, 1883

42

The Orphan II

Kaleva's unhappy son
when first of his mother born
    on five water-rocks
soon as he was three nights old
he broke up his swaddling-bands.
He was seen to promise well
found to be a fine fellow:
he was sold to a stranger
was traded to Karelia
to the smith Köyrötyinen.
He was put to mind a child:
cared for it, dug out its eyes
fed the child, himself ate too
he killed the child with disease
he burned the cradle with fire.

He asked for work at evening
the master for evening work
the mistress for morning work.
Let the serf be told his task
the task be given a name:
he was told to build a fence.
Now he was building the fence:
    tall pines from their place
    he set for a fence
whole spruces from the backwoods
    he drove in for stakes
then he bound them with earthworms
with lizards he fastened them.
Then the smith Köyrötyinen
    came himself to look
at the Kaleva boy's fence
    at the gold-buckle's felling:
well, he saw some heads moving
    heard some skulls rustling
in the Kaleva boy's fence
    in the gold-buckle's felling.

At evening he asked for work
the master for evening work
the mistress for morning work:
he was put to herd cattle.
The smith Köyrötty's mistress
baked a stone inside his loaf
pressed a rock into his cake
    under it laid oats
    over it spread wheat
put it in the herdsman's breast:
    "Don't eat this before
    the cattle come home."

He thrust his knife in the stone
struck it hard against the rock:
"How shall I pay the maid's jeers
the maid's jeers, the wife's laughter
the evil woman's wages?
Go, sun, towards the spruces
roll towards the grove of wheat
break up at the junipers."

He fed the cattle to bears
    drove the bears homeward
and the herd to the bright farm
made a horn out of cow-bones
out of ox-horns a rattle
and he came along playing

came tooting over the heaths.
And Köyrötty's mistress said:
"The Lord God be praised!
The horn blows, the cattle come:
where did the serf get his horn
the blacksmith his smooth whistle?
It is blowing through my ears
shrilling through my head."

And he drove the bears homeward
and the herd to the bright farm
told the dame to tie them up:
"Go and tie the cows up, go
and tether the fully-grown."

"Herdsmen used to tie up cows
herdsmen tether the full-grown."

He put the bears in fetters
tethered the wolves in irons:
he instructed his bears, talked
by word of mouth to his wolves:
"Tear the thigh of the mistress."

A bear seized hold of her heel
tore the thigh of the mistress.
So he avenged the maid's jeers
settled the wife's laughter, paid
the evil woman's wages.

Singer unknown
Kemi, North Ostrobothnia
Copied from the manuscript of an unknown
collector by K. Ganander, ca 1760

43

The Orphan III

My mother brought up
brought up many chicks
a great crowd of swans:
saw them all growing
but not when they were grown up.
She put the chicks on a fence
the swans in river-water:
one she shooed into Finland
one she bore to Karelia.
From the one formed in Finland
Uttamo was formed:
from that grown in Karelia
Kalerva grew up.

Uttamo had a fine ewe.
Now, Kalervainen's fierce dog
ate the ewe of Uttamo.
Utta grew angry and wild
made a war from his fingers
strife from the tips of his palms.
Uttamo went to war, put
small alders in silver belts
adzes on tree-stumps' shoulders.

Kalerva's young daughter-in-law
looked through the window:
now, what was the foggy fog
and what the thick smoke?
It was not a foggy fog
nor was it thick smoke:
Uttamo's war was coming.

It killed the great, killed the small.
Kalerva's one son was left
five or ten years old
swinging in the crib
and rocking in the cradle.
The sturdy cradle thudded
the house of sprucewood rumbled
and the floor of limewood rocked
with the little boy's rocking.

Uttamo pondered:
where now should the boy be put
where be done to death?

Put the baby in the sea:
the boy was put in the sea.

He sent out a serf to look
at the end of two, three nights.
The serf brought word home: the boy
was not dying in the sea.
A gold ladle in his hand
measured water from the sea:
just two ladlefuls were left –
if it were rightly measured
there would be part of a third.

Uttamo pondered:
where now should the boy be put
where be done to death?

Put the baby in the fire –
of ashwood fivescore sledgefuls
fivescore armfuls of tar-wood:
the boy was put in the fire.

He sent out a serf to look
at the end of two, three nights.
The serf brought word home: the boy
was not dying in the fire.
A little hook in his hand
was stirring up the embers
    was poking the sparks.

    Uttamo pondered:
where now should the boy be put
    where be done to death?

Put the boy as a herdsman
in an honest smith's village
for the smith's honest woman.

Now, that smith's honest mistress
    baked a loaf of stone
    cooked a cake of rock
    smoothed the top with flour
for the herdsman's provisions.

The herdsman was a small boy –
he watched the sun lengthening:
now was time for the orphan
the fatherless one's supper.
He drew his knife from its sheath
he took the cake from his bag:
the cake was fair to look on
there was chaff beneath the crust.
He stuck the knife in the stone
struck it hard against the rock.
"O whore of the grey top-knot
O you smith's honest mistress
who have baked a loaf of stone
    cooked a cake of rock
for the herdsman's provisions!
I've wept for my father's knife:
so you'll weep for your blazed cows.
    I'll make a flute of Tiny
a horn out of Thirsty's leg:
    I'll play as I walk
to the marsh, blast on the heath
    the sheep to she-wolves
    all the cows to bears."

Levo Manninen
Repola, Olonets Karelia
A. A. Borenius, 1872

44

The Incest I

It was stern Tuiretuinen
wanton child Lemminkäinen
    came to the market
    to pay his land-tax
    to take in his dues
    to play with a maid.
The maid went bump in the sleigh
descended upon his furs:
"Death be to this sleigh of yours
    a pox on your fur!"

He showed off, he talked about
money-bags with mouths of gold
knives with handles of silver:
the maid went bump in the sleigh
descended upon his furs.
The hand within a mitten
was upon the stallion's rein
the hand without a mitten
was under the maid's nipple
and the foot within a boot
was upon the sleigh-runner
and the foot without a boot
was under the maiden's thigh.

He struck the horse with the reins:
the horse ran, the journey sped
the sledge rolled and the road fled.

    He inquired, he said
at the end of two, three nights:
"Is yours a great family too
are they famous, your people?"
"It is neither great nor small.
There are just my five brothers:
one was stern Tuurittuinen
wanton child Lemminkäinen."

He flung himself off the sleigh
    struck with his two hands
the two sides of his body
like the two planks of the grave
the five gates of Viipuri.

    "Mother who bore me
    put meal in a cloth
lay provisions in a bag
that I may flee my bad deeds
that I may conceal my crimes:
I have shamed my mother's child."

"My offspring, my only son
don't go away and don't stay:
    go to those spruces
    dash off to the pines
while the dogs are on the loose
the townsmen are on the move."

Ondrei Sotikainen
Suistamo, Ladoga Karelia
D. E. D. Europaeus, 1845

45

The Incest II

Now, a boy came from Tuuri
whistled out of Viipuri
he whined from under Narva
after taking in his tithes
after paying his land-tax
after giving his poll-tax.

He saw a maid on a headland
a golden-locks on dry grass
a bead-aproned on the hay.
The stern boy Tuurikkaine
the full-blooded roguish boy
began to talk to the maid
banter with the plaited head:
"Step, maiden, into my sledge
into the back of my sleigh
    to eat my apples
    and to bite my nuts!"

The maiden heavily cursed
    and swore grievously:
"May That One eat your apples
and may That One bite your nuts!"

The stern boy Tuurikkaine
the full-blooded roguish boy
did not know then what to do.

He displayed, he covered up
money-bags with mouths of gold
knives with handles of silver:
the maid flopped into the sledge.

He got the maid in the sledge
    to eat his apples
    and to bite his nuts.
He struck the horse with the reins
stallion with the beaded whip:
he went on a little way
    went a short distance
he travelled a verst or so.
The stern boy Tuurikkaine
the full-blooded roguish boy
began to ask the maiden
to question the plaited head:
    "Where are you from, maid?"

The maid answering replied:
    "I am a maiden
    from where lands are blue
    lands are blue, trees red
    the pine-sprouts are tin
    the fir-tops silver."

The stern boy Tuurikkaine
the full-blooded roguish boy
struck his two palms together
like the two gates of the grave
he stuck out his five fingers
like Estonia's five beams:
"O what a poor boy am I
I have done what I should not:
I've taken my own sister
I've gone with my own sibling
    lured my own berry."

Singer unknown
Hevaa, Kaprio, Ingria
V. Porkka, 1883

46

The Sower I

Sämsä the Pellervo boy
lay with his sister
and slept with his mother's child:
when he knew doom was coming
his day of distress dawning
    he knew he must flee
    to dark Pohjola
among the eaters of men
and the drowners of heroes.

Ahti kept brooding, wanted
something to sweeten his land
something to soften his fields
someone to burn off his grass
to produce a hardy crop
    make a better ear.
And he rattled his money
    jingled his silver
for two, three days: the money
rattled upon the table
Huotola's silver jingled.

    The wolf, the wild boy
was a madman for money
he squandered all for silver
he spent all for Hiisi's gold.

    Who would fetch Sämpsä
win over Pellervöinen
    to sow these lands now
scatter the seed on the fields?
Folk were beginning to brood:
    who would fetch Sämpsä
win over Pellervöinen?

    The wolf, scratcher boy
bought a heavier fur coat
the better to bear the cold:
he went off to fetch Sämpsä
was a madman for money
he squandered all for silver
he spent all for Hiisi's gold
he went off to fetch Sämpsä
win over Pellervöinen.

    Ahti kept brooding
spat into his eyes:
    "Shame, you evil-looking one
when you ate my mother's ewe
in the best season for wool
the sweet time of summer hay
I was lying without milk
was living without butter."

The wolf, the mild-weather boy
did not care much for wages
    did not ask for gain:
he went off to fetch Sämpsä
to win over Pellervi.

He said as he arrived there:
"Ahti keeps wanting, wanting
something to sweeten his land
something to soften his fields
someone to burn off his grass
you to bring forth a hardy
crop and make a better ear."

"Little brother beside me
 you did a good thing
as I was coming this way."

Sämsä the Pellervö boy
 took up a few seeds
 a mixture of seeds
black specks from an ermine's tail
 from a swan's footprints.

 "You did a good thing
as I was coming this way:
you thawed the mouths of rivers
you thinned out the ice on lakes
you sent fish towards the shores
sliding things to the marshes.
From there young men can get them
 catch the best supply.
 Someone was cooking
as I came this way: there is
a fine pike at Kalehva's."

 He came here to sow
 to scatter the seed:
sowed the marshes, heather grew
sowed damp hollows, birches rose
 sowed the hills, pines grew
the fresh lands for birdcherries
narrow lands for junipers
 choice spots for alders.

Ahti would run out of lands
before Sämpsä out of seeds:
 southward he sowed first
 then he flung eastward
he blustered on the north side
 and finished westward.

Singer unknown
Kaavi (?), North Karelia
C. A. Gottlund, ca 1835

47

The Sower II

Why are our oats not growing
our rye not rising
not growing in the clearing
nor springing in the hollow
nor yet on Sämpsä's hummock
nor yet on Pellervoi's hill?

For this our oats do not grow
and our rye is not rising
not growing in the clearing
nor springing in the hollow
nor yet on Sämpsä's hummock
nor yet on Pellervoi's hill:
Sämpsä was lying in bed
the seven-crossed on his back
the ten-buttoned on his side
his legs could be seen in bed
    on slats his red braids.

There were none to raise Sämpsä
    lift up Pellervoi.

The winter-boy, little lad
    rose to raise Sämpsä
    lift up Pellervoi:
he took a stallion of wind
took a colt that was a gale
began to ride on the wind
    flutter on the gale
and he blew the trees leafless
the grass till it lost sweetness
the maids till they lost their bloom.

And he went to Sämpsä's bed:
"Get up, Sämpsä, from your bed
seven-crossed one, off your back
ten-buttoned one, off your side!"

And Sämpsä indeed answered:
"I will not get up for you:
I will for the other man.
    You did well to come
    still better to stay:
you have blown the trees leafless
the grass till it lost sweetness
the maids till they lost their bloom
blown the cabbages headless
    the turnips rootless."

Well now, who would raise Sämpsä
    lift up Pellervoi?
The summer-boy, little lad
    rose to raise Sämpsä
    lift up Pellervoi:
he took a stallion of wind
took a colt that was a gale
began to ride on the wind
    flutter on the gale
and he blew the trees leafy
blew the grass till it was sweet
blew heads on the cabbages
    roots on the turnips
the maids till they were blooming.

And he drove to Sämpsä's bed:
"Get up, Sämpsä, from your bed

seven-crossed one, off your back
ten-buttoned one, off your side!"

Sämpsä answering replied:
"Now I will get up for you
but not for the other man.
You did well to come
still better to stay:
you have blown the trees leafy
blown the grass till it was sweet
blown heads on the cabbages
blown roots upon the turnips
the maids till they were blooming!"

Kati
Soikkola, Ingria
V. Porkka, 1883

48

The Bear

Where was Bruin born
the honey-paw turned over?
There Bruin was born
the honey-paw turned over –
in the upper air
upon the Great Bear's shoulders.

Where was it let down?
In a sling it was let down
in a silver sling
a golden cradle:
then it went to roam the woods
to tread the North Land.

Don't hurt the dung-shank
and don't kill the milk-bearer:
mother has more work
the parent big trouble if
the little boy is naughty.

Olli Timonen
Kitee, North Karelia
O. A. F. Lönnbohm, 1894

49

The Oak I

I hurried to God's revels
Väinämöinen's assizes
the feast of Kalerva's son.
    Beer was brought to drink:
below was yeast, on top foam
    below was fine yeast
    on top was white foam
in the middle was brown beer.
Where shall I pour off my foam
and where get rid of my yeast?
I'll pour at father's window
at my brother's gateway, at
the well-path of my bearer.
There a steadfast oak-tree grew
a tall rowan-tree rose up
    branched out its branches
    straightened out its boughs
    spread abroad its leaves.
There the Creator's birds flew.
I sought one to fell the oak
    cut the tall tree short
    chop down the rowan:
I found none to fell the oak
    cut the tall tree short
    chop down the rowan.

Now, it came into my mind
    caught fire in my heart:
I had an only brother.
On Sundays I fed him grouse
on weekdays I fed him perch
he was brought up on white bread
    kept on buttermilk:
    when he could not eat
    butter, he ate pork.
I went, I sought my brother
searched Finland, searched the Island
searched Turku, feeling about
glancing all over the town
on the two sides of Moscow
on both sides of Kaprio
and there I found my brother
    among the smith-men
among the worthy women
in the street of the splendid:
    he was buying gold
    purchasing silver.

"O brother, my mother's child
for whom are you buying gold
    purchasing silver?"

My brother answering said:
"For no one but my sister."

I gripped him by the upper
arm, clasped him by the shoulders:
    "Come home, my brother
    come and fell the oak
    chop down the rowan!"

    My brother came home
    came and felled the oak
    cut the tall tree short
    chopped down the rowan
felled the oak for sticks and stakes

of the branches made beer-mugs
of the small wood made goblets:
of the pieces left over
he built a bath-house for me.

And the village women said:
"Could it be Kirjamo's church
or else Raisu's Rakvere?"

Maioi answering replied:
"It is not Kirjamo's church
nor yet Raisu's Rakvere:
it is five brothers' bath-house
the chapel of two sisters."

Singer unknown
Soikkola, Ingria
J. Länkelä, 1858

50

The Oak II

There were once four maids
four maids and three men
mowing a meadow:
what they mowed they raked
teased into a swath
piled up a rakeful
gathered in haycocks
and started a rick.

A Lapp came from Turja's land
burnt the hay to ash
and the wind came from the North
bore the ash away
to a mountain slope
on which grew a frightful tree
an incomparable tree
that was bushy with branches
was spreading with leaves:
it stopped the sun from shining
the moon from gleaming
from it cold came to the corn
frightful for the water-fish.

Someone was sought to fell it:
now, a man rose from the sea
who was a thumb long
and three fingers high.
He sharpened his axe
upon three whetstones
on four scraping-stones
on seven oilstones
upon eight boulders.
He struck the tree with the axe
the oak with the even blade:
fire flashed from the axe
and a chip fled from the oak.

Now the oak-tree had been felled
across Pohjoinen's river
a bridge to the timeless place
for a traveller to go
a man to dark Pohjola
to the man-eating village
the village that drowns heroes.
He has an eternal bridge
who was eaten without cause
who was killed without disease
without the Creator done
to death, in dark Pohjola
in the man-eating village:
there is meat without bones there
there is calf without gristle
for the hungry man to eat
a bite for the one in want.

Lari Bogdanov
Uhtua, Archangel Karelia
A. A. Borenius, 1872

51

The Great Ox

The ox grew beautifully
the bull was getting too fat:
its head roared in Häme Land
its tail drooped in Tornio.
All day long a swallow flew
from its neck to its tail's tip
all month long a squirrel ran
between the horns of the ox:
still it did not reach the end
it did not get there at all.

A slaughterer was searched for.
A black man rose from the sea:
first he forced it to its knees
then he turned it on its side
there moved it on to its back.
And there a great kill was made
with a hundred tubs of meat
with seven boatfuls of blood
six barrels of fat:
from this ointments are taken
from this spells are worked
by which hates are hurled away
the burnings of fire burnt up
the power of fire overpowered
the ills of fire healed.

Singer unknown
Ostrobothnia
K. Ganander(?), before 1789

52

The Great Pig

I went visiting
my aunt in heaven.
What was I made to eat there? –
bones from meat and heads from fish
and crusts from hard loaves.
What was I made to do there? –
made to go herding
some great German pigs
some well-formed young ones
and sheep with blazed heads.
The pig swelled to a great size
the porker grew terrible:
it grew to half a cubit
its tail a hundred cubits
its snout to six axe-handles.
Ukko went to slaughter it
with a golden club
a copper hammer
a silver mallet:
the porker turned its snout round
and gaped at its tail.
Ukko fled up a spruce-tree
other gods up other trees
the little lords up pine-trees.
Ukko scolded from the spruce
he nagged from the juniper:
"Patience, patience, poor porker.
When the coming year is come
you'll not root another year
not root at Tora River
nor on Tora River's bank:
I'll hit hard between the eyes
so that the pork will crackle!"

Singer unknown
Sakkola, Karelian Isthmus
A. Ahlqvist, 1854

53

The Elk I

Clever Finn Vuojolainen
handsome Lapp Kauppi
in autumn shaped a left ski
through the winter a right ski.
Himself, Finn Vuoljalainen
glided on what he had shaped
pushed the left ski on the snow
grasped a ski-stick in his hand:
there was nothing in the woods
that they would not overtake.
    He kicked out again:
    the ear did not hear.
    He kicked one more time:
    the eye did not glimpse.
    He kicked a third time
and now he was hard on Hiisi's elk.

Then he uttered, chattered thus:
"What children are in Lapland
will all be picking up sticks
what women are in Lapland
will all be washing up pots
    to cook Hiisi's elk
what men there are in Lapland
will all be sharpening knives
    skinning Hiisi's elk!"
Now the elk happened to hear
as it stood below the wall.
Hiisi gave the elk advice
as a mother would her child:
    "If you're Hiisi's elk
    with one kick away
stretch the bridle of iron!
    With a second kick
break open the pen of oak!"

    The elk trotted off
and the wild reindeer kicked off
across marshes, across lands
across hills of bare brushwood.
I cannot recover suns
    nor can ask for moons:
    turn, sun, to the woods
    twist, moon, in the woods.
I have no load of my own:
the load is Tapio's load.
May an iron hill meet you
may a fiery birch face you
    may a tree bar you
a river run for your drink
    a lake for your rest.

Aleksei Burushka and Iivana Ratinen
Suistamo, Ladoga Karelia
S. Sirelius, 1847

54

The Elk II

Wanton boy Lemmingöine
in autumn shaped a left ski
in winter planed a right ski
in summer he shaped a staff:
he got the left ski to push
the right for the heel to strike
pushed the left ski on the snow
and carried his two ski-sticks
on either side of his skis.
One ski-stick cost him a mark
the other cost a brown fox.

Wanton Lemmingöine said:
"There's nothing now in the woods
that they will not overtake
 whirring on two wings
 running on four feet!"

Now Hiizi happened to hear
the evil spirits to spy:
Hiizi constructed an elk
the evil spirits conceived
snatched the head from a hummock
the body from rotten wood
 legs from a fence-pole
 ears from pond-lilies
the eyes from pond-lily buds.

 Hiizi drove his elk
 the reindeer its rear:
 "Go, run, Hiizi's elk
 reindeer, trot along
to Lapland's timber regions
 Pohjo's sloping yards:
 use your legs, great elk
kick the corner of the hut
and tip over the cauldron
spill the soup in the fireplace
spoil the meat in the ashes!"

Then the dog of Pohjo barked
then the girl of Pohjo wept
then the wives of Pohjo laughed
 then the folk marvelled.
Wanton Lemmingöine heard
 heard the wife laughing
 saw the girl weeping
 heard the dog barking.
 From his skis he said
from his snow-shoes he shouted:
"Why were the wives laughing here
 the girls weeping here?"

The women of Pohjo said:
"Hiizi's elk has run this way
 the reindeer trotted
and the great elk used its legs
kicked the corner of the hut
has tipped over the cauldron
spilt the soup in the fireplace
spoilt the meat in the ashes."

So wanton Lemmingöine
 himself spoke like this
as he set off on his skis:
"There is nothing in the woods
that they will not overtake!"

So wanton Lemmingöine
the first time he kicked
the eye did not glimpse.
The next time he kicked
the ear did not hear.
The third time he aimed
at the loins of Hiizi's elk
at the calves of the reindeer.

So wanton Lemmingöine
was stroking its back
was patting its coat:
he made a shed of maple
he built a stable of oak.
Wanton Lemmingöine said:
"How fitting just to lie here
with a young maiden
under a growing girl's arm
on the back of the blue elk
on the calves of the reindeer!"

Then Hiizi's elk grew angry
grew angry, became inflamed
smashed the maple shed
shattered the oaken stable
then Hiizi's elk fled
the reindeer ran off.

So wanton Lemmingöine
the first time he kicked
the left ski bent at the hole
the ski-stick where the disc is.

Simana Kieleväinen
Jyskyjärvi, Archangel Karelia
A. A. Borenius, 1872

55

Elk and Snake

An elk ran from Hiisi's land
kicked a cowberry on the heath
it gnawed a twig as it ran
drank a lake when it thirsted.
It ran into a new house
into a splendid chamber:
it saw a snake drinking beer
a worm taking refreshment.
It struck the snake on the ribs
the worm under the liver:
the snake wept over its ribs
the poor worm for its liver.

Who would be the snake's milker
the looser of the worm's flood?
Margaret's mother was such:
she would be the snake's milker.
　　The snake gave brown milk
　　the worm a white flood
into the striped milking-pail.
The milk fell upon the ground:
　　there brown trees sprang up
　　brown trees and blue lands
yellow boughs of juniper
　　silver fir-tree tops.

Oute
Hevaa, Kaprio, Ingria
A. A. Borenius, 1877

56

The Fishing

Sturdy old Väinämöinen
was fishing, using
a hand-net, turning about
at a misty headland's tip
at a foggy island's end:
the silver line whined
the copper rod twitched
the golden twine jingled, as
Väinämöinen fished.

A salmon stuck on his hook
a trout on his fish-iron:
he drew it into his boat
guided it on to his planks.
He looked, he turned it over
did not know that fish—
rather smooth for a whitefish
rather pale for a lake-trout
too scaleless for a salmon
not webbed enough for a seal
too unbraided for a maid
too beltless for Väinö's girl
too earless to keep at home.

The old Väinämöinen said:
"In my belt is Väinö's knife
the pot is in the smith's forge:
the salmon is mine to cut
the fish is mine to chop up
into pieces for breakfast
into bits for the morning."

Into the sea the salmon
splashed and the bright fish twisted:
showed a right shoulder
toes of a left foot
showed nameless fingers
upon the seventh water
on the sixth billow
upon the ninth wave.

"You silly old man
you did not know how to keep
Ahti's only child
Vellamo's watery maid.
I was not coming
a salmon for you to cut
a fish for you to chop up
into pieces for breakfast:
no, I was coming
to be an old one's mainstay
support for one who trembles
a bringer of fire homeward
a kindler of light
to lay out your bed
settle your pillow.
Cares have been given to you
a heavy heart has crushed you."

Ontrei Malinen
Vuonninen, Vuokkiniemi, Archangel Karelia
E. Lönnrot, 1833

57

Leavetaking I

A boy was found in a marsh.
No one knew what to name him:
they sought someone to christen
all the people a baptist.

Father called him Ilmori
mother called him her sweet boy
the sisters, gallant warrior
the brothers, mere layabout
the other kin, the nameless.

Old Väinämöinen spoke: "Would
his head were struck with a log
or hammered with a crowbar!"

The half-a-month-old boy spoke
the fortnight-old one sang out:
"O you old Väinämöinen
there was a greater reason
a weightier cause why your
head was not struck with a log
nor hammered with a crowbar
when you lay with your mother
on the shore, on the sea-rock
on the hard, gravelly beach."

Then the old Väinämöinen
was in bad spirits
then he plodded, his head down
looked about, his cap askew
sang a copper-bottomed boat
plunged to the depths of the sea
to the earth-mothers below
up to the heavens above
into the whirlpool's gullet.

Singer unknown
Vuokkiniemi, Archangel Karelia
M. A. Castrén, 1839

58

Leavetaking II

Mariatta, fair youngest child
wore down the timber threshold
with her fine skirt-hems
and the floorboard too
with the heels of her hide shoes
more timber above her head
with her blue silk bands.

Mariatta, fair youngest child
drank milk from no cow
that had been sporting with bulls
sat in the sledge of no horse
that had been among stallions.

The poor one took to herding
and the wretch to driving cows.
Evil Tuurituinen's boy
thereon lay with Mariatta
seduced the tin-breasted one.

Mariatta brought forth a boy
of whom no father was known:
father called him Ilmari
mother called him her sweet boy
the other kin, the nameless
the brothers, mere layabout.

The priest came to christen him
Virokanas to baptise
and Palvonen to hold him.
Now, he put this into words:
"Who will be brought here
to be this evil one's judge?"
The old Väinämöinen said:
"Carry the boy to a marsh
and strike his head with a log!"

The half-a-month-old boy spoke
the fortnight-old one boomed out:
"You silly old man
you have judged badly
misapplied the law."

And the priest sprinkled the child
then he dubbed the child
King of Metsola
Guardian of Rahansaari.

Väinämöinen grew angry
then, was angry and ashamed.
He sang a boat of copper
formed an iron-bottomed punt
he launched out, he sailed away
down into the whirlpool's throat
where the whale's tongue was turning:
there he lodged for all his days
there sank for longer
vanished for ever.

Ontrei Malinen
Vuonninen, Vuokkiniemi, Archangel Karelia
E. Lönnrot, 1833

59

The Messiah I

A berry called from the hill
a cranberry from the heath:
"Come, maid, and pick me
copper-belted one, choose me
before the slug devours me
and the black worm gobbles me."

The Virgin lady Mary
the dear merciful mother
dressed herself and decked herself
prettily adorned her head
with a fair white cloth:
she went to pick the berry
to look for the cranberry.
So she went to the hills – tell! –
found the berry on the hill
the cranberry on the heath:
it was plainly a berry
a natural cranberry:
she was too low to eat it
from the ground, and too high from a tree.

She dragged a pole from the heath
and stood upon it
threw the berry in her lap
from her lap up to her belt
from her belt up to her breasts
from her breasts up to her lip
from her lip on to her tongue:
thence it slipped to her belly.

She was fulfilled, she was filled
by it, grew thickset from it
put on flesh from it:
she carried a heavy womb
a full and troubled belly
she carried for two, three months
for three months, four months
for four months, five months
for seven, eight months
for a round nine months
after old wives' reckonings
and half a tenth month.

So in the tenth month
she was struck by a wife's pain
girl's fire was kindled
woman's trouble came.
She uttered a word, spoke thus:
"Piltti my little lassie
seek a bath in the village
a bath-house in Saraja
where a wretch can be cared for
one in trouble can be helped."

Piltti her little lassie
quick to take orders
easy to persuade
both ran and made haste
bringing down highlands
lifting up lowlands
to the ugly Herod's house.

Ugly Herod in shirtsleeves
ate, drank at the table-head
at table in his shirtsleeves

wearing only his linen
    lived like a rich man.
The ugly Herod's mistress
trod the centre of the floor
bustled at the floorboard-joint.
Piltti her lassie said: "I
seek a bath in the village
a bath-house in Saraja
where a wretch can be cared for
one in trouble can be helped."

The ugly Herod's mistress
uttered a word, speaking thus:
"There's no bath in the village
no bath-house in Saraja:
there's a stable on Tapo Hill
a room in the fir-clump house
where the whores have their babies
scarlet women their children."

Piltti her little lassie
    soon ran and made haste
said when she had come from there:
"There's no bath in the village
no bath-house in Saraja.
Ugly Herod in shirtsleeves
ate, drank at the table-head
at table in his shirtsleeves
wearing only his linen
    lived like a rich man.
The ugly Herod's mistress
trod the centre of the floor
bustled at the floorboard-joint.
And I said in these words: 'I
seek a bath in the village
a bath-house in Saraja
where a wretch can be cared for
one in trouble can be helped.'
The ugly Herod's mistress:
'There's no bath in the village
no bath-house in Saraja:
there's a stable on Tapo Hill
a room in the fir-clump field
where the whores have their babies
scarlet women their children.' "

    Woman's trouble came.
The Virgin lady Mary
said a second time:
    "Both run and make haste
    seek a bath in the village
a bath-house in Saraja
where a wretch can be cared for
one in trouble can be helped."

Piltti her little lassie
    quick to take orders
    easy to persuade
    both ran and made haste
    lifting up lowlands
    bringing down highlands.

Ugly Herod in shirtsleeves
ate, drank at the table-head
at table in his shirtsleeves
wearing only his linen
    lived like a rich man.
Piltti her lassie said: "I
seek a bath in the village
a bath-house in Saraja
where a wretch can be cared for
one in trouble can be helped."

The ugly Herod's mistress
trod the centre of the floor
bustled at the floorboard-joint
uttered a word, speaking thus:
"There's no bath in the village
no bath-house in Saraja:
there's a stable on Tapo Hill

a room in the fir-clump field
where the whores have their babies
scarlet women their children."

Piltti her little lassie
both ran and made haste
said when she had come from there:
"There's no bath in the village
no bath-house in Saraja.
The ugly Herod's mistress
uttered a word, speaking thus:
'There's a stable on Tapo Hill
a room in the fir-clump field
where the whores have their babies
scarlet women their children.'
Just like that, she said."

A little time passed
and still the pain came
pressing forcefully
woman's trouble came
her womb turned heavy
filled her belly with trouble.
She uttered a word, spoke thus:
"Piltti my little lassie
seek a bath in the village
a bath-house in Saraja
where a wretch can be cared for
one in trouble can be helped."

Piltti her little lassie
both ran and made haste
lifting up lowlands
bringing down highlands
to the ugly Herod's house.

Ugly Herod in shirtsleeves
ate, drank at the table-head
at table in his shirtsleeves
lived like a rich man.
The ugly Herod's mistress
trod the centre of the floor
bustled at the floorboard-joint.
Piltti her little lassie
uttered a word, spoke thus: "I
seek a bath in the village
a bath-house in Saraja
where a wretch can be cared for
one in trouble can be helped."

The ugly Herod's mistress
uttered a word, speaking thus:
"There's no bath in the village
no bath-house in Saraja:
there's a stable on Tapo Hill
a room in the fir-clump field
where the whores have their babies
scarlet women their children."

Piltti her little lassie
both ran and made haste
said when she came back from there:
"There's no bath in the village
no bath-house in Saraja
where a wretch can be cared for
one in trouble can be helped.
The ugly Herod's mistress
uttered a word, speaking thus:
'There's a stable on Tapo Hill
a room in the fir-clump field
where the whores have their babies
scarlet women their children.' "

A little time passed
woman's trouble came
her womb turned heavy
filled her belly with trouble.
She took a bath-whisk for ward
in her fists gathered her skirt
in her hands bundled her dress
herself put this into words:
"It is for me to depart

as of old for the hired man
or for the serf, the hireling."

She stepped, tripped along
to the room in the fir-clump
to the stable on Tapo Hill.
She said in these words:
"Now breathe, my good horse
over my troubled belly
let some bath-steam loose
send some bath-house warmth
over my troubled belly
where a wretch can be cared for
one in trouble can be helped."

And the good horse breathed
let some bath-steam loose
sent some bath-house warmth
over her troubled belly.

On Christmas Day God was born
the best boy when it was cold
born upon a horse's hay
at a straight-hair's manger-end.

The Virgin lady Mary
the dear merciful mother
kept her offspring in hiding
her golden apple
beneath the siftable sieve
beneath the portable tub
the sledge-runner as it ran.

Her little offspring vanished
her little golden apple
from beneath the sieve
the sledge-runner as it ran
beneath the portable tub:
she sought her little offspring
her golden apple
in summer in a light craft
in winter on sliding skis.
He was sought but was not found.

The Virgin lady Mary
trudged along the roads
and she met a road.
She bowed to the road
herself put this into words:
"Road, creature of God
have you seen my little boy
my golden apple?"

And the road answered:
"If I knew I would not tell:
your boy created me too
for steeds to be ridden on
for hard shoes to walk upon."

The Virgin lady Mary
the dear merciful mother
kept searching further
and she met the moon.
She bowed to the moon
herself put this into words:
"Moon, creature of God
have you seen my little boy
my golden apple?"

And the moon answered:
"If I knew I would not tell:
your boy created me too
to vanish during the day
to shine during the night-time."

She kept on searching
the Virgin lady Mary
the dear merciful mother
she sought her little offspring
her golden apple
and she met the sun.
She bowed to the sun:

"Sun, creature of God
have you seen my little boy
my golden apple?"

The sun, the creature of God
uttered a word, speaking thus:
"Your boy created me too
to shine during the day-time
to rest during the night-time.
There is your little offspring
your golden apple –
in the highest heaven, in
the place of God the Father:
he will come from there to judge."

Arhippa Perttunen
Latvajärvi, Vuokkiniemi, Archangel Karelia
E. Lönnrot, 1834

60

The Messiah II

Always other things
are recalled, never
the great killing of
God, the Lord's harsh death
how the Creator was killed
the Almighty destroyed
with a hundred spears
a thousand sword-points
no greater number
no smaller number:
a horse stood on the spearhead
a colt ran along the shaft
a barren cow on the sleeve
a cat mewed in the peg-place
a pig where the haft-joint was.
When the Creator was killed
the Almighty destroyed
the rocks were heaped under him
rocks under, the slabs on top
the gravel against the heart.

So the sun, creature of God
flew as a headless chicken
as one cut down, its wing whirred
to the Creator's grave-side.
In tears it drizzled:
"Rise, O Creator, from death
O Lord, awake from the grave
or I too will come
to die beside you
to perish with you!"

And so our great Creator
uttered a word, speaking thus:
"There is no rising from here
as there is hoping from there:
the rocks are heaped under me
the gravel against the heart.
Sun, creature of God
fly as a headless chicken
as one cut down, whirr your wing
to where you once were
to your place of old!
Blaze for one moment sultry
another dimly swelter
for a third with your whole disc
send the wicked crowd to sleep
oppress the pagan people
slump the young on their arrows
the old over their spear-hafts!"

So the sun, creature of God
both flew and made haste
to where it once was
to its place of old:
blazed for one moment sultry
another dimly sweltered
for a third with its whole disc
slumped the young on their arrows
the old over their spear-hafts.

And so our great Creator
the Creator rose from death
and then the rocks sang with tongues
the boulders chattered with words
the rivers stirred, the lakes shook
the copper mountains trembled.

The Creator rose from death
the Lord awoke from the grave
went as poor man to the forge
as beggar to the cellar:
there the iron-men hammered
the smiths of Hiisi pounded.
He uttered a word, spoke thus:
"What do the iron-men pound
the smiths of Hiisi hammer?"

The cruellest of the Jews
the worst of the evil boys
basest of father's sons said:
"Well now, you have eyes as big
    eyelashes as long
    as yesterday's god
whom we buried in the earth
    heaped the rocks on top
rocks under, the rocks on top
the gravel against the heart."

And the great Creator said
    and the pure God spoke:
"This is why I have big eyes
why I have long eyelashes:
long I watched the Creator's
mouth, the beard of who bites off,
the jaws of who grinds and sifts."

The cruellest of the Jews
worst of the evil boys said:
"That was the worst thing I did:
I did not think to measure
how long the Creator's beard
    how long and how thick
    and how wide across
so I cannot hammer that."

So the great Creator said
    and the pure God spoke:

"The Creator's neck is long
    as long and as thick
    and as wide across
    as your own neck is."

The cruellest of the Jews
worst of the evil boys said:
    "My hand will not turn
    nor is my finger
    fit to measure it."

And the great Creator said:
    "My hand would turn it
    my finger would be
    fit to measure it."

The cruellest of the Jews said:
"If I let it be measured
do not lock me in a lock
nor press on a buckle-pin:
the lock is not loosed with hands
the bolts not eased with fingers.
    No key has been made:
only the lock has been formed."

Then he let it be measured.
And so our great Creator
    and so our Lord God
then locked him into the lock
pressed him on the buckle-pin.
So then he put into words:
    "Stay in there, scoundrel
    howl in there, accurst
in the evil you have done
in the fetters you have made
as long as the moon, the sun
the day are fair to look on!"

He bore the end to the rock
himself put this into words:

"From this day forward
fire is to light the heavens
water to temper iron!"

He hardened rock with a shout
tempered iron with a roar.

Arhippa Perttunen
Latvajärvi, Vuokkiniemi, Archangel Karelia
J. F. Cajan, 1836

295

61

The Messiah III

It was Kaija's small woman
carried three wombfuls –
one Maija, the next Kaija
the third little Marjatta.
Marjatta was a fair maid
sat long in her father's house
hung about in Koijola.
Six waist-trinkets she got through
five waist-chains she wore away
sitting in her father's house
pacing in her mother's house
    wore down a floorboard
made a groove with her closed shoe
sitting in her father's house
pacing in her mother's house
wore down a threshold timber
    with her fine skirt-hem
wore down a lintel timber
    with her wide-cut frock
sitting in her father's house
pacing in her mother's house.

She went outside as a mist
to the field beside the yard.
A berry shrieked on the hill
a cranberry on the heath:
    "Come, maid, and pick me
    ring-handed, pull me
    tin-breasted, pluck me!"

    She snatched a basket
slapped a silk scarf on her head:
the hills boomed with her going
mountains bent with her climbing.
A berry in her fingers
she took, from fingers to lips
from her lips on to her tongue:
thence to her belly it sank
was swallowed up in her throat.

She was fulfilled, she was filled
by it, swelled thickset from it
put on flesh from it. She took
the berries to her father:
"Eat a berry, poor father!"

"Where were you, whore, all this time?"
"I was picking a berry."

"You were picking no berry:
you were seeking a bridegroom
brush-headed and silk-belted
looking for a handsome heel
toiling after a red lace."

She took them to her mother:
"Eat a berry, poor mother!"

"Where were you, whore, all this time?
You were seeking a bridegroom
brush-headed and silk-belted
looking for a handsome heel
toiling after a red lace."

She took them to her brother:
"Eat a berry, poor brother!"

"Where were you, whore, all this time?
You were seeking a bridegroom
brush-headed and silk-belted
looking for a handsome heel
toiling after a red lace."

She took them to her sister:
"Eat a berry, poor sister!"

"That's what I yearned for –
a maiden's berries
picked by my sister."

"Wretched harlot that I am:
I've sat in no horse's sledge
that has been among stallions
nor drunk a barren cow's milk
that has been around with bulls
I have eaten no hen's eggs
mounted by a cockerel!
Wretched harlot that I am –
stretched out on a crag
swaying over reeds
sitting in the grass!
This is the Creator's work
begotten by holy God."

She took them to her grandma:
"Eat a berry, poor grandma!"

"That's what I yearned for –
a young maid's berries
picked by my grandchild."

"Take me, stream, lift me, rapids!"

"No, the stream will not take you
nor will the rapids lift you:
you'll have a boy on your knees
the Lord Christ upon your lap."

She had the boy in the porch
the child among the shavings:
she covered her boy
she guarded her boy
beneath the straight-hair's manger.

"O my serfs I bought
drudges I got with money!
Is this the dawn of God's birth
is the sun of God shining?"

"What is the sign at daybreak?"

"The spruces have gold trinkets
the firs silver belts
the earth puts out golden shoots."

"This is the dawn of God's birth
the sun of God is shining
and the wheel of the Lord glows."

She went in search of her boy
and she met the moon:
"Moon, creature of God
can you see my little boy?"

"I can see your little boy:
beneath the straight-hair's manger
the devils are tormenting
the evil crowd conquers him."

And she met the sun:
"Sun, creature of God
can you see my little boy?"

"I can see your little boy:
beneath the straight-hair's manger
the devils are tormenting
the evil crowd conquers him."

Now he went to Tuonela
he called, shouted out:
"Bring a boat, girl of Tuoni
a ferry, Labala's child!"

"Why to Tuonela?"
"I come to Tuonela for a spike
underground for a fighter."
"Will a boat of iron hold?"
"One of sprucewood will float me
of juniper will support:
an iron-bottomed will squeak."

Now he went to Tuonela.
The smith hammered and pounded
in a smithy with no door
with not a window: he'd put
his fur coat as a stopgap
to patch up the bad gateway.

"What are you forging, poor smith?"
"I am forging prison-clamps."

"How thick is the captive's neck?"
"Put them on your neck:
as thick as your own neck is
so thick the Creator's neck!"

Okki Gordeinen
Repola, Olonets Karelia
U. Karttunen, 1897

62

The Messiah IV

Mary the holy woman
the fair-skinned woman
went strolling along:
her fine skirt-hems were swaying
on her bosom a clean shirt
under it a silken cloth
a golden lash in her hand
a silver whip at her belt.
She went to her barley field
to her small oat-rick
saw an apple on that bough
saw a nut upon the tree
took the apple from the bough
took the nut from off the tree
put the apple to her lips
from her lips on to her tongue
from her tongue into her throat.

She was fulfilled, she was filled
by it, grew thickset from it
put on flesh from it.
She went on a little way
went a short distance
went to Pohjola village:
the crone was at the window.

She asked Pohjoi's crone:
"Crone, my good mother
O crone, my old nurse!
Is there room here for the night
room for the night, an earth-lodge
where an earth-woman may lie
a woman with child may stretch
a veiled one may sigh
a delicate one draw breath?"

The crone answering replied:
"Go to the stable on the hill
to the stallion's big manger
to the horse's stall:
there we've other women too."

Mary the holy woman
the fair-skinned woman
went to the stable on the hill
to the stallion's big manger
to the horse's stall
and she gave birth to her son
on the hay sprinkled with snow
on the dung crusted with ice.

On Christmas Day God was born
within a horse's stable
in a stallion's big manger
in a horse's stall
upon hay sprinkled with snow
upon dung crusted with ice.

Tahvana the horse-master
went to give the horse a drink
at the river, the Jordan
at the never-frozen spring:
it would not drink the river
would not lap the water-waves.

Tahvana the horse-master
formed in words, declared by mouth:
"Why will it not drink
from the river, lap the waves?"

The stallion applied its tongue
set its wagger in motion:
"For this I shan't drink
from the river, lap the waves:
the moon's form in the river
shines, the daystar's in the waves
this morning early
the whores have rinsed their head-cloths
the fishermen their towels
the hired men their rags.
For this I shan't drink
from the river, lap the waves."

She went to her barley-field
to her small oat-rick
she searched for the holy boy
for the blessed little fruit:
she went on a little way
and she met the sun.

And she asked the sun:
"Sun, creature of God
have you seen the holy boy
seen the blessed fruit?"

The sun answering replied:
"Had I seen I would not tell:
your good one has got me too
in the morning to come up
in the evening to go down
at midday to be busy."

Mary the holy woman
went a little way further
went a short distance
and she met the moon.

And she asked the moon:
"Moon, creature of God
have you seen the holy boy
seen the blessed fruit?"

The moon answering replied:
"Had I seen I would not tell:
your good one has got me too
in the evening to come up
in the morning to go down
at midnight to be busy."

Mary the holy woman
went a little way further
went a short distance:
Pohjola village loomed up . . .

Well, and then she went to Pohjola village.

What shall I sing, what the song?
I'll sing the Creator's death
the loss of the Almighty.
Where was the Creator killed
the Almighty lost?

In thick willow-woods
dense birdcherry-woods
at the edge of a wide grove
under the narrow wood's arm:
there the sun was not shining
nor was the moon gleaming there.

"Shine, O shine, Creator's sun
glimmer, moon of God
shine on the Creator's tomb
on the grave of God:
free the Creator from death
and the Almighty from loss
melt the nails of tin
loosen the nails of copper
let the nails of wood drop out!"

The Creator's sun shone, shone
    and God's moon glimmered
and melted the nails of tin
loosened the nails of copper
let the nails of wood drop out
freed the Creator from death
and the Almighty from loss.
    The Creator stirred
    God rose to his feet
as the evening fire was lit
as the splint-torch was kindled
as the windows were fastened
    as the doors were shut.

He went to the hill-stable
to the stallion's big manger:
there he took from his stallions
he chose from among his colts
which had a pool on its loins
a ditch on the stallion's flanks
a cold well under its hoofs.
He took it from his stallions
chose it from among his colts
then leapt on the good one's back
hopped upon the horse's flanks.

He rode on a little way
    went about a verst:
a tree fluttered, the earth shook
a black grouse flapped from the wood.
The horse of Jesus startled:
Jesus was thrown to the earth
to a rock upon the ground
and the horse's foot was sprained.

He sought a sage on the road
a mighty man on the ridge
    a singer of spells
a mutterer over salt
and a binder of blue threads
a speaker of red ribbons.

He found no sage on the road
no mighty man on the ridge
    no singer of spells
no mutterer over salt
nor a binder of blue threads
no speaker of red ribbons.
That was when our Creator
    that was when our God
himself became a wise man
    a knowing wise man
    a singer of spells
a mutterer over salt
and a binder of blue threads
a speaker of red ribbons:
fixed the flesh fast to the bones
fast fixed the bones to the flesh
    made the top-side well
    the inside painless
the top-side to feel no ill.

He leapt on the good one's back
hopped upon the horse's flanks:
he went on a little way
    and he met a bridge.
That was when our Creator
    that was when our God
    bowed before the bridge
gave his hand to the bridge-planks.

He went on a little way
    went about a verst
    and he met a church.
That was when our Creator
did not bow before the church
give his hand to the church-planks.

    The holy men smirked
    the angels marvelled:
"What's wrong with our Creator
what's the matter with our God:
he did not bow to the church

give his hand to the church-planks
but he bows before the bridge
gives his hand to the bridge-posts?"

The Creator in reply
for an answer said:
"I stayed underneath the bridge
till the Jews walked openly
the bad ones fled above: so
long I stood beneath the bridge.
I did not bow to the church
because in church I was seized
in a chapel I was sold."

He leapt on the good one's back:
he went on a little way
went about a verst
heard Hiitoila's hammering
the smith of Hiisi pounding.
To Hiitoila's forge he rode
in front of Hiitoila's forge
like any other stranger
stranger, traveller.

He asked, he inquired
right to the bottom he probed:
"What do you forge, Hiisi's smith
smith of Hiisi, what fashion?"

The smith answering replied:
"I fashion the Creator's
gallows-tree, God's strangling-tree
but did not think to measure
how thick the Creator's neck
how thick and how long
and how wide across."

That was when our Creator
that was when our God
formed in words, declared by mouth:
"Measure your own neck:
as your own neck is
so thick the Creator's neck
so thick and so long
and so wide across."

That one measured his own neck:
the Creator locked him up
and secured the latch
and hurled him into the fire
plunged him into hell
to sit for ever.

Taroi, Päntty's daughter
Hevaa, Kaprio, Ingria
V. Alava, 1891

63

St Stephen

Is Stephen at home?
Clever Stephen danced
fed Herod's horses
and tended Herodias' mounts
on noble, pure Christmas night
on high Christmas night, he led
a horse to the spring to drink.
The horse would not drink water
the white-streak-head did not care:
he sought flaws in the water
found no flaws in the water
he saw a star in the sky
the star's likeness in the spring
a dot in a cloud-gap. He
led the horse home from the spring
the club-footed from its well:
its muzzle reached to the clouds
its long tail dragged on the ground
it had no need of blankets
had no need of oats.
I went then to Herod's house
beneath beams, above rafters.
Herod answered from his meal
and Herodias from her board:
"If you don't lessen your noise
indeed I'll shorten your life."

"Now the power of God is born
a better one is swelling:
now I am leaving Herod
taking my faith from Jesus
going to better service."

"I'll believe it to be true
if that cock should crow."

And the cock began to crow:
the cock crowed for six quarters
the son of a hen for eight.

"I'll believe it to be true
if that bull bellows."

The flesh eaten, the bone gnawed
the hide as shoes was worn down:
the bull began to bellow
to crush with its bones
to shake with its limbs.

"I'll believe it to be true
if that knife-point sprouts."

He flung his knife on the floor:
the knife-point began to sprout
and six golden shoots sprouted
with a gold leaf at each tip.

"Dear beer, darling drink
run towards high ground
like a sledge along its tracks
an old crone across the ice.
Half a pint of liquor, half a gallon of beer:
it takes a lot to entertain these people here.

Good was the sign in my mind
as I came to this village

especially to this house
especially this cottage:
one black road leads to the hut
one to the shed on the hill
a third jogged to the cellar.
Yes, there's beer in the cellar
    in an oak barrel
beneath a bung that keeps tight
    behind a birch tap:
    red the master's cheeks
    broad the mistress' hips
    curly the dog's tail
    knotted the pig's tail
    glossy the cat's back."

(*On going out this was sung finally:*)

"Ih ha, ha, ha
everybody's hairy arse."

J. Hepola
Koski, South-West Finland
J. Liipola, 1892

64

St Catherine I

Kitty was weaving
by a little willow-brook
by a dense birdcherry-wood:
the shuttle turned in her hand
like a weasel in a stack
a precious-fur in a cairn
on a pine-branch a squirrel.
Herod the dishonest king
came to Catherine's fireside
said as soon as he arrived:
"Come, Kitty, to me
or else to my son!"

Katie knowingly answered:
"I won't come to you
nor yet to your son:
the bad one has a bad son
the bad one himself is bad.
By the corner you came in
got in at the timber-joint:
the door's creaking was unheard."

Herod the dishonest king
went in search of trees
birches and hardwoods
firs that had shed their branches
rowans that held firm:
Herod the dishonest king
put Catherine on the fire.
The Virgin lady Mary
the dear merciful mother
was reading a book.

Singer unknown
Kuhmo, Kainuu
M. A. Castrén, 1839

65

St Catherine II

A girl was weaving
a wench held the reed:
the village could get no rest
because of the girl's weaving.
Herod the king heard:
he had three strong sons
said straight to his sons:
"We three are going courting
we four to look for the maid."

Old Väinämöinen himself
considered and took his time:
"Will you come to me
or else to my son?"

The girl certainly answered:
"Now, you yourself are ugly:
your sons so much uglier."

King Herod grew angry then:
he heaped up a heap of wood
thirty sledges full
birches and hardwoods
firs that had shed their branches
rowans that were tough
pushed Catherine in the fire
the fine-hemmed into the blaze.

He blew a day, another
soon began a third
looked at the base of his forge
the edges of his furnace:
Katie squeezed out of the fire
the fine-hemmed out of the blaze.
He pushed Katie in again
the fine-hemmed into the blaze.

He set his best son
to blow once again
he blew, his eyes watering:
a stallion squeezed from the fire
flaxen-maned from the furnace.
He considered, took his time:
was the stallion well-behaved?
The horse was not well-behaved:
every day it killed a mare –
even two on many days.

Old Väinämöinen himself
pushed the stallion in the fire
flaxen-maned in the furnace
set the serfs blowing
the hirelings pressing:
the serfs blew and fanned
for three summer days.
Soon upon the third day he
looked at the base of his forge
the edges of his furnace:
a maid squeezed out of the fire
golden-templed from the heat. . . .

Paavo Hukkanen
Kiuruvesi, Savo
A. I. Arwidsson, 1819

66

St Henry I

A ballad about St Henry
first bishop of Turku who
had been born in England

Two holy men there once were
two princes of the people
Christian brothers, noble knights:
one grew up on Swedish soil
the other on foreign soil.
Soon the swaddled ones grew up
together in napkins rose:
the child from the foreign land
was the Lord Henry
while he who rose in Sweden
was Eric the Knight
the famous king of Sweden.

And the Lord Henry
said to Eric his brother:
"Let us go to Häme Land
to the unchristened country
the place without priests
have churches of stone put up
and have chapels built."

Then Eric the Knight
formed in words, declared by mouth:
"My brother, son of woman
there are many who went there
not many who have come back
more who have refused: and yet
I will go, I do not mind.
If I should be killed
the king of the land cut down
one will yet be left behind."

Then the Lord Henry
formed in words, declared by mouth:
"My dear little lad
coachman a span high
take my sleigh out of the hut
and put the sleigh in order
the small bright-worked part behind
fit it on to its runners
fit shafts of oak, stretch
out reins of sinews
put traces of walrus-bones
a harness of beaver-bones
either side of the grey's neck:
take a horse from the barley
a well-built one from the shoots
a sweeping-hair from the malt
put a collar-bow of elm
on the mane of the good horse."

Then the Lord Henry
drove rumbling away:
he startled a herd of deer
into a run behind him
he set a flock of singers
flying overhead
refreshing his brow
there was a bear in fetters
of iron, an iron grouse

cooed in the iron bear's jaws
and he made a white hare dance
before him on the sleigh-rug.

The tiny lad said
coachman a span high:
"Now I am getting hungry."

The Lord Henry said:
"Soon we shall get to a house —
to Lalloi's beyond the bay.
Take a roll from the stove-top
take some beer from the cellar
and leave a coin in their place:
hay from the hay-loft
oats from the oat-bin
and leave a coin in their place."

An evil cursed woman
ill-tempered guzzler
yelled from the hot stove
screamed from the top of the post:
"Wait until Lalloi comes home:
he'll gnaw your bones yet
rattle your heads yet
scatter your sinews!"

Then the Lord Henry
hurried away from the house.
When Lalloi came home
the old bitch told lies:
"My dear boy, my younger one
a Swede to feed, a greedy
foreigner has passed this way:
he took a cake off the stove
he took beer from the cellar
and left ashes in their place
hay from the hay-loft
oats from the oat-bin
and left ashes in their place."

Lalloi tied on his hatchet
his broad, his long axe
pushed his left ski on the snow
like a greased shaving, slammed his
right ski on the frozen ground
like a winter hare:
Lalli skied at frightful speed
his left ski ran fast
and fire puffed in the ski's path
smoke where the stick was.
Then the Lord Henry
formed in words, declared by mouth:
"Lalloi comes skiing
a long spear under his arm."

He could feel his doom coming
his day of distress dawning
and said: "My dear little lad
coachman a span high
keep watch from behind a rock –
no, there's no shield in a rock:
keep watch from behind an oak
in the shade of the good horse.
Whichever way my bones fly
and my sinews are scattered
gather them up in a cloth
bind them with blue threads
tie them all neatly
lay them in the stallion's sledge:
wherever the stallion halts
there let an ox be harnessed
and wherever the ox halts
there let a church be put up
a chapel be built
in the name of Lord Henry."

There the ox halted –
on Nousiainen's sandy soil
on a tip of sandy heath:
there the Lord Henry
he, the first one, was buried

a church also was built there
in the name of Lord Henry.

    But the tiny lad
    coachman a span high
could not spy among the snow
    the holy man's thumb
nor the great master's finger
    with its ring of gold
till in the heart of summer
when the springtime was lovely
the ice on the lake melted
then, in the heart of summer
on a little block of ice
the wind wafted on the waves
the holy hero's finger
    with its ring of gold
    for mankind to see
    and a noble sign
that the great Creator would
not vouchsafe, nor God permit
to sink beneath the water
    nor come to nothing
    the holy man's thumb
nor the great master's finger
    with its ring of gold.

Lalli the worst of pagans
    cruellest of Jews
he who killed the holy man
the bishop, the Lord Henry
    took the tall helmet
off the holy bishop's head
and put it on his own head
    on his wicked skull
    and went proudly home.

The woman, spinning her wheel
formed in words, declared by mouth:
"Where did Lalloi get the cap
the bad man the good helmet?"

Lalli lifted up his cap:
Lalli's hair stuck to the cap
and all the scalp stuck with it.
It slithered loose from the bone
came clean away from the skull:
his snout became defenceless
    his evil head bare
skinless as a cattle-head
and bare the evil one's brow.
The great Creator did that
the strong God permitted that
the Father for a wonder
    and a noble sign.
Now the bishop is in joy–
Lalli in evil torment:
the bishop with the angels
sings, and chants a hymn of joy–
Lalli is skiing in hell.
    His left ski skating
into torment's thick smoke he
    strikes out with his stick:
the devils sorely prick him
    in the heat of hell
and they trouble his poor soul.

Keep us from that, steadfast God
bar the way, true Creator:
see us into heaven's hall
into everlasting joy
free us from the wicked world.

Amen.

Singer unknown
Vaasa, South Ostrobothnia
A. Heikkilä, 1731

67

St Henry II

Long ago two children grew
one grew up in Cabbageland
the other rose in Sweden:
one was Henry of Häme
the other Eric the king.
Henry of Häme
said to Eric his brother:
"Let us go and christen lands
to the unchristened countries
to the places without priests."

Then Eric the king
said to Henry his brother:
"What if the lakes have no ice
the winding river's melted?"

And Henry of Häme said:
"So we circle Kiulo Lake
go round the winding river.
Put the colts into harness
fit the yearlings with bridles
and put the sleighs in order
and line up the struts
to their runners fit wide shafts
the small bright-worked parts behind."

At once they drove off.
So they drove one summer day
two nights in a row
and Eric the king
said to Henry his brother:
"Now we are getting hungry
neither eating nor drinking
no stop for a meal."
"Lalli is beyond the bay
the fortunate on the cape:
there we shall eat, there we'll drink
there stop for a meal."

Then, when they got there
Kerttu the idle mistress
steamed with her vile mouth
used her worthless tongue:
at that Henry of Häme
took hay for the horse
left coins in its place
took bread off the stove
left coins in its place
took beer out of the cellar
and rolled money in its place.
There they ate and there they drank
there stopped for a meal.
And soon they drove off.

Lalli came homeward.
That Lalli's evil mistress
steamed with her vile mouth
used her worthless tongue:
"Men have passed this way:
here they ate and here they drank
here stopped for a meal
took hay for the horse
and left sand-grains in its place
took bread off the stove

and left sand-grains in its place
took beer out of the cellar
and rolled gravel in its place."

A herdsman spoke from the post:
"Now you are just telling lies! –
Don't you believe her!"

Lalli, ill-behaved
from an evil family too
Lalli took up his hatchet
the devil took his long spear
and drove off after the lord.

Then the faithful man
said, the servant to his lord:
"There is a thudding back there:
shall I drive this horse faster?"

Henry of Häme answered:
"If there's a thudding back there
do not drive this horse faster
do not push the steed harder:
hide in the shade of a rock
listen from behind the rocks.
And when I am caught
or else even killed
pick my bones out of the snow
and put them on an ox-sledge:
it will draw me to Finland.
Where the ox grows tired
there let a church be put up
a chapel be built
for priests to preach sermons in
that all the people may hear."

Then Lalli returned homeward.
A herdsman spoke from the post:
"Where did Lalli get the cap
the bad man the good helmet
the gallows-bird the mitre?"

Then Lalli the murderer
snatched the cap from off his head:
his hair came with it.
Pulled the ring off his finger:
his finger-sinews slid off.

So to this ill-behaved one
to the dear bishop's maimer
came the vengeance from on high
payment from the world's ruler.

Singer unknown
West Finland
Collector unknown, ca 1671

68

The Tree

Two Karelians, five
or six Estonians
honed for a day their axes
another the other sides
and for a third the whole blades
and they went in search of wood
to catch an oak-tree:
they found a tree, caught an oak
began to hack the oak-tree.

The oak chattered with its tongue:
"What do you men want of me?"

The men answering said: "I
seek wood for a church threshold
wood for raising an altar
wood where a deacon may sing
wood for Mary to lie on."

The oak answering replied:
"My wood will not serve for that
no wood for a church threshold
wood for raising an altar
wood where a deacon may sing
wood for Mary to lie on:
a wolf has run on my roots
a bear has lain on my foot
a squirrel in my branches
a bird has sung in my top."

Singer unknown
Venjoki, Ingria
H. A. Reinholm, 1847

69

The Forest

The handsome son of Suokas
was out searching for horses:
lay with a widow's daughter
sported with Mari's daughter
under the narrow woods' arm
in the blue backwoods' inside.
Those backwoods began to die
and our forest to wither
leaves on trees and grass in soil
cuckoo calling in the spruce
sun shining on them
moon gleaming on them.
Priests were brought from Paaritsa:
our woods were christened
christened and baptised.
Then the backwoods grew lovely
our forests began to sprout
leaves on trees and grass in soil
cuckoo to call in the tree
sun to shine on them
moon to gleam on them.

Singer unknown
Sakkola, Karelian Isthmus
K. Slöör, 1854

70

The Foundling I

Hanno, melancholy boy
went out in search of horses
    went to catch a mare
the kin's bridle at his waist
the manor's harness on his back.

Marketta, beautiful maid
went out to the grove for broom
to the thicket for bath-whisks:
    Hanno stopped to speak
over the fence gave a kiss
through the fence he gave his hand.

She was fulfilled, she was filled
by it, put to bed by it
and blown out thickset from it:
she had a child on shavings
    a boy on pig's straw.

Elina the smith's mistress
found the child on the shavings
the boy upon the pig's straw.
She brought beer in a flagon:
    who drank up the beer
would be parent to the child.
Where was the boy to be put?
He was tossed in the water.

The boy chattered with his tongue:
    "Hannas' red hat shall
cover me in the water
    Marketta's blue skirt
shall shelter me in the fire."

Singer unknown
Hietamäki – Liissilä, Ingria
D. E. D. Europaeus, 1848

71

The Foundling II

Helina the good mistress
Katro the fair of figure
brought up six daughters:
five were married off
and the sixth was left at home
at home Marketta was left
to be the home-bird.
Marketta the haughty maid
in a silk head-band
wore half the threshold away
with her bright skirt-hems
her six waist-trinkets
frayed down her five chains
on the road to and from church.
Then she dashed away to herd
skipped away after the cows
she found young grass there
young grass on old hay:
and there sleep overcame her
the heat oppressed her
the warmth weighed her down.

Hannus, German of the Isle
the kin's bridle in his hand
and the tribe's trappings
found that maid asleep
found Marketta lying down:
there beside her he stretched out
then he lay with Marketta.

Marketta came home
seemed now strange to her mother:
"What's wrong with our Marketta
and what's up with our home-bird?
She was once slim and slender
now she is thickset and stout:
her backside won't rise from seats
nor her feet from the floor-joint."

She moved into the bath-house
wore no belt around her waist
walked about without leggings.

Helina the good mistress
went to get some beer
and to fetch some ale: she found
a child in the chicken-house
a boy underneath the steps.
She took him to the men's house:
"Whose is this doing
whose is the child's fashioning?"

One swore and another swore
that one swore a stronger oath
more grievously bound himself
who knew it was his doing
knew well it was his getting.

Then to the women's house she
took him: one swore, another
that one swore a stronger oath
who knew it was her doing
knew well it was her getting.
Marketta the red-skirted
swore the strongest oath:
Hannus, German of the Isle

swore the strongest oath
most grievously bound himself.

Then the women considered
where to put the boy
where death might be found:
take the boy to the water
and shove him into the fire.

Jesus then gave him a tongue
Jesus tongue and Mary mind
gave to the three-night-old boy:
"Hannus' grey hat shall
cover me in the water
Marketta's red skirt
shall shelter me in the fire."

Saara and Liisa
Sakkola, Karelian Isthmus
H. A. Reinholm, 1848

72

The Maid and the Dragon I

Let's rock two children
and when shall we get a third?
Fair Jesus shall be the third
the Virgin Mary the fourth
    wise father the fifth
    dear mother the sixth:
there will be a crowd of us!
Let us go to Cuckoo Hill
and learn the cuckoo's language
pull off a long strip of bast
a strip of bast long and wide
    to hang a gallows
at the road's end, the gatepost
    where the kings walk, where
    the mighty lords stroll.

Singer unknown
Eräjärvi, Häme
N. Järvinen, 1853

73

The Maid and the Dragon II

Let's go, young ones, to the vale
summer-blessed to the rock
let's cut down a tall lime-tree
a lime-tree both tall and smooth
pull off a long strip of bast
a strip of bast long and wide:
    let's twine a long rope
a rope both long and supple
where the bridegroom shall be hanged
at the road's end, the gatepost
    where the king walks, the
    castle's elder strolls.

    The king sternly asked
the castle's elder complained:
"Wherefore is this one bound here
this son of woman captive?"
"Because he lay with a maid
    a young maid, a bride."

The poor maiden was condemned
to the jaws of the dragon.
    And the dragon sighed
    it sighed, it drew breath:
"I'd sooner swallow a young
man, a young man with his sword
and a horse with its saddle
and a priest with his church gold
and a king with his helmet
than swallow a young maiden
    a young maid, a bride:
    a maid will have sons
will load a ship with children
for that great war, for the fight
with Martti of Tanikka."

Singer unknown
Karelian Isthmus
E. Lönnrot, 1837

74

The Maid and the Dragon III

Get up, get up and go, go
let's go, young ones, to the vale
summer-blessed to the rock
let's twine a taut rope
a rope both taut and even
let's cut down a tall lime-tree
a lime-tree both tall and broad
on which the wretch shall be hanged
the son of woman captive
at the road's end, the gatepost
right at the fence's corner
where the kings walk, the
lordlings pass by, the
castle's nobles ride.

And the king asked: "Why
is a man bound here
a man bound and wound
his hands fastened hard
fingers knotted fast?"

"Because of a maid he's bound
the man's bound and wound
his hands fastened hard
fingers knotted fast."

And the king asked, the
castle's elder persisted:
"Are you here through your own fault
or through parish injustice?"

"I'm not here through my own fault
nor through parish injustice."

The poor maiden was condemned
condemned and cast out:
she was cast in the snake's jaws
between the pike's teeth.
The dragon slumped on the rocks
the pike flung itself ashore:
"I shall not gnaw a young maid
nor yet a young bride:
for a bride will have a son
will load a ship with shipwrights
for Sweden's great war
the fight with Tanumartti.
I'll gnaw a man with his sword
a hero with his sheathed blade
and a horse with its saddle
a weak lord with his household
and a king with his castle."

Singer unknown
Hevaa, Kaprio, Ingria
V. Alava, 1891

75

Magdalen I

Magdalen, young maid
was long growing up at home
long growing, widely heard of
with her good father
beside her darling mother:
she trampled down the floor-beam
with her high-heeled shoes
wore down a threshold-timber
with her fine skirt-hem
another timber above
with her golden crown
wore away the golden stool
as she washed dishes
wore down the table-corner
with her silver-hafted knife.

Magdalen, young maid
went to the spring for water
a golden pail in her hand
a gold handle on the pail.
She looked where her likeness was:
"O what a poor maid I am!
My form has quite changed
my lovely hue has vanished
my pendant does not glitter
nor does my head-silver gleam
as they glittered yesteryear."

Jesus, a herdsman among willows
a drover in burnt clearings:
"Give me a drink of water!"

"I have no pitcher."

"Then scoop a handful
fetch me some in your two hands."

"What do you say, Finnish slave
Finnish slave, serf of the soil
always my father's herdsman
fed on fishbones left by Swedes
nourished on fish-heads?"
"If not
I'll tell of your evil deeds."

"Tell me all you know."

"Where are your three little boys?
One you thrust into the fire
one you plunged in the water
one you dug into the field.
He you thrust into the fire
would be a knight in Sweden
he you plunged in the water
would be a priest of the best
he you dug into the field
would be a lord in this land."

Magdalen, young maid
only then began to weep
wept the pail full of water
and washed the feet of Jesus
and wiped them dry with her hair:
"Put me, Lord Jesus
put me wherever you will –
to be steps on marshy ground
to be trampled on by whores

blown about by every wind
    swayed by every flame.
    Put me, Lord Jesus
put me anywhere you like –
to be a bridge on the sea
rotten timbers on the waves
tossed about by every wind
    swept by every wave.
    Put me, Lord Jesus
put me anywhere you like:
push like charcoal in the fire
like a brand into the flames
blown about by every fire
    swayed by every flame."

Eriika Haudanmäki
Sääksmäki, Häme
A. A. Borenius, 1879

76

Magdalen II

Magdalen, fair maid
went defiantly to church
purposefully to chapel
in bluish stockings
in a many-coloured hood.
She found a small scrap of cloth
a small piece of silk
took the cloth to the shearer
to the German shoemaker.

She flattered the shoemaker:
"Shoemaker, sweet boy,
governor, lord of Narvoi
make from this a great fur coat
a great garment, a fine cloak!
Fit it close under the arms
make it strong about the bust
and wide lower down!
Sew silk down the openings
with room to spare at the hems!"

The shoemaker, the sweet boy,
governor, lord of Narvoi
sewed from that a great fur coat
a great garment, a fine cloak
fitted close under the arms
sewed it strong about the bust
sewed silk down the openings
a hemmed linen skirt below
with room to spare at the hems.

Magdalen, fair maid
went defiantly to church
purposefully to chapel
saw an apple on a bough
saw a nut upon a tree
took the apple from the bough
reached the nut down from the tree
put the apple to her lips
from her lips on to her tongue
from her tongue down her gullet.

She was fulfilled, she was filled
by it, swelled with child by it
grew thickset from it
put on flesh from it.

Magdalen, sinful woman
went defiantly to church
purposefully to chapel
set one foot within the church
the other on the church steps.

Jesus yelled from the churchyard
the Creator from the bench
sang, God from the footstool-tip:
"Magdalen, fair maid
don't go round the church
don't shame the chapel! There are
three children under your belt:
one by your noble father
one by your supple brother
and one by your godfather.
For two I will grant pardon
but grant no leave for the third –
grant for your noble father's

and for your supple brother's
but not for your godfather's:
from a sponsor graver sins
from a godfather worse come."

Olgoi
Hevaa, Kaprio, Ingria
V. Porkka, 1883

77

Serf and Master I

A poor serf under the sun
grieving sat and grieving stepped
grieving started on his food
cut his cursed bread
from a cursed crust
the serf ate his cursed milk
from a cursed bowl
from a cursed hut
from a cursed pot
ate cursed and drank cursed
lay in cursed sleep
on a cursed bed.

Three men of heaven
came asking, speaking:
"Where is the serf's corner here?"

"At the door, beneath the beam."

So the master's eye glinted
as a snake glints in dry grass
the mistress's tongue
clacked like a dry aspen leaf.

To the serf leave was given
the serf leave, the captive power
to run off home for Christmas
for the long feast of Christmas
in the hardest frost
in a threadbare coat
in a smock falling apart:
there the serf froze on the way
fell on his face in the snow
face in snow and head in snow
his fists in the bitter air.

Three men of heaven
came, the third the Son of God
and the serf's soul was taken
was led into heaven, brought
to the house of Tuonela
with the other souls:
"Sit down here, poor serf:
you had all your standing there
when you were a serf!"

A flagon of mead was brought:
"Drink this, O poor serf:
you had water to drink there!"

And the master's soul was brought
and a fiery chair was brought:
"Sit down here, O great master!"

A fiery flagon was brought:
"Drink this, great master!"

"Wherefore is this done to me?"

"For this it is done to you:
you had mead for drinking there
you drank mead and you drank beer."

The great master stepped
down the streets of Tuonela
a long cubit in his hand

shouldering a roll of cloth
a big gallon beneath his arm:
"Take this, O poor serf
take, take, O poor serf!"

"I'll not, great master."

"Take, take, my dear serf
a still bigger gallon's worth
a still longer cubit's worth!"

"You might have paid at the time
I was in the threshing-house
slamming beneath the rafters
when I ran to drink water
three times in a summer night
and wiped hoarfrost off the trees
and shook the dew off the earth."

Singer unknown
Korpiselkä, Ladoga Karelia
R. Polén, 1847

78

Serf and Master II

I was a serf in Estonia
herdsman in the pagan land.
The poor serf had leave
to go off home for Christmas
in a threadbare coat
in a hempen smock.
The poor serf died on the way:
his soul was borne to the gates.
Jesus asked Peter:
"Whose is the soul at the gates?"

Peter the steadfast replied:
"It is a poor serf's soul there."

"Bring the soul inside
with the other souls."

The soul was taken inside.
Now, a golden chair was brought
and the poor soul sat on it:
"Wherefore is this done to me?"

"For this it is done to you:
you had all your standing up
when you were a serf."

A golden flagon was brought
with mead, with liquor inside:
"Drink this, O poor serf."

"Wherefore is this done to me?"

"For this it is done to you:
you had water for drinking
when you were a serf."

And then the great master died:
his soul was borne to the gates.
Jesus asked Peter:
"Whose is the soul at the gates?"

"It is a great master's soul."

"Bring the soul inside
with the other souls."

Now, a fiery chair was brought:
"Sit here, great master."

"Wherefore is this done to me?"

"For this it is done to you:
you sat at the table-head
when you were master."

A fiery flagon was brought
with fire and with tar inside:
"Drink this, great master."

"Wherefore is this done to me?"

"For this it is done to you:
you had beer to drink
when you were master."

Singer unknown
Central Finland
E. Rudbeck, A. Rothman, 1850

79

Serf and Master III

There was a poor serf
once, a poor serf in Venaa
employed in the evil lands
a slave in the devil's nest.
He spent a year, another
began to ask for wages
to complain of his troubles.

Bad wages were paid
bad were the poor serf's wages –
a tiny handful
a narrow gallon measure
and corn full of dust
chaff to throw to beasts.

To the serf leave was given
the serf leave, the captive power
to run off home for Christmas
to flee at Easter
in his bare shirtsleeves
in just his linen
in the hardest frosts
the most howling chills:
fell on his face in the snow
face in snow, head in water
his fists in the bitter air
flat on his back on the ground.

The Creator came from his
town with six coachmen
and eight footmen too:
five were foreigners
in a gold carriage
with silver wheels. They
saw the serf's soul on the road.

Then the serf's soul was taken
face from snow, head from water
his fists from the bitter air
up off his back from the ground.
The soul was put in the car
in the gold carriage
with the silver wheels:
the soul was borne to heaven
to behind God's door, beneath
the Lord Creator's window.

A short time went by
a little while passed
and God's door opened
the Creator's gate swung out.

To his serfs the Creator
said: "O my own serfs
go out, serfs, and see
what is making the door whine
what is making the gate creak!"

The serfs went to see:
there was the serf's soul
there behind God's door, beneath
the Lord Creator's window.

To his serfs the Creator
said: "Take the serf's soul
lead the soul among the souls!"

Thence the serf's soul was taken
the soul led among the souls
body beside the bodies.
A chair of silver was brought
for the serf to sit upon.

And the poor serf sighed
he sighed, he drew breath:
"Wherefore is this done to me
why this to a wretched boy?"

"For this it is done to you:
you had all your standing up
when you were a serf
hireling of an evil man."

A silver flagon was brought
with mead, with liquor inside
for the serf to drink.

And the poor serf sighed
he sighed, he drew breath:
"Wherefore is this done to me
why this to a wretched boy?"

"For this it is done to you:
you had water for drinking
when you were a serf
hireling of an evil man."

A short time went by
a little while passed
and then the wicked master
was walking and praying down
Tuonela's hill, a gallon
of barley held in his hand
of oats held under his arm:
"Hullo, my own serf!
I'll pay you better wages."

The serf answering replied:
"Since you did not pay at home
payment is bad in Mana
vengeance harsh in Tuonela:
here no triflers are suffered
a careful man is needed
before the true judge
and the law lord's bench."

A short time went by:
it was the wicked master
began to make the door whine
to make the gates creak.

To his serfs the Creator
said: "Go, serfs, and see
what is making the door whine
making the gate creak!"

The serfs went to see:
and there was the master's soul.

The master's soul was taken
from behind God's door, beneath
the Lord Creator's window:
the soul was borne to the souls
the soul among the souls borne.
A fiery chair was brought there.

And the master sighed
he sighed, he drew breath:
"Wherefore is this done to me
why this to a wretched boy?"

"For this it is done to you:
you had all your sitting down
when you were master
and you treated serfs badly
paid serfs bad wages."

A fiery flagon was brought
with fire and with tar inside
as a drink for the master
    as a drink, a meal.

    That wicked master
    now sighed, now drew breath:
"Wherefore is this done to me
why this to a wretched boy?"

"For this it is done to you:
    you had beer to drink
    when you were master
and you treated serfs badly.
For this it is done to you:
    you ill-treated serfs
    paid serfs bad wages
    a tiny handful
a narrow gallon measure
    and corn full of dust
    chaff to throw to beasts."

Taroi, Päntty's daughter
Hevaa, Kaprio, Ingria
V. Alava, 1891

80

Death on the Prowl I

Death was tramping on the marsh
Disease down the winter road
tramping, pondering:
"Were I to kill the master
the house might be lost.
Were I to kill the mistress
would the cattle wander loose?
Were I to kill off the son
would the clearing-axe then fail?
Were I to kill the daughter
the dowry would then be lost.
Were I to kill the daughter-in-law
another would be brought in
and a better one taken."

Maura Marttinen
Vuokkiniemi, Archangel Karelia
I. Marttinen, 1911

81

Death on the Prowl II

Death was skiing on the marsh
Disease down the winter road.
Death the Great spoke thus
Disease the Strong considered
at evening behind the house
behind the sheds of the house:
"Whom shall I kill in the house:
shall I kill off the master?
If I kill off the master
the house may be lost
the nets may remain folded
the boats stay in the water.
I'll not kill off the master."

Death was skiing on the marsh
Disease down the winter road.
Death the Great spoke thus
Disease the Strong considered
at evening behind the house
behind the sheds of the house:
"Whom shall I kill in the house:
shall I kill the son?
If I kill the son
the house may be lost
the clearing-axes vanish
the corn-bins will be half-full
the grain-boxes will run down."

Death was skiing on the marsh
Disease down the winter road.
Death the Great spoke thus
Disease the Strong considered
at evening behind the house
behind the sheds of the house:
"Whom shall I kill in the house:
shall I kill off the mistress?
If I kill off the mistress
the house may be lost
the cow's yield will be cut short
the milk-cups will be drained dry
the woman's pails will spring leaks.
I'll not kill off the mistress."

Death was skiing on the marsh
Disease down the winter road.
Death the Great spoke thus
Disease the Strong considered
at evening behind the house
behind the sheds of the house:
"Whom shall I kill in the house:
shall I kill off the daughter?
If I kill off the daughter
the suitors will be left sad
the young boys in bad spirits.
I'll not kill off the daughter."

Death was skiing on the marsh
Disease down the winter road.
Death the Great spoke thus
at evening behind the house
behind the sheds of the house:
"Whom shall I kill in the house –
the daughter-in-law?
If I kill her off, the son
will get him another wife
another wife by marriage."

Kaisa Liisa Lappalainen
Kiihtelysvaara, North Karelia
A. Rytkönen, 1895

82

The Widow I

"Three the springs in the forest
three the salmon in the spring
three the sons I have:
I do not eat, do not drink
without golden cups
copper-rimmed dishes.
One's a dean in Sweden, one
a bishop in a palace
the third is a lord at home."

Death happened to hear
to be standing by the wall:
it killed the dean in Sweden
the bishop in the palace
and it killed the lord at home.
"Now I eat, now drink
without golden cups
copper-rimmed dishes."

Johan Savolainen
Hankasalmi, Central Finland
I. Oksanen, 1892

83

The Widow II

A house was here once
a house once, a castle of old
where now is booming forest.
Three the springs in the forest
three the salmon in the spring:
one salmon is a young maid's
another is a young bride's
a third is a red widow's.

The widow sang in a grove:
"Nor widow nor demon I
nor a woman without means
a weakling without defence.
Three the sons I have:
one's a dean in Sweden, one
a bishop in a palace
the third is a lord at home.
I've not eaten, I've not drunk
neither indeed have I supped
without golden cups
copper-rimmed dishes."

Death happened to hear
chanced to be standing downwind:
it killed the dean in Sweden
the bishop in the palace
and thirdly the lord at home.

The widow began to grieve:
"Now widow, now demon I
now a woman without means:
now a staff has to be found
now a stick used in my hand.
I must eat, must drink
without copper-rimmed dishes
and now I must sup
without gold-rimmed cups."

Taria Korpuna
Vuole, Ingria
F. Pajula, 1894

84

The Death of Elina

Klavus, Elina's mother, Elina,
Kirsti, Olovi, Jesus

Elina the maid went to the shed
a copper box in her hand
a copper key in the box
when she met Klavus:
Kl: "Might you have a maid for sale
has a girl been kept for me?"

M: "No maid is sold on a hill
and none traded on a farm:
but rooms I have, one
for coming, one for going."

That Klavus went to a room:
Elina's five brothers sat
each one at the table-head
and each one stood up.

E: "O my mother, my darling
do not give me to Klavus!"

M: "How do you know him?"
E: "I know
the stern one by his coming
the swing of his noble foot."

With his sword he pushed the door
open, with his scabbard shut:
Kl: "My good woman, my darling
have you got a maid for sale
has a lass been kept for me?"

M: "Small lasses I have
and daughters half-grown."

Kl: "You have little Elina."

M: "Little Elina cannot
take care of a big family
look after a big stockyard
nor set a hireling to work."

Kl: "See, I have the lass Kirsti
to care for the big family
to set the hireling to work
look after the big stockyard."

E: "Yes, you have the lass Kirsti
who will burn me in the fire
and basely kill me."

But who else but the poor girl
took the gifts and gave her hand
walked at Klavus's manor
hand in hand with him. The lass
Kirsti peered through the window
peeped in at the panes:
K: "Oh! that somebody might come
to spoil that union!"

She went at once to Klavus:
K: "O my Klavus, my darling
Olovi is with my lady."

Kl: "O my Kirsti, my lassie
if you can show to be true
what you have put into words
I'll burn Elina in fire
then keep you in cloth."

K: "O my Klavus, my darling
be as one going far off
to Pohjanmaa assizes
drive to the barn at Ammas
round behind Little Meadows
and then I'll show to be true
what I have put into words."

Kl: "O my little Elina
lay provisions in a bag
put some butter in a box
and a joint of ham
and a bushel of hens' eggs
for me to go far away
to Pohjanmaa assizes."

E: "O my Klavus, my darling
speak with half-words, another
time give the latter half so
that you may survive
among the Pohja wizards."

That Klavus drove off
drove to the barn at Ammas
round behind Little Meadows:
that Kirsti went to wash clothes.
The lady came to the shore:

E: "O my Kirsti, my lassie
do not beat so hard
my beautiful clothes:
they were not got here
but back in my mother's house.
. . . O my Kirsti, my lassie
do not beat so hard
my beautiful clothes:
they were not got here
but back in my mother's house.
. . . Do not beat, Kirsti, you whore
quite so very hard
my beautiful clothes:
because they were not made here
but back in my mother's house."

K: "But I do not count –
I'm only a poor hireling:
what a great mistress you are
who have been with Olevi
on the long-bearded one's breast!
O my lady, my darling
let us have a little feast
as we used to have
when the master was away:
let us take the serfs off work
behind the wicked oxen."

E: "O my Kirsti, my lassie
do just as you wish:
tap all the other barrels
but don't tap the one
which was brewed for me."

And Kirsti thought of this trick:
she tapped that one first.

E: "O my Kirsti, my lassie
make my bed above the gate
in the fair chamber:
set out two pillows
and two linen sheets
two woollen covers.
. . . O my Kirsti, my lassie
you have not done as I said:
one pillow you have set out
and one linen sheet
one woollen cover."

K: "O my lady, my darling
Olovi called you to his room."

E: "But what am I to do there?"

She went there nevertheless
Kirsti hurried after her
and she locked nine locks
and shot a bolt for the tenth.
She went then to Ammas barn
round behind Little Meadows:
K: "O my Klavus, my darling
I have just shown to be true
what I have put into words:
Olovi lay with my lady."

Klavus rushed home, thrust a light
in a corner. Elina
thrust her finger through the pane:
E: "O my Klavus, my darling
do not lose your ring
though you lose the ring's wearer."

Klavus drew his sword
slashed the finger off.
Elina prayed in the room:
"Let all corners burn
but let this one run water
till I see my mother. Go
hired man, to my mother's house
tell her to come here!"

The man came to Suomela:
O: "My good woman, darling, my
lady called you to Laukko."

M: "Woe is me, a wan woman:
when I pull on my stockings
they are always back to front.
How is my daughter?"

O: "Quite well, good woman:
a cock is being scalded
a hen is being plucked there
for a tiny prince's feast."

M: "Woe is me, a wan woman:
when I dress up in my dress
it is always back to front.
Woe is me, a wan woman.
How is my daughter?"

O: "Quite well, good woman."

M: "When I put on my kerchief
it is always upside down.
How is my daughter?"

O: "Quite well, good woman."

M: "Ah, from Laukko smoke rises
smoke from Klavus's manor."

O: "Lambs are being slaughtered there
and pigs are being roasted
for a tiny prince's feast."

The woman went on her knees
before her own son-in-law:
M: "O my Klavus, my darling
take the boy out of the fire
the sturdy wife from the flames:
let her go to other lands
to be ashamed of her deeds
to cover her tracks."

K: "No, do not, my dear Klavus.
Take a pan of bad flour, take
a barrel of tar as well:
perhaps she will burn better.
Throw them here into the fire!"

M: "O my darling Elina
you might have curried favour
with the harlot whore."

E: "There is not the slightest cause
not even a needle-point.
Let this corner burn
now I have seen my mother!"
Nothing henceforth prospered in Laukko:
a stableful of horses
a cowshedful of beasts died
all died with straw in their mouths
perished at their oats.
Klavus Kurki, dreadful man
both sat down and wept.

Jesus as an old man walked:
J: "Why do you weep, Klavus Kurki?"

Kl: "There is good cause for weeping
and trouble for bewailing:
I have burnt, have burnt my spouse
set fire to my good armful
a stableful of horses
a shedful of beasts has died
all died with straw in their mouths
perished at their oats."

J: "Do not weep, Klavus Kurki:
I know Lady Elina."

Kl: "Where is Lady Elina?"

J: "In the highest of heavens
before six candles
a golden book in her hand
a little boy in her lap
Olevi before the door.
And I know Klavus Kurki."

Kl: "And where is Klavus Kurki?"

J: "In the lowest hell:
his spurs are just visible
are faintly gleaming.
And I know the whore Kirsti."

Kl: "And where is the whore Kirsti?"

J: "In the lowest hell:
her plaits are just visible."

That Klavus drove off.
He packed his pipes in his bag
played going over the marsh
drove towards the open sea
with Kirsti cur-like behind.
And that was the young man's loss
and the married fellow's too.

Singer unknown
Vesilahti(?), Häme
Collector unknown, recorded before 1800

85

The Faithful Bride I

Lalmanti, great knight
pledged an infant maid
gave his hand to the cradle
betrothed her with rich presents
bought her with big rings:
"Just wait for five years
five years or six years
eight summers with them
and nine warm seasons
a space of ten years.
When you hear I am
dead, wholly perished
take a better man
no better than me
and no worse than me –
take one like yourself."

Eerikki the little knight
carried false letters
false letters in haste:
Lalmanti conquered in wars
brought to the ground in struggles.
She was led to the wine-house
by force, by force was betrothed
by force could not be wedded –
not by men, by sword
nor by brave fellows
nor by choice women
nor by maids' beauty.

Inkeri the lovely maid
sat on the loft balcony
both sat down and wept:
she looked east, looked west
looked away northward.
She saw a bulge on the sea:
"If you are a flock of birds
then take flight and go
if you are a shoal of fish
then sink in the sea
if you are my Lalmanti
move your boat into haven."

"How do you know it's your Lalmanti?"

"I know the boat by the way
it comes, and its two oars move.
One half of its boat is new
the other half of blue silk –
the silk Inkeri's weaving
the maiden's long fashioning.
My young brother, take
your stallion from the barley
your ever-plump from the shoots
from the malts the short-legged
and drive to meet Lalmanti."

"Hullo, young brother-in-law
how is Inkeri faring?"

"Your Inkeri is faring well:
one week the wedding's toasted
another the gifts laid out
a third the presents given."

Singer unknown
Sääksmäki, Häme
E. Lönnrot, 1831

86

The Faithful Bride II

The rich man Maanitahan
bought a maid in the cradle
into her mouth slipped a ring:
in swaddling clothes the deal was
done, the word on bath-house planks.
The bridegroom must go to war:
the maid groomed her mother's head
    one Sunday evening
by the door at the window.

She looked out of the window:
what was the lump on the sea?
The maid dashed into the street:
"If you are a pile of leaves
    then flutter away
if you are a stook of hay
    fall in a windrow
if you are my son-in-law
    then row to the shore!"

"Hullo there, my son-in-law
hail, my young brother-in-law!
What's happening in the war?"

"Nothing's happening at all:
God has sorted out the wars
brought about eternal peace.
What is happening at home?
Has my own one not been wed
my kinswoman led away?"

The brother answering said:
"Your own one would have been wed
your kinswoman led away
but for your darling mamma.
Have you brought your mother gifts?"

"In the ship's hold I have brought
a box of ready money."

Singer unknown
Tyrö, Ingria
D. E. D. Europaeus, 1848

87

Death of the Bride I

Anterus from Holy River
Holy River's holy son
he came home from school

that is, Andrew from Pyhäjoki, a parish in Ostrobothnia, came home from school; and being asked by his mother

"Why, my son, have you come home?
Is the school where it should be
is the new Turku busy?"

why he had come home: surely yhe school had not been moved, and the new Turku was thriving? He answered that he had come to get a wife, and one from Kokemäki, *Swedish* Cumå. *At first his mother said no, fearing that he would be refused, as certain others, nobles from Sweden and rich Ostrobothnians, had been: to this he promptly replied that he was on intimate terms with the girl. The mother finally yielded; wherefore, well fitted out witgh horses, servants and weapons, among them seven shields, of which*

the bridegroom's shield glittered gold
all the others flashed silver:

the bridegroom's shield glittered gold, all the others flashed silver, thus he set out and was received on his arrival. But after the wedding ceremony had been performed, she happened to perish, leaving the deepest grief for a dowry to Andrew as he returned home.

Singer unknown
South-West Finland
D. Juslenius(?), before 1700

88

Death of the Bride II

Antero, Ylinen's son
son of the high-ranking man
  set up six chargers
  under six suitors
and a seventh for himself
and an eighth for his maiden:
that one he adorned with gold
decorated with silver
upon which he himself sat –
on that one he poured copper
where all his brother's folk sat.

Antero, Ylinen's son
son of the high-ranking man
went off to Korkka to woo
to Kavala to look round
went off to Kontui to woo
the young maid of Kalo Cape.

Father said, mother said no
the middle brothers said no
the youngest sisters said no:
  "Don't go, my offspring
  don't go, you shall not!"

Yet he went, he did not heed
he rode against, did not care
he rode against the fearless
  towards the harsh men.

Antero, Ylinen's son
son of the high-ranking man
bought and bargained for the maid
lifted her on to his steed
leapt upon the good one's back
brought her to his father's house:
one week he laid her on wool
  another on down
a third on eagle-feathers
went to wizards in Estonia . . .
  and came home from there.

Antero, Ylinen's son
son of the high-ranking man
went onward a little way
  went a short distance
  and he met a church:
the church bells began to clang.

  And Antero asked:
"Why are the church bells clanging?"

The sly watchman of the church
the too clever caretaker
formed in words, declared by mouth:
"Antero, Ylinen's son
for this the church bells ring out
  the priest's bugles howl:
those who last came to be wed
a couple in the priest-house
have been brought, the two of them
  buried together."

Antero, Ylinen's son
son of the high-ranking man
bit his lip, twisted his head

came onward a little way
now came near his home. He heard
knocking in the house, something
being shaped within the gates:
"What do you shape, my brother
and what smite, my sweet uncle:
are you shaping a war-boat
a war-ship are you building?"
"I shape a house for the dead
a manor for the perished."

Antero, Ylinen's son
son of the high-ranking man
struck his two palms together
like the two doors of the grave
flung his five fingers up, like
the five levers of Estonia.
Grim, he came into the room:
the maid lay in a corner
the curly-head was groaning.

He drew the knife from his thigh
snatched the grim one from its sheath
the bad one from its leather
    first struck his maiden
    and then struck himself.

They were brought, the two of them
    buried together.

Singer unknown
Hevaa, Kaprio, Ingria
A. Törneroos, T. Tallqvist, 1859

89

The Priest-Killer

Kirsti came, the praiseworthy
well spoken of through the lands
went off to church on Sunday
    well groomed and well dressed
    adorned all over.
    There Riiko's strong son
and Kaleva's handsome priest
preached the sermon in his boots
said Mass with his sword-belt on.

When he'd finished preaching he
demanded her for his wife
enticed her to be his whore:
Kirsti came, the praiseworthy
well spoken of through the lands
drew a knife, bared an iron
bore the grim one from its sheath
plunged it under the man's heart
    into the warm flesh.

She herself went weeping home
    wailing to the farm.
Her mother managed to ask:
"Why do you weep, my daughter
born in my youth, why complain?"

"For this I weep, my mother:
I went to church on Sunday
    well groomed and well dressed
    adorned all over.
    There Riiko's strong son
and Kaleva's handsome priest
preached the sermon in his boots
said Mass with his sword-belt on.
When he'd finished preaching he
demanded me for his wife
enticed me to be his whore.
Kirsti came, the praiseworthy
well spoken of through the lands
drew a knife, bared an iron
bore the grim one from its sheath
plunged it under the man's heart
    into the warm flesh.
I myself went weeping home
    wailing to the farm."

Mother said to her daughter:
    "Don't weep, my daughter
born in my youth, don't complain.
Take the horse from the barley
the big gelding from the rye
and drive it to other lands
    to other strange lands."

The daughter answered surely:
"O my mother who bore me
    I shall feel homesick
    be feeling homesick
when I've gone to other lands
    to other strange lands
    come to lands unknown –
most for her who suckled me
miss the great one who fed me
her most who put me to bed."

Mother said to her daughter:
"Longing won't help now:
you have got to go
to other strange lands."

Then Kirsti the praiseworthy
bought a stallion with barley
bought a big gelding with rye
and then drove to other lands
to other strange lands
came to lands unknown.
She drove to town squares:
the town dogs began to bark
the town boys began to stare!
They spoke to the traveller:
"What kindred are you
and from which people?"

"I must tell it, though
it were the end of poor me:
I was Kirsti, praiseworthy
well spoken of through the lands."

Thereupon Kirsti told from the beginning what had happened to her, and her mother's words who had sent her there, whereupon the town boys said the following words:

"Because you have done so, have
beer and liquor for your drink
bread from fine flour for your food
a closed shoe for your walking."

Anna Leskinen
Suistamo, Ladoga Karelia
S. Sirelius, 1847

90

The Intruder-Killer

The gloomy son of Mantu
the squat man, son of Mantu
played long on his kantele
blew for ages on his pipe
    lulled the young to sleep
    weighed the elders down
and the young began to sleep
the elders to be weighed down:
    greased the doors with wort
moistened the hinges with ale
that the new doors might not howl
nor the canvas hinges creak
as he went in to Kaisu.

He went to Kaisu's chamber
stretched himself at Kaisu's side
lifted Kaisu's covering.

The woman Kaisu, right fair
    answering replied:
"If you are my own husband
then stretch yourself at my side!
If you're a total stranger
    leave Kaisu's chamber
get away from Kaisu's side!"

He was a total stranger:
he was not her own husband.

The woman Kaisa, right fair
snatched the grim one from its sheath
the bad one from its leather
thrust it underneath his heart
    lodged it in his breast.
There was a din in the lane
a loud noise in the farmyard.

Antti with his Anni was
    lying in the loft.
Anni said to her Antti:
    "Go, Antti, and see
what the din is in the lane
the loud noise in the farmyard!"

Kaisa stood out in the lane
in her hand a bloody knife.

Antti said to his Anni:
"Kaisa's the din in the lane
the loud noise in the farmyard."
Antti answering replied:
    "O Kaisa, fair whore
you have done what you should not
brought your brothers a bad name
to your kin a great reproach
to yourself eternal shame."

The woman Kaisa, fair one
    she indeed answered:
"I have freed myself from shame
my brothers from a bad name
my kin from a great reproach
myself from eternal shame."

Kati
Soikkola, Ingria
V. Porkka, 1883

91

The Husband-Killer

The girl Maie, a sweet girl
sat on a hill at Tormio:
who raised Maie off the ground
raised the dear one from the mud
to him Maie would be given
the bead-breasted would be left.
The young lad Jyrki
lifted Maie off the ground
raised the dear one from the mud:
to him Maija was given
the bead-breasted one was left.

Maia made a bed of knives.
The young lad Jyrki
leapt upon that couch:
on it he broke his breastbone
ran his shoulders through.

Mother-in-law forced her up:
"Get up, poor daughter-in-law!
Others' cows have well eaten
well eaten, well drunk:
our cows are tethered."

Where Maie, which way Maie?
Maie ran off to the sea:
"Sea, creature of God
take me, care for me!"

The sea answering replied:
"I dare not take you:
you will be found here
snatched with a net-rope."

Where Maija, which way Maija?
Maija ran off to the well:
"Well, creature of God
take me, care for me!"

"I dare not take you:
you will be found here
drawn in water-pails
taken home on a cowlstaff."

Where Maija, which way Maija?
Maija ran off to the woods
Maija up the highest tree
up the most spreading alder.
There Maija was found:
"Maija, come down from the tree!"

Maije answering replied:
"I dare not come down.
What was coming has happened:
I have made a couch of knives
I have killed my own husband."

Singer unknown
Narvusi, Ingria
J. Länkelä, 1858

92

The Forsaken Maid I

Annikkainen the young maid
sat on the bridge at Turku
cared for the hens of the town
counselled the maids of Turku.
"A cloud rose from the north-west
another from the west came:
that which rose from the north-west
changed into a maidens' boat
that which out of the west came
changed into a Hunnish boat.

I was deceived by a Hun:
he ate the pigs I'd fattened
he drank my Christmas barrels
and the whoreson ruined me.
My little shirt of linen
wanted a skirt made of cloth
    my skirt made of cloth
wanted a gilded girdle
    my gilded girdle
wanted a weight of money
    my weight of money
wanted a young trading man
    my young trading man
wished to go to other lands
    to other strange lands
and he blew where the sail was
bore his wares into the boat."

The elk sweated when it ran
the elk drank when it thirsted
from the never-frozen spring:
    where its slaver dripped
    where it left its hair
there a fine birdcherry grew
on the birdcherry good fruit
there a fine juniper sprang
on the tree a fair berry.
He who took a bough from it
took off an eternal bough
and he who cut love from it
cut off an eternal love.

"Jesus I leave in my place
good Mary in my lodging:
it will be good to come back
to stocks made before
    to foundations once begun
And by whom were the stocks made?
By Jesus the stocks were made
by Mary the keels founded.
It will be good to come back
    better to return."

Singer unknown
Sääksmäki, Häme
E. Lönnrot, 1831

93

The Forsaken Maid II

"I'd sooner leave dainty foods
roasts behind in the priest's house
    than leave my dear one
    than leave my sweet one
    spurn my own good one
    I tamed all summer
    I hugged all autumn.
    Let them nowadays
    young maids nowadays
    and brides nowadays
the chickens just growing up
not carry out a man's will
a man's will, a skylark's word
    as I, poor wretch, did:
I carried out a man's will
a man's will, a skylark's word.
Butter I bought, tobacco
meat I bought and bread I bought
fish I bought of every kind
fetched liquor from Viipuri
and salt from the German town
    beer from the homelands.
What is wrong with my dear one
what with my song-bird, that he
has not come and kept his bond
kept his word and arrived here?
Could liquor have delayed him
or the whores have enticed him
the wayward women charmed him?
Liquor has not delayed him
but the whores have enticed him:
they hold him by the trousers
women by the trouser-legs."

Anni went to look for him:
he was loading up his goods
bearing his wares to the shore
    pushing his boat out
to go off to other lands.
He left the maiden weeping
    his dear one groaning.

    And Annikki prayed:
    "O Ukko, high god
    old man in the sky
bring a cloud from the north-west
from the west send another
from the east strike off a third
toss one from the chilly land:
break that boat on the water
to the backwoods hoist its prow
bear its ribs on to a rock
toss them to the chilly land!"

    And Annikki jeered:
"So there, so there, wretched boy:
the sea-surf for your pillow
the sea-foam for your cover
the waves for your undersheet –
no more Kirtti's bright pillow
nor Anni's woollen cover
nor a fine-spun bed-curtain."

Singer unknown
Suistamo(?), Ladoga Karelia
R. Polén, 1847

94

The Forsaken Maid III

Annikke, Turuinen's girl
girl of Turku, Island maid
burned a fire out in the square
and flames below the mountain
in the new house in Turku.
In summer she kept a Hun
in winter let him drink free
summers fed in the cellar
winters in the oak chamber
months long in the stone dwelling.
Meat she took and bread she took
butter she took, beer she took
fish she took of every kind
    white bread of eight kinds
five kinds of liquor she took
for the Hun's food, the Hun's drink
for the Hun, for the Hun's feast.

    She fed, fed her Hun
but that Hun wanted to run.
The Hun hankered for summer:
"If Jesus made it summer
if Mary melted the snow
I would flee in a vessel
    slip off in a boat
    eat meat in a ship
    fling bones to the waves!"

Now, the Creator listened
    Mary understood
so Jesus made it summer
and Mary melted the snow:
the Hun fled in a vessel
    slipped off in a boat.

Annikke, Turuinen's girl
girl of Turku, Island maid
    prayed upon the shore:
    "Bring, God, some north wind
    give some rain head-on:
    turn the ship over
    shove it on its side
drive its anchors on a rock
    push its masts on land
that the coasts may get money
    the little rocks coins."

Now, the Creator listened
    Mary understood:
    God brought the north wind
    gave some rain head-on
    turned the ship over
    shoved it on its side
drove its anchors on a rock
    pushed its masts on land.

Annikke, Turuinen's girl
girl of Turku, Island maid
    Annikke gloated:
    "There, so there, smart Hun
smart Hun, wanton widower:
you're not eating Anni's food
and not drinking Anni's drink.
No more Anni's butter pats

no more Anni's pancake-rolls
nor Anni's woollen cover
nor Anni's feather mattress:
the sea-foam for your cover
the sea-wind for your fur coat
the sea-wave under your head."

Olgoi
Hevaa, Kaprio, Ingria
V. Porkka, 1883

95

The Wife-Killer I

Hannus Pannus, handsome man
went off to Koski to woo
    Virta's youngest girl
    the boyar's best child.
He said when he had arrived:
"The best for me, not the worst
tallest for me, not shortest!"

    Virta's young girl said
    the boyar's best child:
"Neither the best nor the worst
neither tallest nor shortest.
You have married a mistress:
kill the wife you have wedded
slay the mistress you've married!"

Hannus Pannus, best of men
    went home from Koski
leapt on a two-year's withers
mounted a white-face's flanks
killed the mistress he'd married
slew the wife he had wedded.

He went to Koski to woo.
He said when he had arrived:
"The best for me, not the worst
tallest for me, not shortest!"

    Virta's young girl said
    the boyar's best child:
"Neither the best nor the worst
neither tallest nor shortest!
You have killed your wedded wife
slain someone who was alive:
    you might kill me too."

Hannus Pannus, best of men
    trusted a whore's lures
an evil woman's temptings.

Singer unknown
Tuupovaara, North Karelia
E. Lönnrot, 1838

96

The Wife-Killer II

Iivana, Koijoine's son
he, Iivana Koijoine
went off to Kontu to woo
the maidens of Kontu Cape
plaited heads of Kalla Cape.

The maids of Kontu answered:
"But you have a wedded wife
a mistress already sought.
Kill the wife you have wedded
the mistress already sought:
only then I'll go to you."

Iivana, Koijoine's son
he, Iivana Koijoine
　　came back home from there
　　and asked his children:
"Children, where is your mother?"

The eldest daughter replied
the youngest daughter spoke thus:
"She's in the village bathing
in the parish washing down."

Iivana, Koijoine's son
　　went, said to his wife
said through the bath-house window
from the bath-house door declared:
"O Helena, good mistress
Katteeriina, fair woman
　　bathe in your last steam
and soften your last bath-whisks
　　put on your best things!"

Helleena, the good mistress
Katteeriina, fair woman
　　bathed in her last steam
and softened her last bath-whisks
　　put on her best things
　　fine things on her skin
　　on her sweating skin
　　unscorched by the sun:
　　she came home from there.

Iivana, Koijoine's son
cut off the head of his wife
like the top off a turnip
like a cabbage off its stalk
made her head a marsh-hummock
and her hair dry meadow-grass
her fingers sprigs in a marsh
her ears leaves of a birch-tree
　　her eyes blackcurrants.
　　He came home from there.

The children cried for mother.
Iivana, Koijoine's son
answering replied only:
"I'll bring a better mother
I'll bring one five times wiser
five times, six times more famous."

The eldest daughter replied
the youngest daughter spoke thus:
"You'll not bring us a mother:
you'll bring a wife for yourself
you'll bring us one who tears hair

who shares hair out to the wind
    gives it to the gale.
If she were our own mother
she'd be kind five times a week
she'd be kind eight times a month
kind four times in seven days."

He went to Kontu to woo
the maidens of Kalla Cape.
They answering said only:
"You have killed your wedded wife
your mistress already sought:
    you might kill me too.
    I'll not go to you."

Mari Jämpsäläinen
Serepetta, Ingria
V. Porkka, 1883

97

The Daughter-Killer I

I fitted out my brother
fitted him out, gave him shoes
gave him my mother's stockings
brought a lapful of stockings
and a boxful of toe-rags
    an armful of socks.
I thought he'd go to the town
about the gentry's business:
my brother trod wooers' ways
went and bargained for a maid
stepped in the steps of a maid.

    He came from wooing
put his chestnut at the post
his black gelding in the chaff
rushed like wind into the house
like a gale into the porch
flung his cap on the table
his mittens upon his cap
started weeping over them.

    His mother drew near
    she closed in closer:
"Why do you weep, my offspring:
are you timid in men's games
or pushed out by your sisters
avoided by the chickens?"

"I'm not timid in men's games
nor pushed out by my sisters
avoided by the chickens.
For this I weep, my mother:
the maids will not step my way
the bead-breasted won't jingle
the tassel-bottomed won't drop.
The maids will not step my way
the bead-breasted won't jingle
the tassel-bottomed won't drop
because of many sisters
more mother's children I have
and many shirts are needed
    even more good belts."

The mother with wits of wind-
blown flax, twig-minded magpie
took her girls to the water
bore her children to the waves.

The eldest daughter replied
the middle daughter prattled:
"O mother, my old mother
    old mamma, my nurse
there will still be need for girls
still longing for plaited heads
even only in summer
in midsummer, at hay-time.
Summer has three busy times:
one is the fair oat-sowing
another rush rye-reaping
the third is the hot hay-time."

And the desired daughter-in-law was
got for the desired brother
    the wanted goose was
got for the wanted brother.
Cloth was put upon the loom

flaxen cloth under the beam
linen cloth near the ceiling:
the new heddles did not rise
for the young daughter-in-law
the new reed did not jingle
for the young daughter-in-law.

The cloth spoke up with its tongue:
"In this pain I am stifled
in this heat I am smothered.
Take me down the water-path
bear me along the well-path:
the village passers-by will
weave, travellers tie the ends
beggars will make the shuttles!"

    The cloth was finished.
    Who had a sharp knife?
The daughter-in-law had one
cut a shirt for her husband
another shirt for herself:
the poor old man got nothing
the poor old woman nothing.

She went off to the seashore
called out once for her daughters
she called out once, called out twice.

The elder daughter replied
the middle daughter prattled:
"O mother, my old mother
    old mamma, my nurse
    you're not my mother
    and not my old nurse!
The sea is mother to me
    the sea-foam my nurse
and the sea-waves my parent:
the sand has eaten my face
and the shingle my fingers."

Anni
Narvusi, Ingria
V. Porkka, 1883

98

The Daughter-Killer II

My brother went to Estonia
to take Estonia's money
to pay his land-tax.
My brother came back from Estonia
from taking Estonia's money
from paying land-tax.
Grimly he came to the house
proudly to the table-head:
first he tossed away his cloak
and flung down his cap
he went and sat down
he sat down and wept.

I was the youngest sister
was sweeping the floor.
I asked my brother:
"Why are you grieving, brother
your head down, in bad spirits?"

"For this, sister, I'm grieving:
that I have many sisters
and many shirts are needed
even more good belts
a big sackful of leggings
and a bundle of mittens
and a cornerful of gloves."

Now, the mother heard these words.
The mother with her three girls
went to the seashore:
one she drowned there in a sheet
one she sank there in a gown
one she weighed down with a shirt.

She took the desired daughter-in-law
the desired, the wanted one.

Cloth was put upon the loom:
the desired daughter-in-law won't weave.
The cloth sat there a whole year.
The cloth started with its tongue
the cloth began to argue:
"I have an ache in my hocks
I have a pain in my legs.
Take me to water
carry me to the well-path:
there the wanderers will weave
the travellers will turn me
the Swedes will swirl me.
They'll bring cloth home in a roll
to the beam-end all sewn up
into the room all bordered."

Mother's washing was unwashed:
desired daughter-in-law would not wash.
The mother's cows were unmilked:
desired daughter-in-law would not milk.

Mother went to get water
knocked the end of the cowlstaff
and rapped the rocks of the sea:
"Come, my eldest girl
come and weave my cloth!"

"No, I'll not come, my mother.
You have the desired daughter-in-law
the desired, the wanted one:
why will she not weave?"

She rapped the rocks of the sea
knocked the end of the cowlstaff:
"Come, my middle girl
and wash my washing!"

"No, I'll not come, my mother.
You have the desired daughter-in-law:
why will she not wash?"

She rapped the rocks of the sea
knocked the end of the cowlstaff:
"Come, my youngest girl
come and milk my cows!"

"No, I cannot, my mother.
The clouds are holding my head
the vapours my hair:
Tuoni's son is on my knees
Tuoni's step my only way."

Maria Äijö
Miikkulainen, Ingria
V. Alava, 1894

99

The Daughter

In the bath-house my mother
had me, on the bath-house straw:
my noble father
wore out his new shoes
trampled down his German boots
up and down the bath-house road.
Asked through the bath-house window:
"What has God given you, what
has the merciful given?
Has God made a threshing-hand
the merciful a plough-hand?"

My mother replied:
"God has made no threshing-hand
the merciful no plough-hand:
he has made a house-washer
has given a dish-washer
a weaver of spring cloth, a
washer of winter washing."

Father said: Put in the marsh!
Brother: Push in the water!
Uncle: Dash against a wall!
Uncle's wife: Fix on a pole!

But my mother's heart would not
nor would my nurse's belly –
could not push in the water
nor could dash against a wall:
mother had seen great troubles
had borne grievous pains
lying on the bath-house soil
staying on the straw
resting on the boards.
Mother pushed me in a cot
laid her child in a cradle:
many nights she was sleepless
many evenings supperless
many mornings with no meal
breakfast-times with no breakfast
and she dried the new napkins
in eight napkins swaddled me
in a single summer night.
Other kin were at breakfast
my mother was stuck to me
with both hands in the cradle
with five fingers on the beam
with ten nails at the edges.
She thought there would be support
a shelter would be prepared
but for mother no support
no support for her who rocked
aid for the bountiful nurse.
There was support for pick-mouths
a water-drawer for blabber-mouths
for sluggards a wood-chopper . . .

Singer unknown
Soikkola, Ingria
J. Länkelä, 1858

100

The Son

Laari boy, excellent boy
Laari, excellent laddie
shaped skis one autumn
and sledge-shackles a whole spring:
of wolf's bones he shaped the skis
of bear's bones the sledge-shackles.
One year he saved goat's butter
a month long cock's grease
and with these he greased his skis
smeared them with goose-fat.

He went sliding over lands
lands that had been slid over
that had not been slid over
slid into the great backwoods
to some tall birches
saw a creature on a bough
a brown cuckoo on a gnarl
said by mouth, declared in words:
"Sit still there, bird of the air
wait, eagle of God
until I have wiped my gun
I've cleaned my rusty iron
wiped my gun as good as new
my rusty iron on grass!"

I shot once and I shot twice.
I shot once, I hit too low
I shot twice, I hit too high
but it lodged home the third time:
the pure one fell on the snow
the fat spilled on the snow-crust.

I tied it in my handkerchief
I tied it in my eye-rag
took it to please my mother
as a titbit for mamma:
"My mother, my favourite
my mamma, my sweet berry
has the milk now been paid for
the harsh torment been made good?"

Mother answering replied
for an answer said:
"The milk is not yet paid for
the harsh torment not made good.
You'll pay for mamma's troubles
make good your hatcher's torment
your nurse's troubles, only
if you make mother a coat
a fur coat for her who rocked
out of seven foxes' backs
round paws of ermine
six skins of marten."

He made his mother a coat
a fur coat for her who rocked
put silk down the openings
a hemmed linen skirt below
laid cloth along the edges.

Laari boy, excellent boy
asked his dear mother:
"Has the milk now been paid for
the harsh torments been made good?"

Mother answering replied
indeed she answered:
"Ah, my Laari, my offspring
the troubles will be paid for
harsh torments made good, only
if you build mother a house
build a house for her who rocked
a porch in front of the house
with chambers beside the house
a hut beside the chamber
and new doors to the chamber."

Laari boy, excellent boy
built a house for his mother
built a house for her who rocked
a porch in front of the house
with chambers beside the house
a hut beside the chamber
and new doors to the chamber.

Laari boy, excellent boy
asked his dear mother:
"Has the milk now been paid for
the harsh torments been made good?"

Mother answering replied
indeed she answered:
"Ah, my Laari, my offspring
the troubles will be paid for
harsh torments made good, only
if you bring bread from the grove
brown-crusted from the birch-wood."

Laari boy, excellent boy
brought bread from the grove
brown-crusted from the birch-wood.

Laari boy, excellent boy
asked his dear mother:
"Has the milk now been paid for
the harsh torments been made good?"

Mother answering replied
indeed she answered:
"Now the milk has been paid for
the harsh troubles been made good."

Singer unknown
Tyrö, Ingria
D. E. D. Europaeus, 1853

101

The Mother

I went after berries for mother
cranberries for who bore me
picked cowberries, a sockful
two sockfuls of cranberries
a bushel of raspberries
a sieveful of currants, an
eggshellful of bilberries.
I came home in the evening.

So the village women asked
women among neighbours said:
"Give, Maaroi, of your berries
Katoi, of your cranberries!"

But I answering replied:
"Maaroi's berries aren't to spare
nor are Katoi's cranberries:
Maaroi takes them to mother
Katoi to her who bore her."

Marjukkain my dear mother
took the berries on her knees
put a berry on her tongue.
Then she sank down on her bed
then went limp on the bed-boards:
she was a year in her bed
two indeed under covers.

What am I to do, poor wretch
what to do and how to live?
I'll to Estonia's wizards
to augurs below the town.

The young wizards would not rise
the old augurs would not stand
to care for the old woman.

I gave them this, gave them that
I gave my only linen
    I gave my last corn
I gave gold by the fistful
silver cupped in my two hands:
one son of a wizard rose
    an old augur stood
to care for the old woman.

And I hurried home: I heard
knocking in the house, something
being shaped at the gateway
    chopped at the hinges.

"What do you shape, my brother
and what smite, my sweet uncle:
is it war-boats you're shaping
    war-ships you're building
    war-oars you're fitting?"

My brother indeed answered:
"I am shaping no war-boats
    building no war-ships
    fitting no war-oars:
I shape a house for the dead
and a hut for one gone down."

And I rushed into the house
like a gale into the porch:

mother, washed, was on the bench
was laid out on the platform.
    And I drew nearer
    I closed in closer.

I began to cry aloud
I began to chant a dirge
and in burning words to say:
    "O my dear mother
    you've left me in need
like a bird in need of meat
    you've left me in want
like a magpie wanting blood.
    O my dear mother
give your voice to the orphan
    and chant the last word
now you've gone to Tuoni's land
now you've moved into the sand!
    A church is built high:
on you is a shining cross
upon you a linen shroud."

Uljaana
Soikkola, Ingria
V. Porkka, 1883

102

The Dying Maid I

A maid lay ill in the town
below the Island lay sick.
The dear one said as she died
and declared as she lay ill:
"When I die, a famous girl
when I, a joy-bell, perish
bring the kin before my face
the clan as my breath departs!
If a land-journey is made
let it be made on horseback
upon six gilded horses
another six ungilded!
If a water-journey's made
then let it be made by boat
in six gilded boats
another six ungilded!"

The dear one said as she died
and declared as she lay ill:
"When I die, a famous girl
when I, a joy-bell, perish
don't bury me priestless, set
no stone without a pastor:
bring a priest from Paastue
a pastor from Kiljanta!

Carry me out there
carry me where I command
and where I send you –
to Kaarasta village street!
I cannot lie there
not rest in those sands
for the stamp of villagers
for the splash of the fat-cheeks
for the clop of the horseshoes.

Bury me out there
bury me where I bid you
and where I send you –
beneath my father's window
and beside my brother's wall!
I cannot lie there either
not rest in those sands
for my father's loud weeping
for my mother's long wailing
for my brother's axe hewing
daughter-in-law's stone rumbling
my sister's distaff whirring.

Carry me out there
carry me where I command
and where I send you
to the base of the bright church
under the thick boulder's arm!
I cannot lie there either
not rest in those sands
for the priest's loud howl
for the pastor's roar
the deacon singing the dirge.

Bury me out there
bury me where I bid you
in the graveyard's lovely soil
in the sweet shingle
in the shining sands
where other maids are buried!
Then I can lie there
and rest in those sands."

Heloi
Kaprio, Ingria
V. Porkka, 1883

103

The Dying Maid II

The Estonian maid lay sick
and she said as she lay sick:
"When I die, a famous lass
pine away, a rich daughter
bringer of work for good men
source of money for rich men
  take me to lie down
  press me down to sleep
beneath my father's window!"

But the maid could not lie down
  nor the lass rest long
for her father's whip swishing
the trampling of cattle-hoofs:
her father got up early
  to feed the stallion.

The Estonian maid lay sick
and she said as she lay sick:
"When I die, a famous lass
pine away, a rich daughter
bringer of work for good men
source of money for rich men
  take me to lie down
  press me down to sleep
in my brother's boat haven!"

But the maid could not lie down:
the German ships arrived there
  the Stockholm craft came
and the tar-bowed milled about.

The Estonian maid lay sick
and she said as she lay sick:
"When I die, a famous lass
pine away, a rich daughter
bringer of work for good men
source of money for rich men
  take me to lie down
  press me down to sleep
before my mother's cellar!"

But the maid could not lie down:
her mother got up early
  to rinse out the tubs
  to rattle the churns.

The Estonian maid lay sick
and she said as she lay sick:
"When I die, a famous lass
pine away, a rich daughter
bringer of work for good men
source of money for rich men
  take me to lie down
  press me down to sleep
at the edge of sister's field!"

But the maid could not lie down
for sister's distaff jingling:
her sister got up early.

The Estonian maid lay sick
and she said as she lay sick:
"When I die, a famous lass
pine away, a rich daughter
bringer of work for good men
source of money for rich men
  take me to lie down

lay me down to sleep
at the side of the bright church
beside the hundred-boarded
right inside the tarry porch

on the fat bone-hill
beside the lush grass:
there many silent folk are
crowded together."

Mateli Kuivalatar
Ilomantsi, North Karelia
E. Lönnrot, 1838

104

The Hanged Maid I

The girl Anni, matchless girl
went to the wood for bath-whisks
to the thicket for bath-whisks:
broke off one for her father
another for her mother
a third she gathered
for her youngest brother, the
best in the family.

Osmonen slipped from the dell
Kalevainen from the clearing:
"Grow, maid, to please me
not the other young people
the fair young people:
grow in narrow, in neat things
grow tall in dresses of cloth."

The girl Anni, matchless girl
went weeping homeward
wailing to the farm.

Father was at the window
was whittling an axe-handle:
"Why do you weep, Anni girl?"

"The cross has slipped from my breast
the ring slipped from my finger
my trinkets off my belt's end
the beads from my eyes
the gold tassels from my brows."

Her brothers in the gateway
were adorning a bright sleigh
were building a box-sledge: "Why
do you weep, sister Anni?"

"There is cause for my weeping:
the cross has slipped from my breast."

The girl Anni, matchless girl . . .

Her sisters upon the floor
were weaving a belt of gold
working one of silver: "Why
do you weep, sister Anni
sister Anni, matchless one?"

"The cross has slipped from my breast
the ring slipped from my finger
my trinkets off my belt's end."

Mother on the shed step was
washing butter in a pail:
"Why do you weep, Anni girl
you girl Anni, matchless girl?"

"I went to the wood for whisks
to the thicket for bath-whisks
broke off one for my father.
Osmonen called from the dale
Kalevainen from the clearing:
'Grow, maid, to please me
not the other young people
the fair young people:
grow in narrow, in neat things.' "

"You girl Anni, matchless girl
don't weep, Anni girl.
Three are the sheds on the hill.
Step to the shed on the hill
open the best shed:
there eat butter for a year
and grow plumper than others
another year, pork
and a third, fish pies.
Stand trunk upon trunk
case on top of case:
open the best trunk
make the bright lid slam open
put on the best things
the most gorgeous on your breasts."

The girl Anni, matchless maid
stepped to the shed on the hill
opened the worst shed
became prettier than others
became plumper than others
opened the worst trunk
found six golden belts
eight swaddling-girdles
strangled herself with the belts
choked herself with the girdles
she staggered, she slumped
hanged herself with her own thread:
then she dropped upon the case
fell on the trunk-lid.

Her mother came to the shed
when three years had passed:
the girl Anni was no more.

"Roll, a tear, roll, another
let my brimming waters roll
on my fine skirt-hems
on my gorgeous breasts
roll, a tear, roll, another
on my silk belt-ends
roll, a tear, roll, another
on my silk stockings
lower still than that
on my fine skirt-hems
lower still than that
upon my fair heels
the heels of my golden shoes
roll, a tear, roll, another
lower still than that
to the earth-mothers below
to the earth for the earth's good."

Now three rivers came
and a fiery river came
from one maiden's tears
three birches were bred
on the bank of each river
three cuckoos were bred
out of one person's weeping.

The third called *love, love*
to the nameless child
the first called *joy, joy*
to the joyless child
the second *love, love*
to the loveless child
the third called *joy, joy*
to the child with no father.

Singer unknown
Uhtua, Archangel Karelia
E. Lönnrot, 1834

105

The Hanged Maid II

Alermo, Ylermä's swain
one of all the country's best
he asked his mother:
"Have you seen a maid growing
one with locks rising?"

"Yes, I've seen a maid growing
one with locks rising
but she will not do for you
as a bride for you, young squire."

Alermo, Ylermä's swain
fitted out six ships
and a seventh for himself:
fitted sails, red ones
other sails, blue ones
a third lot all green
set the sails to sail
the tar-bows to tug
went to woo the maid.

The maid groomed her mother's head
by the door, beneath the beam
between two windows
stuck her head through the window
and her face through the big gap:
"O mother, my old mother
old mamma, my nurse
Untomaa's war is coming."

Her mother answering said:
"No, Untomaa's war is not:
they are your wooers coming.
Go to the shed on the hill –
there is chest on chest
box on top of box:
put on the best things
fine things on your skin!"
The maid
went to the shed on the hill
put on the best things
fine things on her skin
took six golden belts
seven silver belts.
She fixed the tips to a beam
the middle part to her neck:
there she choked to death
there she fell towards the grave.

Ylermä, Alermo's swain
he asked his mother:
"Where then is this maid of yours?"

His mother answering said:
"She's in the shed on the hill
in the shed upon the hill:
go to the shed on the hill
to the shed upon the hill!"

Alermo, Ylermä's swain
went to the shed on the hill
to the shed upon the hill
looked at the shed door:
the maiden hung from the beam.

Kati Kähärä
Narvusi, Ingria
J. Ruotsalainen, 1900

106

The Loss I

I went to the marsh to wash
to the field to wring
put my shirt on a willow
my skirt on an aspen bough
my beads on the sandy shore.
A thief watched from the thicket
a wicked man from the scrub:
took my shirt from the willow
my skirt from the aspen bough
my stockings from the bare ground
my shoes from the summer-rock
my beads from the sandy shore.
I went weeping home.

Mother asked at home:
"Why do you weep, my youngster?"
"I went to the marsh to wash
to the field to wring
put my shirt on a willow
my skirt on an aspen bough
my beads on the sandy shore.
A thief watched from the thicket
a wicked man from the scrub:
took my shirt from the willow
my skirt from the aspen bough
my stockings from the bare ground
my shoes from the summer-rock
my beads from the sandy shore."

"Don't weep, my youngster.
There's a chestful of bright things
another of shiny things:
put on the best things
fine things on your skin!"

Helena
Kupanitsa, Ingria
J. Ruotsalainen, 1901

107

The Loss II

I stayed a week with parents
another week visiting
wove a cloak with a gold edge
a sheet with a silver edge
went to the marsh to wash them
to the lake-ice to rinse them.
A ring fell from my finger
    a band from my thumb
and one from my other hand.
    I went weeping home.

My mother managed to ask:
"Why are you weeping, my girl?"

"For this I weep, my mother:
I stayed one week with parents
another week visiting."

"Just wait till our brown cow calves
    we'll get German rings
    and some German bands
and horns a hundred spans long
its muzzle a thousand spans."

Singer unknown
Skuoritsa, Ingria
K. Stråhlman, 1856

108

The Loss III

I went to marshes to tramp
to clearings to drive about:
there woods were full of water
tree-roots of brown beer
the clearings full of dishes
the stump-roots of jugs.
I took a jug, another
started at once on a third
I drank myself drunk
drank myself, gave others drink.

I started to feel sleepy
slept on the good grass
sank on the white ground, beneath
a spruce with its top in flower
underneath an aspen boat:
a thief took my good horse, made
away with the mouse-hued one –
yes, and the ashwood saddle.
I went weeping home
wailing to the farm.

My father was in the shed
my mother on the shed steps.
My father managed to ask:
"Why are you weeping, my lad?"

I answering said:
"For this I weep, my father:
a thief took my good horse, made
away with the mouse-hued one –
yes, and the ashwood saddle!"

Father told me not to weep:
"Do not worry, my offspring.
Yesterday our cow calved: she
has dropped a white calf
slipped forth one with white hocks. If
we take it to Viipuri
there we'll make hundreds
thousands will be pressed on us.
We'll buy a better stallion
or a mare, a young filly.
She'll eat the oats from the eaves
from the clouds she'll suck water."

Singer unknown
Tyrö, Ingria
V. Porkka, 1883

109

The Loss IV

I was a small boy
as tall as my father's knee
as long as mother's distaff.
A small boy, I went ploughing
early furrowing:
ploughed a furrow, another
soon began a third.
Death brought many wolves
carried forest bears:
ate my foal in the furrow
my black gelding on the soil.
I went weeping home.

Father asked: "Why do you weep, my lad
why, my fair-haired one, lament?"

"For this I weep, my father:
Death brought many wolves
carried forest bears.
I had no time for ploughing
for they ate my foal in the furrow
my black gelding on the soil."

Father answering replied:
"Do not weep, my lad
my fair-haired one, don't lament!
We'll go to town in summer
yes, and to market proudly:
we'll buy a stallion
or a mare, a young filly."

Maria Kirppu
Liissilä, Ingria
J. Lorvi, 1914

110

The Dance

I think I will start dancing.
The dance is not my breeding
nor the other's, my partner's:
the dance was brought from yonder
the far side of Novgorod
through the yards of Petersburg
from the White Sea's wide waters –
not even from there either!

A berry grew on a hill
fine grass was rising
horses sweating drew
foals wandered foaming
partridges whistled
on the sapling collar-bows
squirrels ran about
on the maple shafts
black grouse were cooing
on the prow of the bright sleigh
water from the collar-bow
dripped, fat from the traces-tip
the iron sledge creaked
as the dance was led along
as the thing of joy was brought.

The dance arrived in the yard:
all joy was at the window.
Whose leave should I ask
to lead the dance in
lead the dance, my guest?

The dance arrived in the yard:
the cows knocked over their pens
the oxen snapped their tethers
the stone oven moved
the post of curly birch shook.
Whose leave should I ask –
master's at the table-head
the mistress's at the side
or the boy's at the bench-end
to lead the dance in
lead the dance, my guest?

But the dance could not come in
without catching the door-wall:
the door-wall was of bear's bones
the rear wall was of deer's bones
the closet was of sheep's bones
the side wall of bunting's bones
and the ceiling of bream-scales.

Now the dance came in.
To him who will come dancing
may a boy be born
as clever as his father
to go through the assizes
to make a case in public!
To him who won't come dancing
may a girl be born
as lazy as her mother
to be laid below the fence
tumbled among the alders!

Down, down, good lady
for your daddy is dying!
Down, down, good lady

for your mamma is dying!
Down, down, good lady:
your brother is dead
your sister is dead
and your bride is dead!

Up, up, good lady:
your daddy's alive again!
Up, up, good lady:
your mamma's alive again!
Up, up, good lady:
your brother's alive again
your sister's alive again
and your bride's alive again!

Singer unknown
Jyskyjärvi, Archangel Karelia
E. Lönnrot, 1835

111

The Suitors from the Sea I

Kirstinen sat on a rock
hoping for a happy man
lilting for a lucky man.
From the sea a gold man rose
with a hat of gold on his shoulders
mittens of gold in his hand:
"Will you come, Kirstinen, to me?"

"Neither meant nor made
nor bidden at home
for a golden man was I."

Kirstinen sat on a rock
hoping for a happy man
lilting for a lucky man.
From the sea a silver man rose
with a silver hat on his shoulders
silver mittens in his hand:
"Will you come, Kirstinen, to me?"

"Neither meant nor made
nor bidden at home
for a silver man was I."

Kirstinen sat on a rock
hoping for a happy man
lilting for a lucky man.
From the sea a copper man rose
with a copper hat on his shoulders
copper mittens in his hand:
"Will you come, Kirstinen, to me?"

"Neither meant nor made
nor bidden at home
for a copper man was I."

Kirstinen sat on a rock
hoping for a happy man
lilting for a lucky man.
From the sea a bread man rose
with a hat of bread on his shoulders
mittens of bread in his hand:
"Will you come, Kirstinen, to me?"

"Yes, both meant and made
and bidden at home
for a man of bread was I."

Jussi
Heinola, Häme
J. Toppola, 1890

112

The Suitors from the Sea II

Anni, matchless maid
sat upon the Finland Quay
sometimes sat and sometimes wept
waiting for a likely man
for a bridegroom with sweet words.

A man appeared on the sea
rose upon the waves
iron in his mouth, his hand
iron mittens in his hands
iron hat on his shoulders
iron gifts in his mittens:
"Are you kept, maiden, for me?"

"Not for you nor anyone
nor for other young people:
I grow up in narrow clothes
grow tall in dresses of cloth
on father's breadcrusts."

A man appeared on the sea
rose upon the waves
copper in his mouth, his hand
copper mittens in his hands
copper hat on his shoulders
copper gifts in his mittens:
"Are you kept, maiden, for me?"

"Not for you nor anyone
nor for other young people:
I grow up in narrow clothes
grow tall in dresses of cloth
on father's breadcrusts."

A man appeared on the sea
rose upon the waves
tin in his mouth, in his hand
mittens of tin in his hands
hat of tin on his shoulders
gifts of tin in his mittens:
"Are you kept, maiden, for me?"

"Not for you nor anyone
nor for other young people:
I grow up in narrow clothes
grow tall in dresses of cloth
on father's breadcrusts."

A man appeared on the sea
rose upon the waves
gold in his mouth, in his hand
mittens of gold in his hands
hat of gold on his shoulders
gifts of gold in his mittens:
"Are you kept, maiden, for me?"

"Not for you nor anyone
nor for other young people:
I grow up in narrow clothes
grow tall in dresses of cloth
on father's breadcrusts."

A man appeared on the sea
rose upon the waves
bread in his mouth, in his hand
mittens of bread in his hands
hat of bread on his shoulders

gifts of bread in his mittens:
"Are you kept, maiden, for me?"

"Now I'll come to you.
Yes, both meant and meet
and rocked by my dame
lulled by my old one
yes, bidden at home
it is granted, made,
granted, made, made meet
meet by holy God
that black to white be a help
that short to tall be a mate."

Okki Gordeinen
Repola, Olonets Karelia
U. Karttunen, 1897

113

The Suitors from Afar

Kati, a flower, little bird
for ages sat, for long grew
for long she grew up at home
longer at her mother's side:
mother did not take it ill
father did not think it odd
that Katri was long growing.

Katri began to gabble:
"Why won't the young men marry
why will they not marry me?"

'Twas her brother's cunning wife
    she, cunning and sly
    who slily gabbled:
"For this they won't marry you:
you don't wash your hair evenings
    nor brush it mornings."
Katri started washing her hair
    brushing it mornings.
    Three nights wooers came:
some came on the moon's behalf
some came on the sun's behalf
some on further Estonia's behalf
some on her own lands' behalf.
Father wished her for the moon
mother wished her for the sun
the brother for further Estonia
the maiden for her own lands:
"I will not go to the moon.
    The moon has six trades:
sometimes it sinks behind cloud
sometimes behind a cloud-edge.
I will not go to the sun:
    the sun burns much land
    the eyes so much more.
I'll not to further Estonia:
there watery gruel is cooked
which is made to last a week
and a month goes by on it."

She chose those from her own lands
chose the lads of her own part.
Better be in your own lands
drinking water from birch-bark
    than be in strange lands
drinking beer from a flagon.

Uljaana
Narvusi, Ingria
V. Porkka, 1883

114

The Foul Maid

I went to Kontu to woo
in famous Kontu village
in a stern father-in-law's house
at a stern mother-in-law's side.
    I spoke, I spoke up:
"Have you a maiden for sale
    or a hen to trade?"

"Hens are sold beneath a beam
maids in a four-cornered room.
Go that way into the house:
a house is for men to come
a stall for horses to live."

Well, I went into the house:
it was full of button-mouths
and the floor of snub-noses
and the back bench of farters.
Beer was brought into the house
a jug of mead, one of beer:
"I do not care to eat yet
    nor care to drink yet
but I'd like to see the maid:
bring the maid into the house!"

    The maid was brought in
under the wing of sisters
the cloak of her brother's wife
arm in arm with her sisters-in-law:
"There is no man's marrying
    there is no man's bride:
she is black as a cockroach
she has a black ragged shirt
and patched stockings on her feet
her eyes are deep in pig-muck
and her ears in dog-slobber . . ."

Long I stayed in Viipuri
for ages in the salt-town.
Others married pretty girls:
I was left with the dud ones
    dealt the cross-eyed ones.

Niilo Pöyhönen
Juva, Savo
V. Tarkiainen, 1898

115

The Thief as Suitor

On the road a grouse-fence I
built, on the field a hare-fence
by the village a maid-fence:
a maid went into my fence
a red-cheek into my snare.

I began to ask the maid:
"Will you go to my brother?"
The maid answering replied:
"What is your brother?"
"A ploughman and a sower
and a scatterer of seeds."

"I'll not go to a ploughman.
A ploughman has a cold shirt:
there's no lying at his side
getting warm under his chin
no settling under his arm
no chatting under his beard."

On the road a grouse-fence I
built, on the field a hare-fence
by the village a maid-fence:
a maid went into my fence
a red-cheek into my snare.

I began to ask the maid:
"Will you go to my brother?"
"What is your brother?"
"He is a smith, my brother."

"I will not go to a smith.
A smith has a coal-black shirt:
there's no lying at his side
getting warm under his chin
no settling under his arm
no chatting under his beard."

On the road a grouse-fence I
built, on the field a hare-fence
by the village a maid-fence:
a maid went into my fence
a red-cheek into my snare.

I began to ask the maid:
"Will you go to my brother?"
The maid answering replied:
"What is your brother?"
"He's a hunter, my brother."

"I'll not go to a hunter.
A hunter smells of pine-sprigs
and of junipers he stinks:
there's no lying at his side
getting warm under his chin
no settling under his arm
no chatting under his beard."

On the road a grouse-fence I
built, on the field a hare-fence
by the village a maid-fence:
a maid went into my fence
a red-cheek into my snare.

I began to ask the maid:
"Will you go to my brother?"

"What is your brother?"
"He is a thief, my brother."

"I'll go, I'll go to a thief!
A thief has a shirt ready
a shirt ready and whitened:
there is lying at his side
and settling under his arm
and chatting under his shirt!"

Lukeri Melikova
Vuole, Ingria
F. Pajula, 1894

116

The Useless Bridegroom

I sent my fair one for fish
my darling for perch
but my fair one caught no fish
my darling no perch.
I went off for fish myself:
I put the nets on my back
the stone weights upon my breasts.
I rowed headlands, rowed islands:
on each island I caught fish
on each crag salmon
on each headland trout.
I went to land to cook them
with my father's tall wood-piles
my brother's shavings. The skins
I gathered in a knapsack
took for my bridegroom to eat.

My bridegroom ate and praised them:
"Now, this is good food
for a useless man to eat."

I warmed the fragrant bath-house
with fragrant firewood:
bathed my fill myself
and my guests bathed too.
I warmed the fumy bath-house
with fumy firewood:
I sent my bridegroom to bathe.
When he shouted for water
then I added steam.
And I pitied my sweet one
felt a pang for my dear one:
I dragged him down by the hair
threw him on my back, took him
to the marsh for washing-steps
for a bridge to dirty spots
his head for a marsh-hummock
his eyes for marsh-cranberries
set his mouth for a marsh-spring.
I went there to see
after five, six weeks
what my bridegroom was doing:
he was sewing some closed shoes.
Who were those shoes for?
My bridegroom answering said:
"For who else if not for you
as for anyone who's good."

I clasped my bridegroom, carried
him in to the table-head
gave him food and gave him drink
laid my bridegroom down to rest
stretched myself out beside him.

Singer unknown
Sakkola, Karelian Isthmus
H. A. Reinholm, 1848

117

Thc Crane I

Ewe, ewe, an Estonian ewe
sheep, a German sheep
its wool dangled on the ground:
I took the wool for myself
went to the marsh to wash it.

And my ring dropped off.
Go, girl, search for it!
The girl starts to weep.

Do not weep now, girl:
I will go myself.
And I found a crane ploughing
a crow furrowing.

I drove the crane home:
into the bath-house closet
put it, tossed hay before it.

Wash the pot now, girl
and put the crane on to boil!

"Do not put me in the pot:
I will wash the long tables
with my tail I'll brush the stove
with my neck I'll fetch water
with my toes I'll sweep."

Ristiina Kohonen
Lemi, Savo
T. Kohvakka, 1933

118

The Crane II

Once I heard a crane moaning
in the priest's meadow groaning.
I went round to the crane's pen:
it bore a white calf for me.

I put some straw before it
    but it would eat none.
I put some hay before it –
    none of that either.
I put some rye before it –
    none of that even.
I put some wheat before it:
of that it pecked a little
it picked about half a peck.

I put Maija to milk it
but she could not find the teats.
I put Kaija to milk it
but she tore out all its hair.
I went myself to milk it
and I milked a big pail full
    the priest's big pot full
and the deacon's big spoon full
    a beggar's shoe full.

Sofia Siivonen
Pyhämaa, South-West Finland
I. Seppänen, 1928

119

The Early Riser

I made a bet with the sun
I vied with the moon
gave my hand to the daylight
gave it to the daylight's son:
which of us would be first up
    and which first awake –
    the maid or the sun?

    The maid was first up
    and beat him to it:
she made it before the sun
    before the moonlight.
She rose up in the morning
    washed her little eyes
    scrubbed her slender palms
she opened the fire-grate hatch
    shifted the range hatch
took the dried corn from the stove
sifted the corn with a sieve
    with a sieve of steel
poured the corn into a box
    a box of copper
took the corn to the stone hut
bore it to the mortar-room.
She ground the corn, pounded it
with a juniper pestle
    in a fir mortar
ground a knapsackful of corn
a boxful of wheat she dragged
lugged a sackful of hulled grain.

She went to look for the sun
to look out for the moonlight:
but the sun was still lying
    the moonlight resting
    the daylight resting
the sun would not raise its head
yet, nor the moon lift its brows.

    The maiden came home
brought five buckets of water
    six pails she wore out
    washed out the churn-room
    swept out the dairy
took the dirt beyond the gate
over the palings tipped it.
    She stood on her dirt:
she stayed till the dirt was chaff
till the chaff was bran she stayed
she stayed till the bran was dust
till the dust was clear water
till the water was a spring
till the spring was warm water
    an underground spring.

She went to look for the sun
to look out for the moonlight:
but the sun was still lying
and the moonlight whispering
    the daylight resting.
Its legs could be seen in bed
its toes under the cover
plenty of feet in the bed
sides enough under the quilt.

The maiden came home
sheared a bluish ewe
fleeced a yearling sheep:
she carded the blue one's wool
flung the threads upon the reel
and hung the coat on the beam.
She went to look for the sun
to look out for the moonlight:
the sun raised its head only
now, the moon lifted its brows.

Singer unknown
Moloskovitsa – Tyrö, Ingria
A. Törneroos, T. Tallqvist, 1859

120

Finding a Husband

Three sisters-in-law quarrelled
across three thresholds
behind three stove-posts
and the beds of three brothers:
who would have a girl
who a girl and who a boy?
The youngest one had a girl
the youngest, smallest
best in the family.

From where would the priests be got
the scholars be brought?
Priests were got from Paatitsa
the scholars from Luutitsa.
What should she be called?
Call her Palaga:
Palaga is a bad name –
the kin would not stand for it.
Call her Paraska:
Paraska is ill-behaved –
mother would not stand for it.
Naasta? – she might be nasty.
Hoora? – she might be a whore.
Hekko tinkled from the book
flitted from the page.

The girl grew, the girl Hekko
Hekko the wearer of beads
the carrier of mother's coins:
she grew for eight years
she rose for nine years
for more than ten years.

Hekko's mother said:
"What is wrong with our Hekko
what with our blossom-berry
that none comes to woo Hekko
to take the apple
to look for my precious one?"

A blind man from the corner
said, sightless from the hallway
a small child from the stove-bench:
"For this none comes to woo her:
she won't wash her eyes
will not brush her hair
at sunrise won't brush her head
at cockcrow will not dry it.
When Saturday evening comes
she will not wash the benches
nor sweep the floor of the house
and when Sunday comes
she dashes out visiting
will not groom her mother's head
scrub the head of who bore her."

The girl Hekko, a sweet girl
Hekkoi the sweet little maid
now began to wash her eyes
every day she washed her head
at cockcrow dried it:
when Saturday evening came
she washed the benches
and swept the floor of the house
and when Sunday came
groomed her mother's head

scrubbed the head of who bore her
    between two windows
    where three tables met.

A sledge clattered in the lane
a sleigh caught in the wood-joints:
someone came to woo Hekko
to look for the precious one
    to take the apple.

The squat smith of the mainland
came, the Ingrian smith himself:
he put the maid in his sledge
in a corner of his sleigh
    bound her face with silk
covered her feet with wool cloth.
He put the maid in his sledge
in a corner of his sleigh
struck the stallion with the whip
    thrashed it with the knout:
the horse ran, the journey sped
the sledge slid, the way grew short
the sledge of iron rattled
    the golden heath boomed
the rowan collar-bow creaked
as the maiden was taken
the dear one was carried off.

Elina Säkki
Narvusi, Ingria
J. Ruotsalainen, 1900

121

The Unwelcome Visitor

I wretch, washed a linen shift
in which to go home
    cleaned a pair of shirts
two pairs of leggings. I asked
father-in-law for a horse
brother-in-law for a sledge
my own love I asked for reins
mother-in-law for presents:
father-in-law froze to ice
brother-in-law, he blew cold
mother-in-law lunged with a fence-prop.
I used my thighs for a sledge
bottom for a wicker-back
and my straight fingers for reins.
I got to my brother's field:
there the dry spruces were cuckooing
the broad-topped pines were singing:
    "This is not your home:
    this is your birthplace."

Yet I went, I paid no heed.
I drove to my brother's farm –
his children at the window
    his wife at their side:
    "There comes my auntie."

Brother's wife answering said:
    "That is not your aunt:
now the eggs will start to grieve
the hens will start to cackle
and the sheep will be put down
and the cows will be laid low."

Yet I went, I paid no heed.
I drove to my brother's gate
I waited for my brother
    to open the gate:
but my brother did not come.
I drew my knife from the sheath
from my belt the angry iron
with which I opened the gate
    made the gate-bolt crack.
I waited for my brother
    to take the breast-strap
off, to undo the head-strap:
but my brother did not come.
    I took the breast-strap
off, I undid the head-strap
I let down the shafts myself.

Yet I went, I paid no heed.
I went to my brother's porch –
his children on the shavings.
Brother's eldest girl answered:
"Don't go indoors, aunt, before
the rest have eaten their crumbs
    cleared up their portions
    changed their cabbage-bowls!"

Yet I went, I paid no heed.
Went into my brother's house:
he sat at the table-head
    his wife at the side.
At the door, beneath the beam
    where once the serfs were

once the serfs, then the captives
was the daughter of this house.

My brother said to his wife:
"Go and embrace my sister!"
But my brother's wife answered:
"I'd sooner embrace my hearth
    my prong-hooks sooner
than the daughter of the house."

My brother said to his wife:
"Make my sister some porridge!"
"The water's frozen, meal's cold:
colder still are the makers."

My brother said to his wife:
"Make my sister potted egg!"
But my brother's wife answered:
"The egg won't cook in the pot.
There's a thick stone in the grate:
thicker still are the makers."

My brother said to his wife:
"Make my sister butter-crumbs!"
But my brother's wife answered:
"There's thick soot in the saucepan."

My brother said to his wife:
"Bring my sister beer to drink!"
But my brother's wife answered:
"The tap broke in the barrel
a mouse ran over the yeast
    a frog on the foam
a beetle under the froth."

I did not make the eggs grieve
did not make the hens cackle
I did not put the sheep down
I did not lay the cows low:
the magpie made the eggs grieve
and the wolf put the sheep down
and the bear laid the cows low.

Singer unknown
Sakkola, Karelian Isthmus
K. Slöör, 1854

122

The Unhappy Bride I

A maid wept and sobbed
on the well-road wailed
at every flower-tip
at every grass-husk.
Her father stopped to listen
father came to ask:
"Why do you weep, my small one
my youngest one, why complain:
does father-in-law harm you?"

"That is not the source of it
nor the spring of it:
father-in-law treats me there
as my father did at home."

A maid wept and sobbed
on the well-road wailed
at every flower-tip
at every grass-husk.
Her mother stopped to listen
mother came to ask:
"Why do you weep, my small one
my youngest one, why complain:
does mother-in-law harm you?"

"That is not the source of it
nor the spring of it:
mother-in-law treats me there
as my mother did at home."

A maid wept and sobbed
on the well-road wailed
at every flower-tip
at every grass-husk.
Her brother stopped to listen
brother came to ask:
"Why do you weep, my sister
youngest sister, why complain:
does brother-in-law harm you?"

"That is not the source of it
nor the spring of it:
he treats me where I live now
as my brother did at home."

A maid wept and sobbed
on the well-path wailed
at every flower-tip
at every grass-husk.
Her sister stopped to listen
sister came to ask:
"Why do you weep, my sister:
does sister-in-law harm you?"

"That is not the source of it
nor the spring of it:
she treats me where I live now
as my sister did at home."

A maid wept and sobbed
on the well-road wailed
at every flower-tip
at every grass-husk.
Her uncle stopped to listen
uncle came to ask:
"Why do you weep, young maiden

brother's child, why do you writhe
is your bridegroom harming you?"

"It is his fault, my uncle:
my father did not suspect
nor did my mother suspect
nor did my supple brother
nor my own sister.

If I saw him being hanged
I'd pull harder on the rope
if I saw him being burned
I would stir the fire up more
if I saw him being slashed
I would sharpen my knife more
I'd swish my knife-end."

Singer unknown
Sakkola, Karelian Isthmus
A. Ahlqvist, 1854

123

The Unhappy Bride II

A bride wept in the forest
on the grass road grieved
on the well-road wailed.
A stranger stopped to listen
to stand by the wall
look from the shelter:
"Why are you weeping, poor bride:
does father-in-law hurt you?"

"He does not hurt me:
he is like my own father."

A bride wept in the forest
on the grass road grieved
on the well-road wailed.
A stranger stopped to listen
to stand by the wall
look from the shelter:
"Why are you weeping, poor bride:
does mother-in-law hurt you?"

"She does not hurt me:
she is like my own mother."

A bride wept in the forest
on the grass road grieved
on the well-road wailed.
A stranger stopped to listen
to stand by the wall
look from the shelter:
"Why are you weeping, poor bride:
does sister-in-law hurt you?"

"She does not hurt me:
she is like my own sister."

A bride wept in the forest
on the grass road grieved
on the well-road wailed.
A stranger stopped to listen
to stand by the wall
look from the shelter:
"Why are you weeping, poor bride:
does brother-in-law hurt you?"

"He does not hurt me:
he is like my own brother."

A bride wept in the forest
on the grass road grieved
on the well-road wailed.
A stranger stopped to listen
to stand by the wall
look from the shelter:
"Why are you weeping, poor bride:
is your bridegroom hurting you?"

"He is like my own devil:
every rod hates me
every twig burns me!"

Nikit Joro
Suistamo, Ladoga Karelia
I. Härkönen, 1900

124

The Water-Carrier I

The girl Anni, matchless maid
  went to fetch water
took a tub on her shoulder
and a ladle on her arm:
she walked a hill, another
soon she walked a third also.
She looked into the deep well:
  the well had dried up
the tin-bottomed had dwindled
the copper-rimmed drained away.

She took water from the ditch
went for water downriver
  for drinking water:
she brought some to her father.
Father with an axe-handle:
"Get away from here, harlot,
  yonder, scarlet whore:
you were not fetching water
you were searching for suitors
toiling after a red lace
looking for a fancy shoe."

She brought some to her mother.
Mother at her with a hook:
"Get away from here, harlot,
  yonder, scarlet whore:
you were not fetching water
you were searching for suitors
toiling after a red lace
looking for a fancy shoe."

The girl Anni, matchless maid
brought water to her brother.
Her brother with a rake's end:
"Get away from here, harlot,
  yonder, scarlet whore:
you were not fetching water
you were searching for suitors
toiling after a red lace
looking for a fancy shoe."

The girl Anni, matchless maid
brought water to her sister.
Sister struck her with a clasp:
"Get away from here, harlot,
  yonder, scarlet whore:
you were not fetching water
you were searching for suitors
toiling after a red lace
looking for a fancy shoe."

She brought some to her uncle.
Uncle with a spear-handle:
"Get away from here, harlot,
  yonder, scarlet whore:
you were not fetching water
you were searching for suitors
toiling after a red lace
looking for a fancy shoe."

The girl Anni, matchless maid
brought some water to her aunt.
Her aunt with a rolling-pin:
"Get away from here, harlot,
  yonder, scarlet whore:
you were not fetching water
you were searching for suitors

toiling after a red lace
looking for a fancy shoe."

The girl Anni, matchless maid
brought water to her grandad.
Grandad once with a distaff:
"Get away from here, harlot,
yonder, scarlet whore:
you were not fetching water
you were searching for suitors
toiling after a red lace
looking for a fancy shoe."

The girl Anni, matchless maid
brought water to her grandma.
Grandma took water to drink.

The girl Anni, matchless maid
her head down, in bad spirits
her cap all askew
stepped to the shed on the hill:
she lifted trunk upon trunk
case where case had been.
It was a dirge-case she drew:
she found a small length of lace
strangled herself, slumped
she hanged herself by the breast
by the neck she slumped.

Three nights she was not looked for.
Her mother went to the shed.
She looked, she turned her over:
Anni had been, gone
the tin-breasted snapped
was hanged by the breast.

"O girl Anni, matchless maid
rise as a young one from death
a fair one from perishing
red-cheeked from rolling away!"

"I cannot rise, I will not:
you condemned me for a whore
damned for a village harlot."

Mother came into the house
put this into words:
"Anni is long dead
the tin-breasted snapped
is hanged by the breast."

Father went off to raise her
the parent to revive her:
"O girl Anni, matchless maid
rise as a young one from death
a fair one from perishing
red-cheeked from rolling away!"

"I cannot rise, I will not:
you condemned me for a whore
damned for a village harlot."

Father came into the house
put this into words:
"Anni is long dead
the tin-breasted snapped
is hanged by the breast."

Brother went off to raise her:
"Anni, matchless maid
rise as a young one from death
a fair one from perishing
red-cheeked from rolling away!"

"I cannot rise, I will not:
you condemned me for a whore
damned for a village harlot."

Brother came into the house
put this into words:
"Anni is long dead
the tin-breasted snapped
is hanged by the breast."

Sister went off to raise her:
"Anni, matchless maid
rise as a young one from death
a fair one from perishing
red-cheeked from rolling away!"

"I cannot rise, I will not:
you condemned me for a whore
damned for a village harlot."

Sister came into the house
put this into words:
"Anni is long dead
the tin-breasted snapped
is hanged by the breast."

Uncle went off to raise her:
"Anni, matchless maid
rise as a young one from death
a fair one from perishing
red-cheeked from rolling away!"

"I cannot rise, I will not:
you condemned me for a whore
damned for a village harlot."

Uncle came into the house
put this into words:
"Anni is long dead
the tin-breasted snapped
is hanged by the breast."

Her aunt went off to raise her:
"Anni, matchless maid
rise as a young one from death
a fair one from perishing
red-cheeked from rolling away!"

"I cannot rise, I will not:
you condemned me for a whore
damned for a village harlot."

Her aunt came into the house
put this into words:
"Anni is long dead
the tin-breasted snapped
is hanged by the breast."

Grandma went off to raise her
grandma went weeping:
"O girl Anni, matchless maid
rise as a young one from death
a fair one from perishing
red-cheeked from rolling away!"

"My darling granny
though I would rise, I cannot:
the grave is holding my hand
Tuoni commands the other.
You condemned me for no whore
damned for no village harlot."

Hoto Lesonen
Vuokkiniemi, Archangel Karelia
A. Berner, 1872

125

The Water-Carrier II

Eeva, poor maid of Riga
went from town to the water
    through town to the spring
with an iron milking-pail
    with a tin teacup
    a copper-rimmed pan.

The crones of the town asked: "Maid
who do you fetch water for?"

"For my father, eye-water.
Will you drink, father, or thirst
or else will you wash your eyes?"

Her father answering said:
"I will neither drink nor thirst
nor yet will I wash my eyes.
    Curst is your water.
You dallied on the well-path:
you were watching the well's height
were reckoning the sea's depth
along the field-edge lying
across the field-edge resting."

Eeva, poor maid of Riga
went from town to the water
    through town to the spring
with an iron milking-pail
    with a tin teacup
    a copper-rimmed pan.

The crones of the town asked: "Maid
who do you fetch water for?"

Eeva answering replied:
"For my mother, eye-water.
Will you drink, mother, or thirst
or else will you wash your eyes?"

Her mother answering said:
"I will neither drink nor thirst
nor yet will I wash my eyes.
    Curst is your water.
You dallied on the well-path:
you were watching the well's height
were reckoning the sea's depth
along the field-edge lying
across the field-edge resting."

Eeva, poor maid of Riga
went from town to the water
    through town to the spring
with an iron milking-pail
    with a tin teacup
    a copper-rimmed pan.

The crones of the town asked: "Maid
who do you fetch water for?"

Eeva answering replied:
"For my brother, eye-water.
Will you drink, brother, or thirst
or else will you wash your eyes?"

Her brother answering said:
"I will neither drink nor thirst
nor yet will I wash my eyes.

Curst is your water.
You dallied on the well-path:
you were watching the well's height
were reckoning the sea's depth
along the field-edge lying
across the field-edge resting."

Eeva, poor maid of Riga
went from town to the water
through town to the spring
with an iron milking-pail
with a tin teacup
a copper-rimmed pan.

The crones of the town asked: "Maid
who do you fetch water for?"

Eeva answering replied:
"For my sister, eye-water.
Will you drink, sister, or thirst
or else will you wash your eyes?"

Her sister answering said:
"I will neither drink nor thirst
nor yet will I wash my eyes.
Curst is your water.
You dallied on the well-path:
you were watching the well's height
were reckoning the sea's depth
along the field-edge lying
across the field-edge resting."

Eeva, poor maid of Riga
went from town to the water
through town to the spring
with an iron milking-pail
with a tin teacup
a copper-rimmed pan.

The crones of the town asked: "Maid
who do you fetch water for?"

Eeva answering replied:
"For my bridegroom, eye-water.
Will you drink, bridegroom, or thirst
or else will you wash your eyes?"

Her bridegroom answering said:
"Yes, I will both drink and thirst
and I'll wash my eyes also.
Blest is your water!"

Singer unknown
Toksova, Ingria
K. Slöör, 1854

126

The Maid and the Boat I

I looked up, looked down:
the sun was shining above
a boat was rowing below
and in the boat my own father sat.
"Take me, father, in your boat!"

"No room, no room, poor daughter:
I myself sit in the stern
I have my feet in the prow."

I looked up, looked down:
the sun was shining above
a boat was rowing below
and in the boat my own mother sat.
"Take me, mother, in your boat!"

"No room, no room, poor daughter:
I myself sit in the stern
my feet, they are in the prow."

I looked up, looked down:
the sun was shining above
a boat was rowing below
and in the boat my own brother sat.
"Take me, brother, in your boat!"

"No room, no room, poor sister:
I myself sit in the stern
my feet, they are in the prow."

I looked up, looked down:
the sun was shining above
a boat was rowing below
and in the boat my own sister sat.
"Take me, sister, in your boat!"

"No room, no room, poor sister:
I myself sit in the stern
I have my feet in the prow."

I looked up, looked down:
the sun was shining above
a boat was rowing below
and in it the daughter-in-law sat.
"Take me, my own, in your boat!"

"Come, come, poor sister-in-law:
I am sitting in the stern
but you shall sit in the prow."

Singer unknown
Nyebelitsa, Novgorod District
V. Petrelius, 1892

127

The Maid and the Boat II

Two Karelians came driving,
three shopkeeper-lads.
I was a tiny maiden:
began to weed the blueflower
to trim the flax-plant.

A shopkeeper said to me:
"If you knew a bit
guessed but a little
you would not weed the blueflower
nor trim the flax-plant:
you, maiden, are sold to us
made over to us, chicken."

"Who has sold poor me
who made over the chicken?"
"Father sold poor you
he made over the chicken."

"What did father get for me?"
"Your father got a stone church
your mother the cow Damsel
your brother a war-stallion
your sister got a blue ewe."

The Russian, a tricky boy
lured the maid into the boat
got the maid into the boat.
The little maid lamented
in the Russians' boat
in the Redbeard's craft:
"Row towards that shore:
there a fire twinkles
a flame is showing
too big for a herdsman's fire
and too small for a camp fire.
That fire is my father's fire."

The maid called out, shouted out:
"Ransom me, father!"

Father answering replied:
"What shall I ransom you with?"

"You have a stone church
for the release of my head
for the ransom of my life."

Father answering replied:
"I'd sooner give up my child
than my church of stone."

The Russian, a clever boy
rowed along, idled along
to Finland's great sea
Sweden's reedy shore.
The little maid lamented:
"Row towards that shore:
there a fire twinkles
a flame is showing
too big for a herdsman's fire
and too small for a camp fire.
That fire is my mother's fire."

The maid called out, shouted out:
"Ransom me, mother!"

Mother answering replied:
"What shall I ransom you with?"

"Well, you have the cow Damsel
for the release of my head
for the ransom of my life."
"I'd sooner give up my child
than my cow Damsel."

The Russian, a tricky boy
rowed along, idled along
to Finland's great sea
Sweden's reedy shore.
The little maid lamented
in the Russians' boat
in the redbeard's craft:
"There a fire twinkles
a flame is showing
too big for a herdsman's fire
and too small for a camp fire.
That there is my brother's fire."

The maid called out, shouted out:
"Ransom me, brother!"

Brother answering replied:
"What shall I ransom you with?"

"Well, you have a war-stallion
for the release of my head
for the ransom of my life."

Brother answering replied:
"I'd sooner yield my sister
than my war-stallion."

The Russian, a tricky boy
rowed along, idled along
to Finland's great sea
Sweden's reedy shore.
The little maid lamented
in the Russian's boat
in the redbeard's craft:
"There a fire twinkles
a flame is showing
too big for a herdsman's fire
and too small for a camp fire.
There, that is my sister's fire."
The maid called out, shouted out:
"Ransom me, sister!"

Sister answering replied:
"What shall I ransom you with?"

"You have a blue ewe
for the release of my head
for the ransom of my life."

Sister answering replied:
"I'd sooner yield my sister
than yield my blue ewe."

"May my father's church of stone
fall down to the ground
may my mother's cow Damsel
be barren of milk
may my brother's war-stallion
drop on the church-road
while racing on the church-road
and may my sister's blue ewe
flop down with its wool
and be worn out with its lambs!"

Sohvi
Vuole, Ingria
V. Alava, 1894

128

The Maid and the Boat III

A Russian, a bloody-ear
    was rowing, idling:
a maid sat in the cabin
    weeping and sighing
her hands on the vessel's side
her knees on the sea's bottom
saw her father walking on the shore.
"Dear father, darling father
    ransom me from here!"

"What shall I ransom you with?"
    "You have three horses:
Give the best one for a pledge."
"I'd sooner yield my daughter
than the best of my horses."

A Russian, a bloody-ear
    was rowing, idling:
a maid sat in the cabin
    weeping and sighing
her hands on the vessel's side
her knees on the sea's bottom
saw her mother walking on the shore.
"Dear mother, darling mother
    ransom me from here!"

"What shall I ransom you with?"
    "Well, you have three cows:
Give the best one for a pledge."
"I'd sooner yield my daughter
than the best one of my cows."

A Russian, a bloody-ear
    was rowing, idling:
a maid sat in the cabin
    weeping and sighing
her hands on the vessel's side
her knees on the sea's bottom
saw her brother walking on the shore.
"Dear brother, darling brother
    ransom me from here!"

"What shall I ransom you with?"
    "Well, you have three swords:
Give the best one for a pledge."
"I'd sooner yield my sister
than the best one of my swords."

A Russian, a bloody-ear
    was rowing, idling:
a maid sat in the cabin
    weeping and sighing
her hands on the vessel's side
her knees on the sea's bottom
saw her sister walking on the shore.
"Dear sister, darling sister
    ransom me from here!"

"What shall I ransom you with?"
    "Well, you have three crowns:
Give the best one for a pledge."
"I'd sooner yield my sister
than the best one of my crowns."

A Russian, a bloody-ear
    was rowing, idling:
a maid sat in the cabin
    weeping and sighing

her hands on the vessel's side
her knees on the sea's bottom
saw her bridegroom walking on the shore.
"Dear bridegroom, darling bridegroom
    ransom me from here!"
"What shall I ransom you with?"
"Well, you have three rings:
Give the best one for a pledge."
"I'd sooner give up my rings
    than yield you, my bride!"
"May my father's horses die
in the best sowing season
may my mother's cows dry up
in the best milking season
may my brother's swords snap off
in the best season for war
may my sister's crowns melt down
at the great moment in church
may my bridegroom's rings hold good
every moment of my life."

Singer unknown
Ylöjärvi, Häme
B. Paldani, 1852

129

Boy and Cloud I

One boy went for cowberries
another for bilberries
a third hare-hunting:
one boy came with cowberries
the second with bilberries
the third did not come.

His father went seeking him
with some barley beer
with a crust of oats
with a loaf of rye:
but he did not find his son
his golden apple.

His mother went seeking him
with some barley beer-water
with a crust of oats
with a loaf of rye:
she did not find her offspring
her little golden apple.
She went weeping home
wailing to the farm.

His brother went seeking him
with some barley beer-water
with a crust of oats
with a loaf of rye.
His sister went seeking him
with some barley beer-water
with a crust of oats
with a loaf of rye:
"Where are you, my dear brother?"

"Here I am, my dear sister:
a cloud is holding my head
a vapour my hair
another my other foot."

Singer unknown
Uhtua, Archangel Karelia
E. Lönnrot, 1834

130

Boy and Cloud II

One boy went for nuts
another for game
a third went for summer-fish
a fourth went tracking a hare
a fifth went trapping a wolf:
    one boy came with nuts
    the second with game
the third came with summer-fish
the fourth from tracking a hare
but not from trapping a wolf.

    Who misses the boy
wants to look after the child?
The father misses the boy
wants to look after the child.

The father went out searching –
searched great forests like a wolf
    spinneys like a hare
high forests like a lamb, flew
through the air like an insect.
"Come away, my little boy!"

"I cannot, my kind father:
the clouds are holding my head
    the vapours my hair.
    Take a sheaf of straw
    a bundle of splints
with which burn the cloud-edges
break up the cloudy vapours."

Jerla's Oute
Metsäpirtti, Karelian Isthmus
A. Koskivaara, 1913

131

Maid and Cloud

Marjukkain, mother of mine
Karjukkain, she who bore me
brought forth six daughters
cared for five children:
five she saw to the altar
but the sixth she kept at home –
kept Maije for a daughter
to spend the gold and
to guard the silver.

And she spent her father's gold
guarded her brother's silver
set the gold upon her brows
the blue threads upon her eyes
copper threads on her figure
at her belt the silver threads.

She took the birchwood cowlstaves
the handles from the stove-post
went to the well-way
to the field past the village
went through six new towns
through eight parishes:
and there Maijoi was stolen
on the water-road was snatched.

Who will seek her, who will search?
Well, no one but her mother:
mother sought her first
after her the family sought.

The mother put on her shoes
shod one foot on the threshold
the other on Maije's trunk
went in search of her Maijoi
trod the great woods like a wolf
the fine forests like a bear
the tree-boughs like a squirrel
and the lakeshores like a hare.

She went up on a great hill
up on a high heath
yelled at the top of her voice
let fly a mouthful:
"Come home, my Maijoi!"

Maijoi answering screamed out:
"I cannot come home, mother:
a cloud is holding my head
a cloud's son my knees
a vapour my hair.
You go home, mother
brew some barley beer
some tasty malted water!"

The mother rushed home
brewed some barley beer
some tasty malted water
gave a glassful to the cloud
another to the cloud's son
two to the whole crowd of them:
so Maijoi reached home.

Tatiana
Soikkola, Ingria
V. Porkka, 1883

132

The Lost Brush

My mother gave birth to me
and I bore my hair,
father brought me up:
I was rearing locks.

Long the locks I grew
long the locks and tough the hair
as long as a length of flax
as white as sea-foam:
brush could not brush it
pig-bristles could not groom it.

My brother went to Estonia
to take the tithe-corn
to pay the land-tax.
I said to my brother: "Bring
a brush from Estonia, brother
pig-bristles from the manor."

He brought a brush from Estonia
pig-bristles from the manor.

I went down to the seashore
I sat on an island-stone
I put a board on my knees
I shook my sad hair
out over my sad shoulders
I began to brush my head
and to groom my hair.
The brush slipped into the sea:
I bent down to look for it
had to pick it up
I leaned out to look for it
I slipped after it
to my neck in fish-water
up to my throat in fish-spawn.

A sword was caught in my tail
a scabbard-sling round my neck:
I carried the sword to land.
Which way the sword, where the sword
what was the sword useful for?
I took it to my brother.
Where the sword, for what the sword?
He took it to the manor.
The masters marvelled
the mistresses considered:
"This sword has been eating man
has eaten man, has drunk blood
the iron has hurt heroes
the steel has snatched men away."

My brother answering said:
"The sword has not eaten man
not eaten man, not drunk blood
nor the iron hurt heroes
nor the steel snatched men away:
this sword was brought from the sea
was taken from the seabed."

Singer unknown
Narvusi, Ingria
D. E. D. Europaeus, 1853

133

The Lost Goose I

I frisked, I frolicked
I skipped, I scampered
on hoppers of tin
on toes of copper
down a lane of gold
a road of silver.
Now, I met a ditch:
by the ditch was a hummock
by the hummock was a hut.
I knocked upon the hut door
rattled the eaves-wood:
a girl came weeping.
"Why are you weeping, poor girl?"

"She who weeps has cause
she who laments has trouble:
my brother has been taken
to war, tall as father's knee
and long as mother's distaff."

"Do not weep, poor girl:
your brother's coming from war -
down on the sea his oars flash
above the town his head shows."

"What shall I give my brother?
I'll give him a linen shirt
which won't dig under his arms
itch below his ribs.
What will my brother bring me?
He'll bring a goose for the gift.
But where shall I put my goose
my favourite bird?
Put it in my wool-basket
it will mat my wool
put it in my barley-bin
and it will catch on the spikes
put it into my rye-bin
and it will catch on the rye
put it on the threshing-house eaves
it will stifle in the smoke
put it on the cowshed eaves . . .
yes, upon the cowshed eaves.
I stayed a day, another
soon I stayed a third as well:
I went to look at the bird
but my bird had gone.
Where had my bird gone
my favourite bird?"
"She got iron boots
a crutch for a third."

She went in search of the bird
she travelled a little way
walked a short distance.
Listened: heard a hum.
Looked: Katti at the roadside.
She was weaving cloth
a girl was holding the reed
the goose there winding.

"There I found my goose
put it in a better place."

Katti Nykänen
Akonlahti, Kontokki, Archangel Karelia
A. R. Niemi, 1904

134

The Lost Goose II

I went to the marsh to scrub
in the marsh found a hummock
on the hummock found a hut.
I knocked upon the hut door
rattled the eaves-wood:
a maiden slunk out
a cur with the maid.

That maid put in words:
"What is it you seek, young maid:
is it red trappings you seek
or do you seek German boots
or do you seek Finnish rings
or ribbon-heads from the town?"

That maid put in words:
"No, I don't seek Finnish rings
nor yet German boots
nor ribbon-heads from the town:
I'm seeking my young brother.
Why has he gone to war young
to battle as a milk-mouth?"

"Do not weep, young maid:
your brother is coming home –
birds are chirping in his hand
geese honking under his arm."

"Where to put my brother's birds?
I'll make a pen in the yard
and a coop on the hard ground:
I'll put a cock to listen
a black bird to mark
and a tarry stump to know.

I myself went to grind corn:
ground a boxful, another
ground a little of a third.
I went to look at the goose
but my goose had fled:
that cock had not heard at all
nor the black bird marked
nor had the tarry stump known.

I went in serach of the goose:
I ran a verst, another
slid a span on my belly.
I met the washerwomen:
'Washerwomen, my sisters
my mother's children
have you seen my goose?
It flew, it fluttered this way.'
'What marking did your goose have?'
'Patches of tin on its mouth
of copper between its toes.
It flew, it fluttered this way:
one wing parted the water
the other reached for the sky.'
I ran a verst, another
ran a little of a third
came upon a new village
and came upon a new house:
the goose, boiling in the pot
was wagging its tail
was beating its wing."

Singer unknown
Narvusi, Ingria
J. Lukkarinen, 1909

135

The Lost Brother I

There were three of us brothers
three brother-lads, we:
one went skiing after elk
the second hunting a hare
and the third to snare a fox.
Back came one brother
with a hare's paw in his hand
back came the second brother
a fox-skin under his arm
but the third did not come back.

I waited a day, two days
soon I waited a third too.
And I asked the village crones:
"You have heard from messengers:
have you seen my dear brother?"

"I saw him at this time yesterday
upon the clear open sea:
he sat upon a big rock
brushing his sorrowful head
grooming his dejected head.
The brush plopped into the sea
the bristles fell from the rock.
He leaned out to look for it
he stretched out to pick it up
and he plopped in after it:
'My darling mother
do not make dough, don't
sprinkle it with seawater!
As the seawater
so also my blood
as the brushwood on the shore
so also my bones.' "

Singer unknown
Suistamo, Ladoga Karelia
R. Polén, 1847

136

The Lost Brother II

A week I sought my brother
a month sought my precious one
I searched Finland, the Island
both sides of Moscow
the two sides of Kaprio:
did not find him there at all.

I went down to the seashore
saw a ship cleaving the waves
a red-keel sailing
a war-boat pitching
a war-craft rolling. Promptly
I changed into a salmon
turned into a water-fish
set myself up as a perch:
I swam to the ship's ladder
to the ship's bows I darted.

And I asked the ship's master:
"Is my brother here
is my mother's child?"

Slowly the ship's master spoke
with his head trembling
and his hair gone grey:
"No, your brother is not here
your mother's child is not here."

And I asked the ship's master:
"Why then is the water red
the white foam bloody?"

The ship's master made reply:
"For this the water is red
the white foam bloody:
a pike's belly has been slit
a whitefish's belly stabbed
the guts cast into the sea
the entrails borne to the land."

From the water my brother
spoke, from the waves mother's child:
"No pike's belly has been slit
no whitefish's belly stabbed:
brother's belly has been slit
his guts cast into the sea
his entrails borne to the land."

My sister took the tidings
to mother: "May my mother
never burn wood from the sea:
if she burns wood from the sea
she'll burn her son's bones.
And may my father
not drink water from the sea:
drinking water from the sea
he'll drink his son's blood.
And may my mother
never wear a lace bonnet
bear a gold headband
and may my sister
never tie on a silk scarf
and may my brother
never dress in a cloth cloak
and may my father
never eat fish from the sea:
if he eats fish from the sea
he'll eat his son's flesh."

Singer unknown
Tyrö, Ingria
D. E. D. Europaeus, 1853

137

The Warrior's Departure I

Kulerva, Kalerva's son
went with music off to war
plucking joy to other lands
merrily to Karelia
said these words to his father:
"Fare you well, my good father
my provider all my life:
    will you weep for me
when you know that I am dead
    left on the sea-ice
    lost to my people
taken away from my folk?"

"No, I will not weep for you:
another boy will be got
    one mark better still
and one daler more skilful."

"My dear mother, my darling
    fair one who bore me
    my nurse all my life
    won't you weep for me?"

"My little son, my darling
don't you know a mother's heart?
    Yes, I'll weep for you –
    weep the snow to slush
    the slush to soft soil
    and the soil to bloom."

Singer unknown
Juva, Savo
C. A. Gottlund, before 1871

138

The Warrior's Departure II

Anterus the handsome boy
the young bridegroom in his prime
harnessed the fiery gelding
    in the fiery field
in front of the fiery sledge –
blood boiled from the collar-bow
and fat from the traces-tip –
    to go off to war.

Anterus the handsome boy
the young bridegroom in his prime
fair beginning of a man
sent out letters from the town
papers from the evil land:
"Will you weep, father, for me
    if I'm felled in war
    and shot below the castle?"
"I will weep, my sweet offspring."

Anterus the handsome boy
the young bridegroom in his prime
fair beginning of a man
sent out letters from the town
papers from the evil land:
"Will you weep for me, maiden
    if I'm felled in war
    and shot below the castle?"

The maiden answering said:
"And why should I weep for you?
If I saw you being burned
I would stir the fire up more
if I saw you being slashed
I would sharpen my knife more
    I'd swish my knife-end
if I saw you being hanged
I'd pull harder on the rope."

Matti Sutelainen
Metsäpirtti, Karelian Isthmus
A. A. Borenius, 1887

139

The Warrior's Departure III

A wolf ran over the marsh
a bear wandered on the heath.
The marsh rose at the wolf's feet
and the heath at the bear's paws:
    iron shoots sprang up
    in the wolf's great tracks
and where the bear's paws had been.

'Twas that smith Ilmarinen
    took the iron shoots
    snatched the steel-blended
    from the wolf's great tracks
from where the bear's paws had been.

Now, the smith Ilmarinen
the everlasting craftsman
    hammered, tapped away
    beat, clattered away
    in the forge without
    doors, without windows.
He hammered a likely sword
and a shield, the best of all
for the hand of Kaleva's son:
now, the moon shone from its point
and the sun glowed from its hilt.

That fair son of Kaleva
went with music off to war
rejoicing off among men
playing joy into battle
said as soon as he'd arrived
upon the great battlefield
on the slaughter-lands of men:
"Even the demons will guard
a hero with their war-gear
will cover him with their cloaks
upon the great battlefields
on the slaughter-lands of men."

    Now destruction came
    evil days befell:
now Kullervo was conquered
Kaleva's son was struck down
upon the great battlefields
on the slaughter-lands of men.

Mishi Sissonen
Ilomantsi, North Karelia
D. E. D. Europaeus, 1845

140

News of Death I

Kinerva, Kanerva's son
went with music off to war
striking joy to other lands.
He thrust whistles in his bag
played as he went through the marsh
    echoed on the heath:
the marsh hummed and the ground shook
the heath echoed in reply.

The word was brought after him:
"Your father at home has died!"

"I'll get a father like him –
a body of rotten wood
    legs of forked sallows
a skull of a worn-out pot
belly of a beggar's bag
    and eyes of flax-seeds
    and ears of birch-leaves."

Kinerva, Kanerva's son
went with music off to war
striking joy to other lands.
He thrust whistles in his bag
played as he went through the marsh
    echoed on the heath:
the marsh hummed and the ground shook
the heath echoed in reply.

The word was brought after him:
"Your mother at home has died!"

"If she has died, let her die!
I'll get a mother like her –
a body of rotten wood
    legs of forked sallows
a skull of a worn-out pot
belly of a beggar's bag
    and eyes of flax-seeds
    and ears of birch-leaves."

Kinerva, Kanerva's son
went with music off to war
striking joy to other lands.
He thrust whistles in his bag
played as he went through the marsh
    echoed on the heath:
the marsh hummed and the ground shook
the heath echoed in reply.

The word was brought after him:
"Your brother at home has died!"

"If he is dead, let him die!
I'll get a brother like him –
a body of rotten wood
    legs of forked sallows
a skull of a worn-out pot
belly of a beggar's bag
    and eyes of flax-seeds
    and ears of birch-leaves."

Kinerva, Kanerva's son
went with music off to war
striking joy to other lands.
He thrust whistles in his bag

played as he went through the marsh
echoed on the heath:
the marsh hummed and the ground shook
the heath echoed in reply.

The word was brought after him:
"Your sister at home has died!"
"If she's dead, then let her die!
I'll get a sister like her –
a body of rotten wood
legs of forked sallows
a skull of a worn-out pot
belly of a beggar's bag
and eyes of flax-seeds
and ears of birch-leaves."

Kinerva, Kanerva's son
went with music off to war
striking joy to other lands.
He thrust whistles in his bag
played as he went through the marsh
echoed on the heath:
the marsh hummed and the ground shook
the heath echoed in reply.

The word was brought after him:
"Now your wife at home has died!"

"Poor boy that I am:
she who made curtains grew tired
she who worked mantles sank down.
Poor boy that I am
wretched, downcast boy!
What shall I wash my wife with?
I'll wash her with German soap.
What shall I wrap my wife in?
Wrap her in German linen.
Where shall I bury my wife?
Under the church floor
under the altar put her."

Singer unknown
Suistamo, Ladoga Karelia
R. Polén, 1847

141

News of Death II

I went to Estonia
for liquor from Osmeroi
and the word rolled after me:
"Your father has died."

What shall I wash father with?
I'll buy German soap:
with it I'll wash my father.
What shall I dress father in?
I'll buy Silesian linen in town:
with it I'll dress my father.
What make father's coffin of?
I'll shape the coffin in gold
work it finely in silver
tap in silver nails.

I went to Estonia
for liquor from Osmeroi
and the word rolled after me:
"Your mother has died."

What shall I wash mother with?
I'll buy German soap:
with it I'll wash my mother.
What shall I dress mother in?
I will bring an ell of silk:
in it I'll dress my mother.
What make mother's coffin of?
I'll make it of Fleetfoot's bones:
in it I'll put my mother
tap in wooden nails.

I went to Estonia
for liquor from Osmeroi
and the word rolled after me:
"Now your stern husband has died
your bedfellow has sunk down
your bedmate fallen."

What shall I wash my man with?
With a yellow chicken's shit.
What shall I dress my man in?
In the village ploughing-rags.
What make my man's coffin of?
I sought a trough in the village
to put my stern husband in –
got no trough from the village.
I took a log and rolled it:
there I put my stern husband
tapped in iron nails.
Cats I set to read the book
and dogs to keep school.
I brought him down the hill: go
into the hands of Hittoi
to seven devils!

Kati, Kirilä's wife
Soikkola, Ingria
V. Porkka, 1883

142

The Warrior

A bird flew from below the castle
a white-feathered one wandered:
it brought news of war
tidings of war it trundled
with bells of war its tongue sang.

Who shall go to war?
The sister shall go to war:
the brother shall stay at home.
Mother fell to bad spirits
to sadness of heart:
father fell to good spirits
to a warmth of heart.

Lords began to gasp
kings too to marvel
and powers to ponder:
"These things were not heard before
heard before or seen before –
ringed fingers at war
ribbon-heads at the castle."

A bird flew from below the castle
a white-feathered one wandered:
it brought news of war
tidings of war it trundled
with bells of war its tongue sang.

Who shall go to war?
The brother shall go to war:
the sister shall stay at home.
Father fell to bad spirits
to sadness of heart:
mother fell to good spirits
to a warmth of heart.

The sister warmed the bath-house
heated the warrior's bath-house
for the warrior, her brother:
she took water, carried wood
she took her brother to bathe.

Brother bathed upon the boards
sister advised on the step:
"O brother, my mother's child
when you get to war
do not be valiant in war
nor very keen in battle:
don't go before the others
don't lag behind the others
cling to those in the middle
close to the standard-bearer!
The standard-bearer is sly:
if the standard slips to earth
slip into the standard's place!
O grey, my dear horse
father's oldest white gelding
when you get to war
don't leave my brother
or forsake my mother's child!"

Five, six nights went by
eight nights passed away.
A horse neighed in the lane. I
thrust my head through the window
and my face through the big gap:

"O grey, my dear horse
father's oldest white gelding
where have you left my brother
forsaken my mother's child?"

The grey indeed answered: "Your
brother was valiant in war
and very keen in battle:
he drove before the others
at times lagged behind others
nor clung to those in the midst.
He tore my mouth with bridles
broke my legs with spurs."

Anni Porissa
Narvusi, Ingria
V. Porkka, 1883

143

Duke Charles

The good lord Duke Charles
Sweden's precious king
Finland's strong ruler
the fatherland's great master
got his craft ready
he laid out his ships
prepared the tillers
set out for Finland
dressed the tallest masts
on the shoulders of great craft
hoisted the red sails
put up his brightly-worked yards.

Grimly the boats came
eagerly too the great craft
hard those of large size
swiftly over the long lakes
through the waves they sailed
in order through tight places
in line over the great lakes
edging past the deepest sounds
the rocks they skirted
skirting the cliffs more widely
they ran beyond the firm hills
beside the steadfast mountains.

He put in to shore
came to Turku as a guest
to Finland as a great good
to the castle unbidden.

When he arrived in Finland
reached Papinluoto
set out for Ruskiakallio
and came below the castle
he pitched his camp in a field
put it up by the seashore
dropped his anchors in the sea
landed his pieces
fastened his ships on the waves
sat his boats on the water:
the shore rang and the sea rocked
and the rocks loudly echoed
the craft eagerly trembled
and guns roared at the gunwales.

He stepped on to the mainland
he sat on Isponen's Hill
to get his breath back
and to rest his feet.

He sent a letter in haste
a scrap of paper early
his good news quickly
his fair precious speech to the
villages of Finland's sons
to the halls of great heroes
the houses of governors
the huts of the town's strongest:
"I have not come here for war
nor yet for battle
but to bring peace to Finland
to settle the fierce
to interrupt fights
to break up quarrels
to turn wrongs to rights
to scold the heedless."

Then the town's evil masters
outcast sons of priests
Turku cobbler-kin
reared by cattle-dogs
harshly the harsh spoke
wickedly shameless
bleakly bleak answered
ill the ill-behaved
bit their lips and wagged their heads
waved their skulls about
twisted their faces
against Sweden's war:
"We'll throw the Duke in the sea
chop up his craft for firewood
smash his boats on the water!"

The good lord Duke Charles
Sweden's precious king
indeed addressed his children
and spoke to his sons:
"Let us be going
strongly on our way."

He walked then to Kupitsa
strode to Hanhenpajusto
scrambled up the Turku cliffs:
now they reached Tallimäki
on to which he moved his flock
laid, spread out his camp
moved a war-band to one flank
another to his other.
There he put the wheels
placed his artillery too
transported his copper guns
settled his brazen pieces.

The good lord Duke Charles
Sweden's precious king
let the guns bellow
the great arrows fly
and the long chains creak:
the copper resounded loud
with it all the brazen horns
the wooden pipes shrilled as well
and the drum-skins strongly boomed
with all the drum-slats.
Stallion whinnied, heath echoed
and armour on men's shoulders
the iron men on horseback
strengthened with their strong weapons.

The good lord Duke Charles
Sweden's precious king
took fire out of his fire-fork
power out of his side
hempen cord from his shoulders
from his belt a cord
lifted gunpowder
put it in the pan.

Hard then the sparks hopped
shot came flying out
smoke poured after it:
then the men were torn apart . . .

Singer unknown
Turku, South-West Finland
Collector unknown, early 18th century

144

Jacob Pontus

Jacob Pontus, noble lord
wise master of Viipuri
laid out some ships for the sea
put some boys inside:
he loaded the ships
and he trimmed his sails
set the winds to be windy
to blow on the sails
and drove below Riga town.

First he fired cannon
made falconets roar:
the castle began to shake
towers to tumble to the ground
walls to roll in the water.

Thus spoke Poland's lord
the castle's eldest answered:
"Don't wreck my Riga
nor yet Narva town:
come quietly inside
have a drink of beer
eat some sweet honey."

Many a man and many a horse
many a feather-hatted lord
many a golden-hilted sword
lie outstretched in Riga's stream.
An old man up a spruce-tree
scolded, up a young fir nagged:
"There are hats now on the heath
on the stubble bits of rags."

Jacob Pontus, noble lord
wise master of Viipuri
drove the wives below Narva
the lasses to the long war
who did not know how to fight
nor to draw a bow.

The Lord, gracious God
held assizes in the clouds
filled the air with iron hail
so the powder did not burn
nor the cannon boom.

Singer unknown
Liperi (?), North Karelia
E. Lönnrot, 1839 (?)

145

Ivan

Ivan, great master
our famous golden buckle
put his war-band in order
as a scaup-duck its ducklings
or as a teal its children
and he launched ships on the sea
as a scaup-duck its ducklings
or as a teal its children:
the wives wept for their husbands
the matrons wept for their sons
as men went under the sword
to the game of bright iron
the mercy of white iron.
The widows fell to joking
daughters went about joyful:
"Now there are some likely men
some different-looking bridegrooms!"

He launched the ships on the sea
raised the sail to the mast-top
the cloth into the mast's care
    sailed steadily off
to Inari the evil
to the bold land of Sweden.
He wrote a letter in haste
and a demanding paper:
"Is there meat in the castle
    butter in Volmar
    for Ivan's supper
    the Russian's tribute
for the hungry man to eat
    that the needy needs?"

Back indeed came the answer:
"There's no meat in the castle
    butter in Volmar:
    a white horse dropped down
and is left at the lake-end
    for Ivan's supper
    the Russian's tribute."

    Ivan, great master
twisted his mouth, tore his head
    tugged at his black hair:
    made his guns thunder
    his great bows rumble.
    He shot once – too high
    he shot twice – too low
shot a third time – on target:
    now the eaves rattled
the sheets of birch-bark fluttered.

    "Russian, my brother
    fair-shod Karelian
you've killed father, killed mother
    killed my five brothers
    my seven sisters:
take now a fistful of gold
a felt hatful of silver
for the release of my head
for the ransom of my life!"

"I piss, villain, on your gold
evil one, on your silver:
Sweden's gold has gone rusty
tarnished is Savo's silver.
You'd take the brains from my head."

Poavila Sirkeinen
Uhtua, Archangel Karelia
K. Karjalainen, 1894

146

Charles XII

Charles went from the town
for the tax, the bloody-pawed
the Swedish cut-throat for food
the wrecker to Petersburg
to turn the place upside-down.

Russia's stout forces
the king's famous men
choice men of the earth
Cossack regulars
evenings and mornings waited
once at midday too.
Harshly they treated their guests:
Bake a loaf of stone
make a cake of rock
for the coming guest
the intending visitor.
Harshly they treated their guests.

Charles was seen far off
the blue-hoofed yonder
in between two crags
over Atimo Island:
some way off was Koroinen.
The guns were set thundering
the open-throated shooting
the great bows twanging
the bowstrings trembling
towards Charles's boat
against Redbeard's craft:
then the steering-oars dropped in
the masts smacked into the sea
as the arrow of steel wrenched
as the iron arrow tore
the sails were thudding
to be carried by the wind
driven by the squall.

And Charles took to flight
as the fiery arrow came
as the shaft of iron tore
as the arrow of steel wrenched.

"Russian, poor brother
give me a drink of water!"

But the Russian said
the hard-hearted snapped:
"There's water beneath your boat
underneath the ship to lap."

Charles indeed answered:
"Bloody is the seawater:
the shores are heaped with Swedish
corpses, capped heads overthrown
round heads have been rolled around."

Trohkimainen Soava
Akonlahti, Kontokki, Archangel Karelia
E. Lönnrot 1832

147

The Conscript

Our curly-haired king
the wax-haired castle-captive
sat and considered
upon a bench-end of iron
wrote letters in haste
demanding papers
sent them to our lands
to our lovely lands.

Who should look at the letter
who spread out the leaf?
The parish elder
the cool parish dean
he should look at the letter
should spread out the leaf.

What's written in the letter
and set out on the paper?
"Let us take soldiers
let us choose captives!"

The parish elder
its most famous chief
drove to the village
by night-light, moonlight
and in white daylight
on a mouse-hued horse
of a pike's colour
called the village together
drove the parish to the field.

He asked the old village men:
"Does the parish have a thief
any petty wrongdoers
frequenters of the tavern?"

The old parish men answered:
"No, the parish has no thief
and no petty wrongdoers
frequenters of the tavern."

Our curly-haired king
the wax-haired castle-captive
sat and considered
upon a bench-end of iron:
"Poor me, what am I to do:
shall I strip rich men
or pick on wretches?"

A rich man happened to hear:
the rich man went quarrelling
quarrelling, fighting.
Where the rich men drive abreast
the poor men walk arm in arm:
where the rich man's money flows
the poor man's head wears away.

Which lot would be drawn?
The lots of five men were cast
the lots of three men were drawn:
the lot of the orphan leapt —
the fatherless, the luckless
the motherless, the last lot.
The fatherless boy was bound
his hands with harsh ropes
the motherless boy was bound

his feet were clapped in irons
led from village to village
escorted from house to house
to the doors of the takers
the lanes of the governor
the farm of the selectors
the windows of the drivers.
They went towards Kolkanpää
the captives going in front
irons clanking on their feet
and the guards going behind
with iron rods in their hands
with which the captives were hurt
the little ones tormented:
they went towards Kolkanpää
beside Väärnoja village.
A captive took to his heels:
    drops of blood rolled down
and a fiery tear spurted
from the lively captive's eye.
The poor captive was seized, led
to the door of the taker.

The king came into the lane
    and the king asked him:
"Are you here through your own fault
or through parish injustice
    or village anger?"

The boy answering replied:
"There are many of us boys
    and all plough-bearers:
the lot of poor me leapt up
    mine was the last lot."

    The great plumed lord said:
    "Here are boys enough:
    even if they're weighed
    measured with steelyards."

To the measuring-room he
was led, measured, tried for size
reckoned up with a yardstick:
he was too long by an inch
and too tall by a straw-stalk.
He was seated on a chair:
    there his hair was clipped
    his tresses were cut
    his golden curls shorn
his locks were showered to the ground
    his locks to God's wind
    the gracious one's squall.

They brought a hat for his head
they brought a blue overcoat
    brought a black tunic
they brought a shirt on their knee
they brought pants under their arm
they brought an armful of socks
and a boxful of toe-rags
they brought boots with copper heels
    copper heels, gold legs:
the poor boy was tossed about
his eyes were washed, his head shorn
fitted to be a soldier
worked on to be a sailor.
They brought him a fiery gun
they fetched him a bloody sword
gave the gun to be his wife
the sword to be his pleasure.

They took the apples to be
trained, took the wretches walking
    the berries marching
    through six new castles
    through eight towns, took them
    over a great plain:
he was no good at learning
    could not keep in step.

A skein of geese flew that way.
The captive said to the geese:
    "When you reach the land
    where my mother is
take tidings to my mother
who had me in the bath-house:
    may my mother weep
    she who hatched me grieve!
I am no good at learning
    cannot keep in step.
It is wretched enough here:
on Sundays it's gun-cleaning
on weekdays it's out shooting.
    Come the holy day
    and that best feast day
then the angry lash whistles
and the willow rod presses
the rowan lashes whistle
and the birch truncheons press down
on the shoulders of poor me."

A week rolled by, another:
    the wretch was walking
    the berry marching.
A flock of swans flew that way.
    "My dear swans, my flock
    when you reach the land
    where my mother is
take tidings to my mother:
    may mother not weep
may she who hatched me not grieve!
It's good to be a soldier
fine to be a sword-bearer:
the bread is smooth, the clothes white
    there are rusks to eat
    seawater to drink.
    It is worse in war:
on Sundays it's gun-cleaning
on weekdays it's out shooting."

Stepu
Narvusi, Ingria
V. Porkka, 1883

148

Epilogue

What so oppressed a strong voice
a strong, handsome voice
brought down a sweet voice, that it
does not as a river run
as a stream sparkle
as rapids by a village
as a pool ripple?

*

Quickly the small one wearies
soon the tiny one is tired
the horse also gasps for breath
having run a long journey
the scythe too grows weak
having cut the summer hay
water also rolls away
having passed the river curve
dying fire flashes
having burned all night.

*

All, that's all, enough, enough
joy for this evening
song for this sunset.

*

Singing is the poet's job
cuckooing is the cuckoo's
pressing is the Blue Girl's job
weaving the Loom Girl's:
singer, though good, does not sing
his fill of verses
nor do rapids, though swift, come
to their water's end.

*

We will stop, we will leave it
we will round off, we will end
for better singers
more skilful poets:
I'll wind my verse in a ball
I'll arrange it in a coil
put it up in the shed loft
inside locks of bone
whence it shall never be freed
nor ever get out
unless the bones are shaken
the jaws are opened
the teeth are parted
the tongue set wagging.

---

8 – 17 *Singer unknown*
Karelian Isthmus
E. Lönnrot, 1837

21 – 28 *Mooses Ahonen*
Latvajärvi, Vuokkiniemi, Archangel Karelia
A. A. Borenius, 1877

29 – 42 *Singer unknown*
Kemi, North Ostrobothnia
Z. Topelius, 1803 or 1804

NAME INDEX

Names are identified by reference to poem and in some cases to line. Where a person or place plays a central role in a poem, only the number of the poem is given. Where the name does not occur at the beginning of a poem, but plays an important role after entry, the reference is given to the line where it first appears followed by *ff*. Names that occur only sporadically are referred to by both poem and line. Etymologies are given where they have a connotative relevance to the occurrence of a name; in the case of first names, an etymology is provided when the surface form of the name is unfamiliar. The term 'parallel' denotes an alternative name in successive lines, while 'epithet' is an elaboration or extension of of the same name.

The entries are arranged in Finnish alphabetical order, i.e. *ä* and *ö* are treated as separate letters that follow *y*.

Aboa → Turku

Ahti
1 water deity (parallels: Hirska, Vellamo) 9:40; 26:56; 56:40
2 rich land-owner: seeks help to bring fertility 46
3 warrior: invited to feast 34:49, 51, 54; (epithet: the Islander/Saarelainen) prefers adventures at sea to life at home 39; 40 (→ Kauko 2, Veitikki)
4 (shaman-)chieftain (epithet: the Islander/Saarelainen): fights Lemminkäinen 34:153*ff*

Alermo
(epithet: Ylermä's swain/Ylermän yrkkä) suitor 105

Alimo → Alue

Alje
place-name, possibly the Estonian village of Haljala 36:11

Alue
? < *alava* 'low-lying'
mythical primeval lake (parallel: Alimo) 9:16, 48

Ammas
place-name (more commonly Aumas), Laukko (→), West Finland 84:58*ff*

Anderus → Vipunen

Andreas → Antero 2

Andrew → Antero 2

Ann St/Santta Anna
in Finnish folk poetry she occurs frequently in hunting and birth incantations: in a storm 27:59*ff* (here a corruption of St Andrew → Antero)

Anna → Ann St

Anni (-kkainen, -ikke, -ikki)
1 Ilmarinen's sister: brings news 15:6,49; 16
2 daughter of otherworld ruler (→ Tuoni): wooed 18
3 Joukahainen's sister: given as ransom 29:149, 157
4 Ahti's sister: divulges secrets 39:10
5 villager: disturbed 90:32*ff*
6 rejected lover: takes revenge 92; 93 (parallel: Kirtti); 94 (epithet: Turuinen's girl)
7 wooed girl: commits suicide 104
8 wooed girl: chooses husband 112
9 girl falsely accused: commits suicide 124

Annikkainen → Anni

Annikke → Anni

Antero, Andreas, Andrew, Anterus, Antti
1 sailor: understands weather 26:55
2 young nobleman (epithet: Ylinen's son): widower 87; kills wife and commits suicide 88
3 villager: disturbed 90:33*ff*
4 young soldier: sets off to war 138

Anterus → Antero 2, 4

Antervo → Vipunen

Antti → Antero 3

Atimo
?corruption of *Satamasaari*
island-harbour, possibly Kronstadt 146:21

Blue Girl/Sinetär
tutelary spirit of dyeing 148:23

Bothnia → Eastern Bothnia

Cabbageland/Kaalimaa
a reference to the common belief in medieval Scandinavia that the staple diet of the English was cabbage: St Henry's birthplace 67:2

Catherine St/Kaia, Kaio, Katie, Katro, Kitty, Pyhä Katri(i)na
her martyrdom (307 AD) was a popular theme in medieval church art: burned on a pyre 64; 65

Charles/Kaarle, Kaarlo
1 Duke of Södermanland until 1599, then Charles IX of Sweden-Finland (1550–1611): suppresses rebellion in Finland (1597) 143
2 Charles XII of Sweden-Finland (1682–1718): campaigns against Russia 146

Christ → Jesus

Creator → God, Jesus

Cuckoo Hill/Käenmäki
fictitious place-name 72:8

Cumå → Kokemäki

Eastern Bothnia/Bothnia orientalis
area corresponding approximately to present-day Ostrobothnia (Pohjanmaa) (→ map) 87

Eerik(ki) → Eric

Eeva
young girl (epithet: maid of Riga): falsely accused 125

Elina, Helina
derivations of Helena (→)
1 woman: finds abandoned child 70:17; (parallel: Katro) 71:1, 40
2 Klavus Kurki's wife (→): falsely accused and murdered 84

Eric/Eerik(ki)
1 Eric IX Jedvardsson of Sweden (murdered 1160, later canonised): crusades in Finland 66; 67
2 knight: attempts to obtain wife by subterfuge 85:17

Estonia[n]/Viro
1 place-name 22:2; 24:2,27; 36:10; 98:1,2,4,5; 103; 132:11,15,17; 141:15,29
2 distance symbol 45:53; 88:74; 113:22*ff*; 117:1
3 home of workers of magic 88:36; 101:27
4 poverty symbol 25:1,13;, 78:1

Finland [Finnish]/Suomi
in folk poetry usually the province of Varsinais-Suomi (South-West Finland, → map); in Ingrian poetry it generally refers to the southern coast of Finland
1 place-name 43:8, 10; 67:85; 75:33, 34; 112:2; 143
2 wealth symbol 23:35; 134:12,15
3 distance symbol 38:126*ff*; 49:36; (parallel: Sweden/Ruotsi) 127:46,66,88; 136:3

German[y]/Saksa
for a singer of folk poetry in the Finnish area *Saksa(-lainen)* 'Germany', 'German 'referred to language-usage, i.e. an area, or an object pertaining to that area where German dialects were spoken. In the North-East Baltic region such areas were clearly defined. The Hanse merchants had made German the common language in the ports, and often in centres of trade in the hinterland. North of the Gulf of Finland the derivative *saksalainen* denoted variously 'foreigner', 'travelling merchant', 'shopkeeper', and 'townsman', while *saksa-*, as the first component of a compound, usually denoted excellence or greatness of size. Hence a clearly defined area of usage in folk poetry concerns wealth and splendour, i.e. imported goods, or goods made by a professional craftsman in contrast to cruder, home-produced wares. South of the Gulf of Finland, in West Ingria and Estonia, *Saksa* had the same use but was also associated both admiringly and deprecatingly with the local gentry, who spoke German as their first language (just as those of comparable social position in Finland spoke Swedish). A further factor that has to be considered, especially in the Russian Orthodox areas of Ingria, is the use by Russians of 'German' to mean 'foreign(er)', a usage that dates from the influx of skilled and professional men at the time of Peter the Great
1 place-name 25:12; 103:26
2 wealth, size, or splendour symbol (i.e. made to order by a craftsman or imported) 12:189; 52:8; 99:5; 107:17,18; 117:2; 134:11,16; 140:88,90; 141:6,20
3 urban 76:9; 93:21
4 foreign (probably Hanse) 66:85–86; 71:22,60

God, Creator/Jumala(inen), Jumma(a)la, Jumalut, Luoja, Luojo(-i), Luojut
cognate forms of Fi. *jumala* 'god' in dialects and related languages meaning 'worker of magic', 'lightning', 'heavens', 'supreme deity' suggest that *jumala* was originally a general term of reference for supernatural powers or persons. The word was adopted as the name of the Christian deity by the early missionaries in the Finnish area, when it also acquired the parallels *Lord, Creator, Jesus* (→). In the minds of the early Christian converts the difference between the pagan and the Christian god was not always distinct and confusion of the two is common in folk poetry, particularly in incantations from the Middle Ages.
1 Christian deity 7; 14:145,146; 27; 32:6,84; 34:108; 49:19; 50:45; 59:253*ff*; 61:80*ff*; 62:82*ff*; 91:24,32; 99:8*ff*; 100:20; 112:68; 147:105; raises wind 3:17; help sought 26:82*ff*; 66:194,195; 94:36*ff*; performs miracle(s) 33; 66:150*ff*; 79:26*ff*; 94:27*ff*; 144:36; praised 42:65; birth of son (→ Jesus) 63:27; reveals sins 76:49,50; merciful in heaven 79:41*ff*; ends war 86:23
2 Jesus (→) 59:227; 60; 61:105*ff*; 62:47,111*ff*; 77:33
3 pagan deity (parallel: Väinämöinen) 49:1

Hanhenpajusto (lit. 'Goose Willow Patch')
unidentified place-name, near Turku, South-West Finland 143:85

Hannus, Hannas, Hanno
1 young man (epithet: German of the Isle): seducer: denies fatherhood 70; 71
2 married man (epithet: Pannus): murders wife in order to remarry 95

Hein(i)rikki, Heinärikki → Henry St

Hekko(-i)
1 young girl: ungrateful 22:24,26
2 maid: learns to attract suitors 120

Hel(le)ena
wife (parallel: Katteeriina): murdered by husband 96

Helina → Elina 1

Henry St/Henrik Pyhä, Hein(i)rikki, Hentrikki, Heinärikki
Englishman (d. 1156), Finland's patron saint, first bishop of Finland, later canonised: murdered while travelling in South-West Finland 66; 67

Hentrikki → Henry St

Herod/Ruotus, Ruatus
1 Herod the Great (c. 73–4 BC), client king of Judea under the Romans at the time of Jesus' birth, associated with Gospel legends of the Magi and the Massacre of the Innocents: ill-treats the Virgin Mary 59:57*ff*; loses stableman, St Stephen (→) 63; burns St Catherine (→) 64; 65 (parallel: Väinämöinen)
2 chieftain: killed in a duel 137:99*ff*

Herodias/Kiiva, Tiiha
wife of Herod Antipas (son of Herod the Great), the ruler who ordered the execution of John the Baptist and received Jesus from the Romans after his arrest. In Finnish folk poetry Herodias is treated as the wife of Herod the Great (→ 1): ill-treats the Virgin Mary 59:63*ff*; loses stableman, St Stephen (→) 63

Hiisi, Hiito(-i, -la), Hiizi, Hittoi, Iitto(va)
the word originally denoted a place associated with the deceased, from which it came to denote variously a sacred place, the otherworld, a distant, often hostile mythological place, a supernatural being (e.g. forest tutelary spirit), all of which were associated with destructive powers and the deceased. The name was later applied to Christian concepts of the devil and hell.
1 distant, often hostile mythological place, or its ruler 14:14,102; 19,98*ff*; 31:29; concealed sun and moon 32; guardian of treasure 46:24,38; possesses elk 53; 54; 55:1 (cf. 17; 23:55; 24:11,55; 139:31)
2 hell 60:69,72; 62:221*ff*; cf. 66:187
3 Devil 141:49

Hirska → Ahti 1

Holy River/Pyhäjoki
parish in West Finland on the coast of the Gulf of Bothnia 87

Honkela
(parallels: Tapio →, Salakaarto →) mythical place-name derived from the personification of *honka* 'fir' + locality formative *-la*, i.e. 'Fir forest realm' 6:2 (cf. Metsola, Tapi(v)ola)

Hoora
< *Houra* < Ru. cf. *Aurora*
name rejected for daughter 120:22

Huotola
possibly a corruption of Luotola, South-West Finnish archipelago
place-name 46:20

Häme
province (→ map) 51:3; 66:15; 67

Iivana
1 husband (epithet: Ko(i)jo(i)ne(n)'s son; parallels: Ilmorini, Kojo): murders wife and bakes pie from her parts 19; 20; murders wife in order to remarry 96 (cf. Hannus 2)
2 → Ivan

Iki Turso → Iku Turso

Iku Tiera, Niera's son
mythical hero: accompanies Väinämöinen to steal *sampo* 12:223*ff*

Iku Turso, Äiö's son
cf. MFi. *tursas* 'sea-monster; creature living in water' < OSc. cf. Old Norse *Þurs* 'giant, monster'
Leviathan: tries to capsize boat in which Jesus is sleeping 27:91*ff*

Ilmari (-nen), Ilmolline, Ilmollini, Ilmori(-nen), Ilmorini, Ismaro
possibly a derivative of *ilma* 'air'
as a deity variously associated with the air and the wind his role is more commonly that of the smith-culture hero. In the oldest poems it is not always possible to separate these two roles, while later the name was frequently applied to any kind of smith
1 smith-god/smith-culture hero: shapes the sky 8 (cf. 7); strikes primeval spark 9:1 (cf. 15:134); shapes *sampo* and helps to steal it 12:109*ff*; 14; 15; makes bride from gold 21; 22; tempers sword 139:8,13 (→ Ingrian smith)
2 smith-culture hero: suitor 16; 17
3 name given to a child found abandoned in a marsh 57:5, 58:20
4 → Iivana 1

Imandra Island/Imandran saari
mythical place-name, sometimes associated with Manala (→) and Tuonela (→) 4:27,33

Inari
small market town and administrative area in Lapland: distance symbol 145:22

Ingrian smith/seppä Inkeroine
corruption of Ilmarinen
Russian Orthodox Ingrian of Karelian descent: marries 121:71

Inkeri
maid: faithful to her betrothed 85 (cf. 86)

Island/Saari
unspecified place, sometimes mythical
1 place-name 22:1; 39:3; 94; 102:2
2 refuge place 37:206*ff*; 38:143*ff*
3 distance symbol 49:36; 71:22, 60; 136:3 (cf. also 16)

Ismaro → Ilmari

Isponen's Hill/Ispostenmäki
Ispoistenmäki, hill near Turku, South-West Finland 143:44

Ivan/Iivana
1 Tsar Ivan III (1440–1505) or Ivan IV (1530–1584): at war with Sweden 145
2 → Iivana

Jacob/Jaakko **Pontus**
a legendary figure based on two historical characters: the Swedish generals Pontus de la Gardie (1520–1585) and his son Jacob de la Gardie (1583–1652): attacks Riga and Narva 144

Jesus, Christ/Jeesus, Jessus, Jiessus, Kiesus, Kristus
son of God (parallels: God, Creator) 33:9,39, 58; 72:3; 77:33; 92:41,47; 94:21,29; in a boat, overcomes sea monster 27; birth and youth 59:227*ff*; resurrection 60; conception, life and works 61; 62; works miracles 62:158,159; 71:68,69; 94:29, birth revealed 63:27*ff*; follower acquired 63:30; conceals identity and confronts people with their sins 75; 76:48*ff*; 84:203; at gates of heaven with St Peter 78:9,31

Jompainen → Joukahainen

Jouka(ha)ine(-n), Jompainen, Jougamoine, Joukamoi(-ne), Joukavainen
? ~*joukea* 'tall'; a second theory links the name to *joutsen* 'swan' (cf. Ostrobothnian dialect *joukhainen*), in which case the animal might be a personification of a shaman's familiar
1 young shaman: competes against Väinämöinen 10; 11; 15:159*ff*; 29:41*ff*
2 young warrior: helps to steal *sampo* 13; 14
3 possible husband 19:3, 4

Jordan/Jortanainen
river that never freezes 62:55

Jumala (-inen), Jumma(a)la, Jumalut → God

Jyrki
young man: murdered by wife 91

Kaalimaa → Cabbageland

Kaaras(t)a
place-name, possibly Oranienbaum, near St Petersburg 41:10, 13; 102:28

Kaarle, Kaarlo → Charles

Kaia, Kaio → Catherine St

Kaija, Kaisa, Kaisu, Katoi(-nen), Katri, Katro, Katteeriina, Katti
1 girl: kills seducer 90
2 girl: one of three sisters 61:3
3 girl: tries to milk crane 118:16
4 girl: prefers local suitor 113
5 woman: finds abandoned child 71:2 (parallel: Helina)
6 woman: weaves 133:53, 54
7 grandmother: has three grand-daughters 61:1
8 → Helena

Kaisa, Kaisu → Kaija 1

Kale(r)va(-inen), Kalehva, Kalervo(-i), Kalervikko
one of the oldest Baltic-Finnish names, possibly cognate with the Balt god-smith *Kalevias*, cf. Balt *kalwis* 'smith'
1 (shaman-)chieftain: kills sister and brother-in-law 36
2 chieftain: attacked by brother Untamo (→) 41; 43
3 warrior: killed at feast 38
4 intruder (parallel: Osmonen): drives girl to suicide by his attentions 104:10,50
5 epithet and parallel name 'K.'s handsome priest', Riiko's son/Riion poika (→) 89:7,29
6 name of unidentified person 46:79

Kale(r)va, Kanerva, son of/Kale(r)van, Kanervan poika
in West Finnish and Estonian tradition a giant, destructive hero (principal character in the Estonian epic *Kalevipoeg*)
1 orphan: survives massacre 41:43; avenges 42; 43
2 epithet: Väinämöinen (→) 5:8; 49:3; Lemminkäinen (→) 35:189*ff*; Kullervo (→) 137; 139; 140

Kalla, Kalo Cape/Kalla-, Kalonniemi
unidentified place-name: home of wooed girl 88:17; 96:5,67 (parallel: Kontu Cape →)

Kanerva, son of/Kanervan poika → Kaleva, son of

Kankahatar → Loom Girl

Kaprio
district in Central Ingria (→ map): distance symbol 49:40; 136:5

Karelia/Karjala
area comprising regions of several provinces situated partly in Finland, partly in the USSR (→ map). In folk poetry Karelia is a region loosely associated with those parts of historical Karelia that lay within the sphere of influence of the Russian Orthodox Church 42:9; 43:9, 12; 137:4

Karjukkain → Mai(j)a 10

Katie → Catherine St

Katoi(-nen) → Maija 6

Katriina → Catherine St

Katri → Kaija

Katro → Kaija; Catherine St; Elina 1

Katteeriina → Kaija; Helleena

Katti → Kaija

Kaugo → Kaukamoinen

Kaukamieli → Kaukamoinen

Kaukamoinen, Kaugo, Kaukamieli, Kauko(-i)
possibly a personification of a word meaning 'far-sighted' or 'proud'
1 smith-culture hero (parallel: Estonian Smith/Viron seppä): makes *kantele* 24:1,26
2 adventurer: invited to feast 34:49*ff* (→ Ahti 3); kills host, flees, sexual prowess 37; 38

Kauko(-i) → Kaukamoinen

Kauppi
male name, possibly derived from Sw. *Jakob*
Lapp hunter (parallel: Vuojolainen): catches Hiisi's elk 53

Kavala
(parallel: Korkka) unidentified place-name 88:15

Kemi
North Ostrobothnian port (→ map): distance symbol 34:192

Kerttu
Lalli's (→) wife: lies 67:37

Kiesus → Jesus

Kiiva → Herodias

Kiljanta
(parallel: Paastue) unidentified place-name 102:24

Kinerva → Kullervo

Kirjamo
village in Narvusi district of Ingria (→ map) 49:67, 70

Kirsti(-nen), Kirtti
~ *Christine*
1 serving maid: falsely accuses mistress 84
2 virtuous girl: kills priest who tries to seduce her 89
3 girl: wooed 111
4 → Anni 6

Kitty → Catherine St

Kiulo
dialect form of Köyliö, lake near Turku, South-West Finland 67:16

Klavus → Kurki, Klavus

Ko(i)jo(i)ne(-n) (< Ru. *Godinovich*) → Iivana 1

Koijola
unidentified place-name, home of Kojonen (→ Iivana 1) 61:7

Koivisto
district on Karelian Isthmus (→ map) 18:2

Kojo → Iivana 1

Kokemäki/Cumå
district in South-West Finland (→ map) 87

Kolkanpää
village in Soikkola district of Ingria (→ map) 147:66, 73

Kommi
father: sets impossible tasks for suitor 19:12*ff*

Kontu(-i)
(parallels: Narentka, Kalla Cape/Kallaniemi) unidentified, place-name component ('homestead') common throughout Ingria and Karelia: home of wooed girl 20; 88:16; 96; 114:1,2

Korkka
(parallel: Kavala) unidentified place-name: home of wooed girl 88:14

Koroinen
unidentified place-name, possibly near Turku 146:22

Koski
unidentified, place-name component ('rapids') common throughout Finnish area: home of wooed girl 95 (→ Virta)

Kristus → Jesus

Kullervo, Kinerva, Kulerva
? < *kulta* 'gold'
warrior (epithets: Kale(r)va's son, Kanerva's son): asks relatives whether they will mourn his death 137; killed in battle 139; hears of relatives' death while at war 140 (cf. Kalervainen)

Kupitsa
Kupittaa, near Turku, South-West Finland 143:84

Kurki, Klavus
legendary murderer. The name is compounded from two historical characters: *Klaus Kurki*, judge of Ylä-Satakunta (West Finland), fifteenth century owner of the Laukko estate, and *Klaus Djäkn*, an officer of the Swedish crown in Finland: marries, believes false rumours about wife, burns her alive 84

Kuuro → Teuri

Kyllikki
? ∼ *kyllä* 'sufficient'
Ahti's (→ Ahti 5) wife: breaks promise, left by husband 39; 40

Käenmäki → Cuckoo Hill

Köyrötyinen, Köyrötty
smith: sets Kullervo (→) to work 42:10*ff*

Laari
< Sw. *Lars* << Lat. *Laurentius*
son: tries to please mother 100

Labala → Manala

Laisa
unidentified place-name 16:5

Lalli, Lalloi
pagan peasant: murders St Henry (→) 66:65*ff*; 67:32*ff*

Lalloila
Lalli's home 66:65

Lalmanti
Finnish adaptation of Sw. *lagman* 'sheriff'
warrior: saves his betrothed from marriage to another man 85 (→ Maanitahan)

Lapland/Lappi
in Finnish folk poetry a geographically undefined area generally referring to the lands beyond the more northern Finnish settlements at any given time
1 place-name 31:22 (parallel: Pohjola); 53; 54:30 (parallel: Pohjo)
2 poverty symbol 1:15

Lappi → Lapland

Laukko
manor in West Finland owned by the Kurki (→) family 84

Lehenlemmykkäine
Ingr. corruption of *lieto* 'wanton' + *Lemminkäinen*
spiteful hostess: killed by brother 36 → Lemminkäinen 1

Lemmasterva
Ingr. corruption of *Lemmin(käinen)* + *terva* 'tar' (an allusion to 'tarry objects', one of the magic devices used by a shaman)
spiteful host: killed by brother-in-law 36
→ Lemminkäinen 1

Lemmenlahti → Lempi Bay

Lemminkäin(-en), Lemmingäin(-e), Lemmingöine
1 shaman-chieftain: skill at magic 1:45; uninvited guest, kills host 34 (cf. 36); killed by host, goes to otherworld 35
2 hunter: catches Hiisi's elk 54 (cf. Kauppi)
3 Tuiretuinen (→) 44:2,34
→ Lehenlemmykkäine, Lemmasterva

Lempi Bay/Lemmenlahti
unidentified place-name, possibly Lemlax in Parainen, South-West Finland 17:130

Little Meadows/Pienet, Pikku niittuset
unidentified place-name, Laukko (→), West Finland 84:59*ff*

Loom Girl/Kankahatar
tutelary spirit of weaving 148:24

Luoja, Luojo(-i), Luojut → God, Jesus

Luutitsa
unidentified place-name, possibly *Luushitsa* in the Kattila district of Ingria 120:13

Maanitahan
Ingr. corruption of the West Fi. line of poetry Lal*manti* iso ri*ta*ri (cf. 85:1)
warrior: saves his betrothed from marriage to another man 86

Maariain, Maarja, → Virgin Mary

Maaroi → Maija 6

Magdalen/Mataleena, Mateliina
sinful woman: confesses and repents 75; 76

Mai(j)a, Maaroi, Mai(j)e, Mai(j)oi, Mari, Marjukkain
∼ *Mary*
1 mother: daughter dissatisfied 22:25, 27
2 girl: brother builds bath-house 49:69

3 Marjatta's (→) sister 61:3
4 mother: daughter raped 69:4
5 young wife: kills husband 91
6 girl (parallel: Katoi): tries to save dying mother 101
7 mother: dies after eating berries 101:18
8 girl: tries to milk crane 118:14
9 girl: abducted by cloud 131
10 mother (parallel: Karjukkain): looks for lost daughter 131

Mana(la), Labala, Manula
? < *mana* 'loss, destruction' + locality formative *-la*: otherworld (commonly with parallels: Tuonela, Tuoni →) 9:6,13; 15:139; 16:29; 17:207*ff*; 34:212; 35:93,191,243*ff*; 79:94; source of spells 29; 30; 61:126

Mantu
tutelary personification of *mantu* 'hard, barren earth', the earlier usage of which is reflected in incantations addressed to local earth spirits *mannun isäntä ja eukko* 'earth master and dame'
son of Mantu killed by woman he tries to seduce 90

Margaret (St)/Marketta
her mother milks snake 55:15

Mari → Mai(j)a

Mariatta
girl: bears child 58 (cf. 57)

Marjukkain → Mai(j)a 6, 9

Marketta
~ *Margaret*
girl: denies parenthood of illegitimate child 70; 71
→ Margaret (St)

Martti → Tanumartti

Mataleena, Mateliina → Magdalen

Metsola
(parallel: Rahansaari →) mythical place-name derived from the personification of *metsä* 'forest' + locality formative *-la*, i.e. 'Forest realm' 58:40 (cf. Honkela, Salakaarto, Tapi(v)ola)

Moscow/Moskova
distance symbol 49:39; 136:4

Naari → Na(a)rva 2

Na(a)rva, Naari, Narvoi
fortified North-East Estonian town, important trading centre in the Middle Ages
1 distance symbol 45:3
2 urban symbol 3:32; 76:12,21
3 threatened and attacked 144:18,32

Naasta
< Ru. cf. *Anastasia*
rejected as name for daughter 120:21

Narentka
(parallel: Kontu →) unidentified place-name: home of wooed girl 20:9

Niera → Iku Tiera

North Land/Pohjanmoa
area, probably comprising the whole of the Arctic North, beyond the more northern Finnish settlements at any given time (cf. Lapland/Lappi, Pohjola): size symbol 48:12

Nousiainen
district in South-West Finland where St Henry (→) is thought to have been buried 66:128

Novgorod/Uusi linna
singers of Finnish folk poetry frequently punned the components of the name (a calque: 'new town/castle'). Where the pun is more important than the place-name, the components of the name have been translated
1 distance symbol 110:5
2 pun and distance symbol 131:20; 147:127

Nurmi-Tuomas → Turf Thomas

Oapsu
? < *Absalom*
father: sets impossible tasks for suitor 20

Old Man of the Air/Ilman Ukko
corruption of Ilmari(nen) (→ 1) + Ukko (→) smith-god: strikes primeval spark 15:134

Olevi, Olovi
hired man: falsely accused 84

Oljona(-inen)
< Ru. cf. *Olyena*
daughter of Kommi (→), wife of Iivana 1 (→) (parallel: Palaka(-inen): murdered by husband, baked in pie and given to father 19:182

Osmeroi
unidentified place in Estonia 141

Osmonen
male name, probably mythological
intruder (parallel: Kalevainen): drives girl to suicide 104:9, 49

Osmotar
female name of uncertain origin, possibly personification of materials used in the fermentation process
brewer 34:5, 32

Ostrobothnia → Eastern Bothnia/Pohjanmaa

Paaritsa
village in the Kolppana district of Ingria 69:13

Paastue
< Ru. cf. *pogost* 'parish'
(parallel: Kiljanta) unidentified place-name 102:23

Paatitsa
place-name, possibly a variant of Paaritsa (→) 120:12

Palaga, Palaka(inen)
< Ru. cf. *Pelagiya*
1 name rejected for daughter 120:15,16
2 daughter of Kommi (→) wife of Iivana 1 (→) (parallel: Oljona(-inen)): murdered by husband, baked in pie and given to father 19:183

Palvonen, Pavannainen
< Fi. *palvoa* 'to worship', i.e. 'one who is worshipped'
deity often associated with Ukko (→) and Virokannas (→). It is uncertain whether Palvonen is an epithet of Ukko or a separate deity: parallel of Ukko (→) 12:46; baptizes illegitimate child 58:26

Papinluoto (lit. 'priest's rock')
place-name, near Turku, South-West Finland 143:30

Paraska
< Ru. cf. *Paraskeviya*
name rejected for daughter 120:18, 19

Pavannainen → Palvonen

Pedro → Peterkin

Pellervi, Pellervoinen, Pellervöinen → Sampsa

Pentti
castle lord: inhospitable to travellers 26:110,111

Peter St/Santta Pietari
helmsman 27; at gates of heaven 78

Peterkin/Pieni Pedro
i.e. St Peter's day, 29th June, a major feast in the Russian Orthodox calendar, traditionally the date on which burn-beat clearing was started (see Plate 13): date of departure to search for wood 26:3

Petersburg/Pietari, Piiteri
1 distance symbol 110:6
2 attacked 146:4

Pienet niittuset → Little Meadows

Pieni Pedro → Peterkin

Pietari, Piiteri → Peter; Petersburg

Piltti
< Sw. cf. *pilt* 'small boy'
its occurrence as a proper name is exceptional
serving maid: looks for place for the Virgin Mary's (→) confinement 59

Pohja → Pohjola

Pohjanmoa → North Land

Pohja, Pohjanmaa, Pohjo(-inen, -la)
1 land in the North, destination of dangerous journeys (an analogue of the *Nordheim, Nordbotn* of the *Fornaldarsögur*) 4:11; 5:65; 12; 13; 14; 15; 16
2 otherworld 17:183, 195; 31:20*ff*; 50:36*ff*
3 strange land: as refuge 46:7; 62:23*ff*
4 South Ostrobothnia 84:57*ff*
5 parallel of Lapland 54:30*ff*

Poland/Puola
attacked by Jacob Pontus (→) 144:15

Pontus → Jacob Pontus

Puola → Poland

Pyhä Anna → Ann St

Pyhäjoki → Holy River

Pyhä Henrik → Henry St

Pyhä Katriina → Catherine St

Pyhä Pietari → Peter St

Pyhä Tapani → Stephen St

Päivölä
mythical place-name derived from personification of *päivä* 'sun' + locality formative *-lä*. In Finnish incantations *Päivölä* functions as the antithesis of *Pohjola* (→ Pohja 1), which was associated with darkness and evil; in epic poetry, however, the antithesis does not occur and the name generally refers to the place where heroes meet to feast 34:74*ff*; 37 (parallel: Sariola →)

Rahansaari
(parallel: Metsola →) mythical island-name derived from the primary meaning of *raha* 'fur pelt' (< Sc.), hence 'island on which there were (many) fur-bearing animals' 58:41

Raisu
understood by the Ingrian singer as an Estonian place-name (but more likely a misunderstanding of the Estonian expletive *rauda, raibe* 'rotten') 49:68,71

Rakkavuori, Rakkavuuri → Rakvere

Rakvere/Rakkavuori, Rakkavuuri
town in North Estonia (German: Wesenberg): size symbol 49:68,71

Riga/Riika
Baltic port (now capital of Latvian SSR)
1 epithet 125
2 threatened and attacked 144

Riika → Riga

Riiko's son/Riion poika
? < *Fredrik*
priest (epithet and parallel: Kaleva's (→) handsome priest): killed by girl he tries to seduce 89: 6,28

Riion poika → Riiko's son

Ruotsi → Sweden

Ruatus, Ruotus → Herod

Ruskiakallio (lit. 'brown rock')
Ruskeakallio in the district of Raisio near Turku, South-West Finland 143:31

Russia/Venäjä
its army attacked by Charles XII 146:6

Saari → Island

St Ann → Ann St

St Catherine → Catherine St

St Henry → Henry St

St Peter → Peter St

St Stephen → Stephen St

Saksa → German[y]

Salakaarto
(parallels: Tapio →, Honkela →) possibly a tutelary personification of *salon kaarto* 'winding forest way', the earlier usage of which is reflected in incantations addressed to *salon kaarron kaunis vaimo* 'the beautiful female spirit of the winding forest way'. An alternative theory explains S. as a corruption of *Santa Kaaren* 'St Catherine' 6:3 (cf. Honkela, Metsola, Tapi(v)ola)

Sampsa the Pellervo boy/ Säm(p)sä Pellervo(-inen), Pellervö(-inen)
Sampsa ? ∼ *St Samson* or *Sämpsä*(*heinä*) 'forest-rush') + *pellervo* (< *pelto* 'field')
deity associated with fertility: builds a boat for God 27:1, 58; his help is sought to start growth in spring 46; 47

Santta Anna → Ann St

Santta Pietari → Peter St

Saraja
< *sarajas* 'sea', later sometimes associated with Jerusalem
mythical place-name: no place in S. village for the Virgin Mary to deliver her child 59:48*ff*

Sariola
mythical place-name, variant of Saraja (→): (parallel of Päivölä →) place where heroes meet to feast 37

Savo
province (→ map) 4:12; 145:61 (parallel: Sweden → 1)

Siimet Isle/Siimetsaari
place-name, identified by some scholars as Simasalo, an island in the Sipoo Archipelago, Gulf of Finland 17:133 (cf. Lempi Bay/Lemmenlahti)

Sinetär → Blue Girl

Sinivermo
? < *siniverka* 'blue cloth' → Väinölä

Stephen St/Pyhä Tapani, Tahvana
Herod's stableman: sees star in stream 62:53, 59; reveals the birth of Jesus 63

Stockholm/Tukhulmi
port, capital of Sweden 103:27

Suokas, son of/Suokkaan poika
young man: rapes a girl 69:1

Suomela
birthplace of Elina (→), estate near Laukko (→), 84:150

Suomi → Finland

Sweden [Swedish]/Ruatsi, Ruotsi, Ruotti, Svecia
the area understood by 'Sweden' varied from singer to singer and depended largely on where the singer had grown up and on the political circumstances that prevailed both when the original poem was composed and when each redaction and variant evolved. Seen from Finland, particularly from the western regions, the name referred either to Sweden, approximately within its present-day frontiers, or to Sweden-Finland, a territory that diminished in size during the 18th and 19th centuries. For a Russian Orthodox Karelian or Ingrian, 'Sweden' probably denoted an area where the Lutheran Church of Sweden-Finland predominated; hence to an Ingrian it could sometimes refer to certain close, even neighbouring districts (pastors in the Lutheran parishes of Ingria were often trained in

Turku and spoke Swedish amongst themselves), while to a Karelian it was more likely to mean an area corresponding approximately to present-day Finland. For the few Karelians and Ingrians with a wider knowledge of geography, 'Sweden' corresponded approximately to Sweden-Finland of the 17th and 18th centuries and may have continued to have the same meaning even after the union of the Grand Duchy of Finland in 1808–1809.
1 Sweden (without Finland) 25:11 (parallels: Estonia[n]/Viro →, German[y]/Saksa →); 66:4*ff*; 67:3; 74:40; 75:45; 87; 142:2 (parallel: Finland/Suomi →), 74*ff*; 145:23, 60 (parallel: Savo); 146: 3, 48; wealth symbol 3:31; splendour symbol 82:7, 12; 83; 143:2; distance symbol (parallel: Finland/Suomi →) 127:47*ff*
2 Sweden-Finland 74:40; 127:47,67,89; 143; 145: 23,60; 146:3,48

Tabie → Tapio

Tahvana → Stephen St

Tallimäki (lit. 'stable-hill')
hill near Turku, South-West Finland 143:87

Tanikka, Martti of, Tanumartti/Tanikan Martti, Tanumartti
folk personifications of forms of the name *Denmark* (< **Danamark*) that entered 15th century Fi. dialects in several forms (e.g. *Tanamarkki*, *Tanumartti*): enemy 73:33; 74:41

Tapio, Tabie
possibly a personification of 'trap, snare' > 'area where trapping took place'
1 male supreme forest deity 6:1 (parallel: Honkela →, Salakaarto →); 53:44
2 → Väinämöinen 29:57

Tapi(v)ola
mythical place-name < *Tapio* (→) + locality formative *-la*, i.e. 'Tapio's realm', often personified as 'forest'
otherworld (parallel: Pohjola → 2) 15

Tapo Hill/Tapomäki
mythical place-name derived from Tapiomäki (→ Tapio), i.e. 'hill in a forest'
place where outcast women deliver their children 59:75*ff*

Tapomäki → Tapo Hill

Teuri
? < Sc. cf. Sw. *djur* 'animal' or cognate with male name *Tiera* (→ Iku Tiera)
newly married warrior: prefers adventures at sea to life at home (→ Ahti 3) 40

Thomas → Turf Thomas

Tiera → Iku Tiera

Tiiha → Herodias

Tora River/Torajoki
mythical place-name 52:30,31

Torajoki → Tora River

Tormio
dialect form of Est. *Torma*, district in the Tartu (Dorpat) administrative area 91:2

Torni(v)o
port in North Ostrobotnia (→ map): size symbol 34:191,51:4

Tukhulmi → Stockholm

Tuomas → Turf Thomas

Tuonela
mythical place-name < *Tuoni* (→) + locality formative *-la*. Originally *Tuonela* meant 'place of death', i.e. 'grave' from which evolved the secondary meaning of 'place, home of all the dead', i.e. 'otherworld'
1 otherworld 34:211 (parallel: Manala); 61:123*ff*; source of spells (parallel: Manala) 30
2 heaven 77:36,54; 79:87,95 (parallel: Manala)

Tuoni
origin unknown, possibly cognate with a Lapp word meaning 'smell of a starved reindeer'
1 ruler of the otherworld, personified as death 9:43,44; 15:26*ff*; 16:28; 17:181*ff*; 23:58,59; 30; 98:75,76; 101:72; sets impossible tasks for daughter's suitor 18; will not allow girl to visit relatives 124:181
2 otherworld 29:8*ff*; 35:92,233*ff* (parallel: Manala); 61:125*ff* (parallel: Labala)

Turf Thomas/Nurmi-Tuomas
i.e. Thomas who is buried beneath the grass, death personification: takes girl 3:34

Turja
cape on the White Sea Peninsula, often confused in folk poems with Ruija (the southern region of Lapland in Norway and Sweden)
1 White Sea coast 5:89, 108
2 Lapland 50:9

Turku/Aboa
city, former capital of Finland, South-West Finland (→ map)
1 place-name 87; 92:2,4; 94
2 distance symbol 49:37
3 attacked 143

Turso → Iku Turso

Turuinen → Annikki 6

Tuulikki
? < *tuuli* 'wind'
Tapio's (→) daughter: wooed 6

Tuuri
< Sc. cf. *Thor*
unidentified place-name, probably mythical 45:1

Tuurikkaine, Tuiretuinen, Tuurit(t)uinen
< Sc. cf. *Ture*
1 wealthy young man: unwittingly seduces his sister 44 (parallel: Lemminkäinen); 45
2 father: his son as seducer 58:15

Ukko
possibly a back-formation and personification of *ukkonen* 'thunder'
god of thunder, supreme Finnish pagan deity: determines weather 2:26; 12:45*ff* (parallel: Pavannainen); 93:42; fails to slaughter great pig 52 → Ilman ukko

Umanto, Umento
< *uvanto* 'area of slow-flowing water'
mythical place-name, home of Väinämöinen; epithets 'man from U.', 'bridegroom from U.': Väinämöinen (→) 12:7; 16:25

Untamo (-inen), Unto(-i), Untomaa, Uttamo
male name, originally possibly associated with stranger, often hostile
1 vaguely sketched character, sometimes attributed with supernatural powers 33:46*ff*; master of ferocious animals 37:74,91; guest at feast 38:30
2 ship's captain (epithet: Ylermö's son) 26:63*ff*
3 chieftain: attacks and believes he has destroyed brother and brother's family (→ Kale(r)va 2) 41; 43; 105:26,28
4 → Väinämöinen 12:76,84

Veitikki, Veitikkä
? < *Vetrikka*, cf. Est. *Vidrik*, Fi. *veitikka* 'rascal, scamp, rogue' or *Friedrich*
adventurer: guest at a feast 34:50*ff*; 38:34 (→ Ahti 3)

Vellamo
? < *velloa* 'to undulate (of water)'
parallel of Ahti (→ 1) 56:41

Venaa
place-name, probably the village of Vena in the Narvusi district of Ingria (→) 79:2

Vento
vaguely sketched male character, possibly possessing supernatural powers 33:46*ff*; guest at feast 38:30

Venäjä → Russia

Viena(n vedet) → White Sea

Viipuri
city, port and market on Karelian Isthmus 45:2; 144:2,31; market 93:20; 108:35; 114:34; size symbol 44:39

Vipunen, Antervo, Virone, Anderus
possibly a derivative of *vipu* 'lift-trap'
ancient shaman: Väinämöinen visits his grave in search of spells 28; 29:18,19

Virgin Mary/Ma(a)ria(-in), Maarja, Marjatta
as mother of Jesus: 26:4; 64:28; 68:16,22; 71:69; 72:4; 92:42, 48; 94:22*ff*; bears child 59; 61; 62; searches for lost child 59:238*ff*; 62:75*ff*

Viro → Estonia

Virokannas
deity associated with fertility: baptizes illegitimate child 58:25

Virone → Vipunen, Antervo

Virta
unidentified, place-name component ('river; current') common throughout the Finnish area: home of wooed girl 95 → Koski

Volmar/Volmari
fortified town near Riga, present-day Valmiera Latvian SSR: attacked 145: 27,34

Vuojolainen, Vuoljalainen → Kauppi

Väinämöi(-nen), Väinämöini, Väinö
< *väinä* 'broad, deep, slow-flowing river'
the most commonly mentioned character in ancient Finnish epic poetry, Väinämöinen also appears in incantations and has often replaced characters in poems in the early versions of which he did not feature. Whether his original role was that of a deity or a culture hero is uncertain. In the earliest stratum of poems he is probably a water-spirit. In later poems he is variously attributed with the role of a creator, a deity, and a culture hero; usually his role becomes that of a shaman or sea-hero in a coastal fishing milieu
1 god/culture hero: takes part in creation of world 4; 5; 15:145*ff*; strikes primeval spark 9:2; 15:135; rejected by mankind, departs for otherworld 57; 58
2 shaman-singer: sings Joukahainen into swamp 10; 11; 15:159*ff*; 29:130*ff*; sings Lemminkäinen into otherworld river 35:149*ff*; enters mouth of ancient shaman 28; visits otherworld in search of spells 29; 30; releases sun from rock 31; makes and plays *kantele* 23:53*ff*; plays *kantele* 24:23*ff*; 29:107*ff*
3 wizard-chieftain: wounds knee 5; 6:31*ff*; suitor 6; 15; 16; 65:10 (parallel: Herod →); steals *sampo* 12 (parallel: Untamoinen); 13; 14; 15; holds feast (parallel: God) 49:2; catches water spirit 56; burns

St Catherine (parallel: Herod) 65; makes maid from gold 65:43*ff*

Väinölä
mythical place-name, Väinämöinen's home 35 (parallel: Sinivermo)

Väärnoja
Vääräoja, village in the Soikkola district of Ingria (→ map) 147:74

White Sea/Viena(n vedet)
→ map, distance symbol 110:7

Ylermä → Alermo

Ylermö → Untamo 2

Ylinen → Antero 2

Äiö → Iku Turso

MOTIF INDEX

The arrangement of the motif types occurring in the Anthology and their codes are based on the system published by Stith Thompson in his *Motif-Index of Folk-Literature.* An asterisk preceding a code number indicates that the motif is not included in Thompson's Index. In most cases reference is given only to the number of the poem. Line numbers are given where it would be otherwise difficult to identify the part of the poem where the motif is introduced.

A. Mythological Motifs

A13.2 Bird as creator – 2–5
A142 Smith of the gods – 2 7–9 12:106 14–19 21–22 24–25 31 139
A284 God of thunder – 12:45 15:134 52:16 93:41
A430 God of vegetation – 46–47
A527.1 Culture hero precocious – 8 31
A605.1 Primeval darkness – 32–33
A625.2 Raising of the sky – 10:32
A641 Cosmic egg – 2–5
A652 World-tree – 49–50
A661.0.1.2 Saint Peter as porter of heaven – 78
A661.1.0.4 Deer and the fountain – 92:28
A671.2 Horrible sights in hell – 34–37
A672 Stygian river – 30–31
A677.1 Smith of hell – 60–62
A713.1 Sun and moon from belly of a fish – 5
A714.2 Sun and moon placed in top of tree – 32–33
*A733.6 Sun melting the grave of Christ – 60 62
A734 Sun hides – 31–33
A736 Sun as human being – 33:105 113 119
A737 Causes of eclipses – 31
*A739.8.1 Sun placed evenly over rich and poor – 32–33
A753.1 Moon as wooer – 113
A811 Earth brought up from bottom of primeval water – 5:79 15:146
A814.9 Earth from egg breaking on primeval water – 3–5
A911 Bodies of water from tears – 104:87
A1012.3 Flood from blood – 5–6
A1071.1 Underground monster fettered by trick – 60–62
A1115 Why the sea is salt – 13
A1251 Creation of man from tree stump – 11:16 **41:7**
A1414 Origin of fire – 9 15:134
*A1415.2.2 Fire carried in sea by fishes – 9:21
A1425 Origin of seed – 46
A1432.1 Origin of iron – 139
A1447 Origin of metal-working – 7–8 31 139
A1457.3 Origin of the net for fishing – 9:36
A1461.2 Origin of lyre – 23–25
A1836 Creation of bear – 48
A2602 Planting the earth – 46:80
A2681 Origin of trees – 46:80 55 92
A2681.2 Origin of oak – 49–50

B. Animals

B11.8 Dragon as power of good – 73–74
B16.1.5.1 Monster ox killed – 26:123 51
B31 Giant bird – 12–15
B81.13.11.1 Mermaid caught by fisherman – 56
*B91.8 Flying serpent – 31
B102 Animals of precious metal (gold) – 21–22 65
B130 Truth-telling animals – 62–63 142
B155.1 Building site determined by halting of animal – 66–67
B184.1.4 Magic horse travels on sea or land – 11–12 18 20 62:143
B184.4 Magic deer – 53–55
B211.1.3 Speaking horse – 142
B264.2 Fight between eagle and fish – 5:88 17:218
B401 Helpful horse – 59:215
B437.3 Helpful squirrel – 34
B463.3 Helpful crane – 117–118
B531.2 Unusual milking animal (viper) – 55
B575.1 Wild animals kept as dogs – 35–37
B576 Animal as guard – 15–17
B845 Wild animals herded – 42
B871 Giant beasts – 26 51 52 107
B872.1 Giant eagle – 12:344 14:113
B875.1 Giant serpent 34:115 35:30
B877.1.2 Giant sea monster overpowered by saint – 27

C. Taboo

*C102 Extreme abhorrence of sexual intercourse – 58:8 61:69
C451–452 Boasting of wealth/children – 82–83
C623 Forbidden well – 62–63
C949.2 Baldness from breaking taboo – 66:157 67:91
C998 Trees wither because of broken taboo – 69

D. Magic

D152.2 Transformation: man to eagle – 12 14–15 17:218
D154.4 Transformation: bride to gull – 17:246
D191 Transformation: man to snake – 30
D412.2.1 Transformation: herd of cattle to wolves – 43
D523 Transformation through song – 10–11
D615.1 Transformation contest between magicians – 34
D672 Obstacle flight – 12:323 14:91 32:38
*D705.2 Forest disenchanted by priests – 69
*D763.3 Disenchantment by scorching cloud – 130
*D764.9 Disenchantment by giving beer to cloud 131
*D791.2.3 Disenchantment by enchanter – 10–11 15 29
D853 Magic object forged by smith to order – 2 12 15 18–19 25
D945 Magic hedge – 34 36 42
D950.2 Magic oak tree – 27 49–50 68
D1121 Magic boats – 5–6 14 26–29
D1175 Magic match – 12:322 14:91 15:131
D1208 Magic whip – 14:171
D1222 Magic horn – 42–43
D1273 Magic formula (charm) – 5–6 48
D1275 Magic song – 10–11 14–15 28–29 34–35 37 58:44
D1311.4.0.1 Oracular twig – 63
D1311.6 Moon and sun answer questions – 59 61–62
D1364 Object causes magic sleep – 12:233 32:24
D1419.3 Magic object prevents ship from moving – 12 14 23 27 29
D1441.1.3.2 Magic harp calls animals together – 23–25 29
D1503.1 Magic song heals wound – 6 62
D1562 Magic object removes obstacles – 33
D1610.9.1 Speaking sword – 36
D1810.13 Magic knowledge from the dead – 28–30
D1812.5.1.2 Bad dream as evil omen – 39:20
D2141 Storm produced by magic – 93–94
D2142.1 Wind produced by magic – 12:47 31:35
D2143.3 Fog produced and dispelled by magic – 14:155
D2153.1 Rock in sea created by magic – 12 14

E. The Dead

E32 Resuscitated eaten animal – 63
E168.1 Roasted cock comes to life and crows – 63
E186 Failure at resuscitation – 35
E363.3 Ghost warns the living – 35:275 135–136
E366 Return from dead to give counsel – 30:94
*E420.1 Appearance of deceased expressing manner of death – 30
E481.2.1 Bridge to land of dead – 50:35
E481.2.2 Boat to land of dead – 30 61:123
E741.1.1.2 Star as sign of birth of hero – 62–63
E761.1.7 Life token: comb drips blood – 35

F. Marvels

F81.1.2 Journey to land of dead to visit deceased – 28–29
F87 Journey to otherworld to secure bride – 17–18
F93.1 River entrance to lower world – 29–30 61:123
F95.5 Tree as roadway to underworld – 50:35
F112 Journey to island of women – 37–38
F141.1 River as barrier to otherworld – 29–31 33
F142 River of fire as barrier to otherworld – 34–35 37
F152.1.6.1 Bridge to otherworld covered with knives – 28:31, cf. 19:65
F167.11.1 Serpents in otherworld – 30 35–36
F343.3 Fairy smith gives knight a magic sword – 139
*F492.1 Death on skis – 81
F521.3 Men of metal – 111–112
F531.2.6 Giant lies underground with trees growing all over his body – 28–29
F535.1 Thumbling – 50:23
F610.2 Dwarf-hero of superhuman strength – 50:23 51:12
F614 Strong man's labours – 42
F663 Skilful smith – 7–8 21–22
F735 Island rises up in sea – 3–4 15:146
F771.5.1 Castle guarded by beasts – 34–37
F833 Extraordinary sword – 36 132 139
*F838.3 Knife handle with golden leaves – 63

F841 Extraordinary boat – 6 26–29
*F849 Extraordinary skis – 53–54
*F859 Extraordinary rake – 2 35:248
F871 Sampo – 1:44 12–15
F911.5 Giant swallows man – 28
F960.1 Extraordinary nature phenomena at birth of holy person – 61–63
*F967.5 Child caught by cloud – 129–131
F979.23 Trees wither when tragic things happen – 69
F989.15 Hunt for extraordinary animal – 17 53–54
F1021.1 Flight on artificial wings – 12:344
F1041.1.11.3 Suicide from fright of evil prophecy – 84:230
F1041.21 Reactions to excessive grief – 101 104 124

G. Ogres

G61 Relation's flesh eaten unwittingly 19–20
G500 Ogre defeated – 27

H. Tests

H252 Act of truth – 63
H335 Tasks assigned suitors – 6–7 15 17–20
H335.0.1 Bride helps suitor perform his tasks – 17:168
H373 Bride test: performance of tasks – 20:68
H1021–1022 Task: construction from impossible kind/amount of material – 6 20
H1131.1 Task: building bridge over land and sea – 18:74
H1154 Task: capturing animals – 17 19
H1188 Task: ploughing field of vipers – 17:155
H1347 Quest for lost comb – 132 135
H1382.1 Quest for unknown magic words – 28–29
H1385.2 Quest for vanished daughter or son – 59 61–62 130–131
H1385.8 Quest for lost brother – 129 135–136
H1386.3 Quest for lost bird (goose) – 133–134
H1510 Vain attempts to kill hero – 41 43, cf. 70–71

J. The Wise and the Foolish

*J868 Consolation by dreams of future compensation – 107–109

K. Deceptions

K1335 Clothes of bathing girl stolen – 106
K1340 Entrance into girl's room by deceit – 90
*K1851.2 False message of death – 85
K2112 Woman slandered as adulteress – 84 124–125
*K2127.3 Bishop falsely accused of usurpation – 66–67

L. Reversal of Fortune

L111.4.4 Mistreated orphan hero – 41–43 70–71
*L112.4.1 Dirty girl advised and wooed – 120
L113.6 Smith as hero – 7 15–18 21–22
*L213.3 Man of bread preferred to suitors of precious metal – 111–112
*L213.4 Neighbour's son preferred to celestial suitors – 113
L412 Rich woman made poor to punish pride – 82–83

M. Ordaining the Future

M114 Oath taken on sacred object – 39
M205 Breaking of bargains or promises – 39–40
M411.20 Curse by spouse – 122 138
*M464.1 Curse of a woman against her former family – 127–128

N. Chance and Fate

*N126.3 Lots cast to determine life or death – 101
N365.3 Unwitting brother-sister incest – 44–46
*N381.2 Ant urinating on leg of crane causes chain of accidents – 12:269 14:64
N542.1 With one-night-old colt on one-night-old ice – 11:29 18:89
*N770.1 Leaving the home as occasion for the beginning of adventures – 89 95–98 101 104 106–109 124–125 129–132 134–135
N774.2 Adventures from seeking domestic beast (horse) – 23
N818.1 Sun as helper – 60 62
*N819.5 Summer boy helper – 47
N825.2 Old man helper – 5–6
N855 Helpful smith – 2 19 25 139

P. Society

P11 Choice of king – 58:38
P19.4.1 King as judge – 72–74

P173.2 Killed enemy's son as slave – 41–43
P231 Mother and son – 35 97–98 100 137
P232 Mother and daughter – 101 131
P233 Father and son – 130
P551 Army – 142 147
P677 Customs connected with duelling – 34 37–38

Q. Rewards and Punishments

Q87 Reward for preservation of chastity – 89:80
Q172 Reward: admission to heaven – 66:183 77–79 84:215
Q243.2.1 Attempted seduction punished – 89–90
Q413 Punishment: hanging – 72–74 122 138
Q414 Punishment: burning alive – 64–65 84 122 138
Q451.9 Punishment: woman's breasts cut off – 19–20
Q560 Punishments in hell – 35 66:184 77–79 84:222

R. Captives and Fugitives

R12.4 Girl enticed into boat and abducted – 127–128
*R90 Ransom refused – 10–11 145
R111 Rescue of captive maiden – 127–128
R153.4 Mother rescues son – 35
R225 Elopement – 15:113
R310–317 Refuges: forest, meadow, well, sea, island – 38 91
R345 Cities of refuge – 89

S. Unnatural Cruelty

*S12.2.4 Mother drowns childen – 97
S62 Cruel husband – 7:38 84 95–96 122–123
S139.2.2.1 Heads of slain enemies impaled upon stakes – 37:22
S139.7 Murder by slicing person into small pieces – 96
*S177 Mutilation: breasts cut off – 20:81
S322.1.1 Father who wanted son will expose daughter – 99
S341.1 Exposure given up on account of newborn son's protest – 57–58 70–71

T. Sex

T52 Bride purchased – 12:124 15:64 16:71 127–128
T61.4 Betrothal ceremony – 84 88
T61.5.1 Betrothal in cradle – 85–86
T65 Betrothal restrictions – 85
*T75.4.1 Lady humiliates lover who killed wife for her – 7 95–96
T81 Death from love – 88
T117.11 Marriage to a statue – 21–22 65
*T131.0.2 Maiden has restricted choice of husband – 111–113 115
T173 Murderous bride – 91
T210.1 Faithful wife – 85 90
T211.9 Excessive grief at wife's death – 87–88 140
T311 Woman averse to marriage – 58:8 61:66
T320.2 Girl kills man who threatens her virtue – 89–90
T326.3 Martyrdom to preserve virginity – 64–65
T415 Brother-sister incest – 35 44–46
T475.2.1 Intercourse with sleeping girl – 71
T511.1.1–2 Conception from eating apple or berry – 59 61–62 76
T581.4 Child born in stable – 59 62
T585.2 Newborn child speaks – 57–58 70–71
T596 Naming of children – 57–58 120

U. The Nature of Life

*U62 God places the sun evenly over rich and poor – 33
*U90 Wealth and poverty: exchange of roles in otherworld – 77–79

V. Religion

V10.1 God prevents suicide – 61:87
V111.3 Place where a church must be built miraculously indicated – 66:121 67:86
*V138 Bridge preferred by Christ to church – 62:187
*V211.2.1.3 Christ disguised as poor man – 60:66 75:27 84:203
V211.7 Christ's descent to hell – 60–62
V211.8 Christ's resurrection – 60 62
V223.3 Saint can reveal hidden sins – 75–76
V229.1 Saint commands return from dead with supernatural information – 35:275
V515.1.1 Chairs in heaven – 77–79

W. Traits of Character

W115.1 The slovenly fiancée – 114 120
*W155.6 Hospitality refused – 59 121

X. Humour

*X201 Thief preferred as suitor to farmer, smith and hunter – 115

X1201 Lie: the great animal – 26 51–52

*X1259 Lies about crane – 117–118

Z. Miscellaneous Groups of Motifs

Z111–112 Death/Sickness personified – 80–83

*Z129 Dance personified – 110

Z216 Supernatural origin of hero: magic conception – 59 61

Z252 Hero at first nameless – 57–58

Z356 Unique survivor – 41 43

KALEVALA AND KANTELETAR CONCORDANCE

The poems in the present work are closely related to many of those used by Elias Lönnrot to compile the *Kalevala* and its companion volume the *Kanteletar*. The concordance shows the relationship between the genuine oral tradition and Lönnrot's compilations. The bold numbers refer to the poems in the 1849 edition of the *Kalevala* and the 1840–1841 and 1887 editions of the *Kanteletar* and are followed by a reference to the relevant poems in the present work

Kalevala (1849)

1: 1–5. **2**: 46–47, 49–50. **3**: 10–11. **4**: 104, 135–136. **5**: 56. **6**: 4–5, 12. **7**: 7–8, 12. **8**: 5–7. **9**: 139. **10**: 12. **11**: 39–40. **12**: 34–35, 37, 39–40. **13**: 53–54. **14**: 17, 35. **15**: 35, 59. **16**: 26–28, 30, 35, 61. **17**: 28–29. **18**: 15–17. **19**: 5, 17, 19. **20**: 26, 34–35, 37, 51–52. **23**: 121. **24**: 12. **25**: 1, 30. **26**: 34–37. **27**: 34–38. **28**: 37–38, 91. **29**: 37–38. **30**: 40. **31**: 41–43. **32**: 42–43. **33**: 42–43. **34**: 137. **35**: 44–45. **36**: 137–141. **37**: 21–22, 65. **38**: 19. **39**: 12–14, 23, 139. **40**: 23–25. **41**: 23–25. **42**: 12–15, 27. **43**: 12–15. **44**: 23–25. **46**: 48. **47**: 9. **48**: 9. **49**: 31. **50**: 1, 57–59, 61–62, 75–76, 148.

Kanteletar (1840–1841), Book III

1: 113. **2**: 53–54. **3**: 64–65. **4**: 77–79. **5**: 75–76. **6**: 59–63. **7**: 66–67. **8**: 84. **9**: 85–86. **10**: 145. **11**: 144. **12**: 146. **13**: 92–94. **14**: 90. **15**: 104–105. **16**: 95–96. **17**: 70–71. **18–19**: 44–45. **20**: 49–50. **21**: 127. **23**: 124–126, 128. **24–25**: 7, 18–20. **26–27**: 128. **28**: 126. **29**: 113. **30**: 137–138. **31**: 133–134. **32**: 92–94. **33**: 116. **34–37**: 106–109. **38**: 111–112. **39–40**: 122–123. **41**: 102–103. **42–43**: 135–136. **45–46**: 120. **47**: 72–74. **48**: 124–125. **49**: 116. **50**: 115. **53–54**: 129–131. **55**: 102–103. **56**: 114. **57**: 109, 114. **60**: 80–81.

Kanteletar (1887), Book III

2: 32–33. **23**: 68. **25**: 82–83. **36**: 87–88. **51**: 100. **52**: 143. **59**: 147. **105**: 101. **120**: 142. **127**: 132. **130**: 119. **137**: 69.

SOURCE INDEX

The numbers in the left-hand columns refer to the poems in the present work, those in the right-hand columns to the volume (in roman) of *Suomen Kansan Vanhat Runot* and the number of the poem in that volume.

1:1–14	I_3 1280
1:15–22	XII_1 332
1:23–47	I_3 1278
1:48–52	VII_2 1687: 7–11
2	IV_2 1821
3	V_1 541
4	VII_1 18
5	I_1 305
6	XII_1 62
7	VII_1 478
8	I_1 136
9	I_4 250: 1–88
10	I_1 185
11	IV_2 1855
12	I_1 54
13	VII_5 10
14	VII_1 679
15	I_1 441
16	I_1 492
17	VII_1 435
18	III_1 1218
19	I_1 562
20	V_1 256
21	I_1 529
22	III_3 4033
23	XII_1 75
24	VII_1 547a
25	V_1 158
26	III_3 4250
27	I_1 339
28	I_1 399
29	II 161
30	I_1 370
31	XII_1 99
32	III_1 1150
33	IV_2 1838
34	I_2 716
35	VII_1 835
36	III_2 2247
37	I_2 759
38	IV_1 1319
39	II 232
40	I_2 907
41	III_2 1284
42	XII_1 122
43	II 237
44	VII_1 892
45	IV_2 2011: 1–58
46	VII_3 273
47	III_1 1139
48	VII_5 3932
49	III_3 4041
50	I_4 870: 1–71
51	XII_1 110
52	XIII_1 254
53	VII_1 859
54	I_2 858
55	IV_2 1807
56	I_1 262
57	I_1 697a
58	I_1 689
59	I_2 1103
60	I_2 1105a
61	II 323a
62	IV_3 4022, 4023, 4024, 4025
63	VIII 1255
64	XII, 136
65	VI_1 41
66	VIII 990A
67	VIII 993A
68	IV_1 651
69	XIII_1 1075
70	IV_1 329
71	XIII_1 786
72	X_1 46
73	XIII_1 654
74	IV_3 4048
75	IX_1 102
76	IV_2 2052
77	VII_2 1420
78	IX_2 13
79	IV_3 4041
80	I_2 1032
81	VII_2 948
82	IX_2 10
83	V_1 453
84	X_1 4
85	IX_1 90
86	IV_1 316
87	VIII 1011
88	IV_1 1155
89	VII_1 209
90	III_2 1340
91	III_3 3669
92	IX_1 91
93	VII_2 934
94	IV_2 2084
95	VII_1 489
96	IV_2 1934
97	III_1 812
98	V_1 985
99	III_3 4244: 1–53
100	IV_1 551
101	III_2 1372
102	IV_2 2074

103	VII_2 1367	120	III_3 2703	137	VI_1 30
104	I_1 233	121	XIII_1 928	138	XIII_1 11
105	III_3 2725	122	XIII_1 969	139	VII_1 654
106	IV_3 2931	123	VII_2 1256	140	VII_1 904
107	IV_2 1504	124	I_2 1206	141	III_2 1442
108	IV_2 1867	125	V_1 1035	142	III_1 979
109	IV_3 3927	126	II 1420	143	VIII 1006
110	I_2 1188	127	V_1 697	144	VII_2 1361
111	IX_1 10	128	X_1 58	145	I_2 1054
112	II 351	129	I_2 1170	146	I_2 1064
113	III_1 687	130	XIII_1 978	147	III_1 987
114	VI_1 179	131	III_2 1358	148:1–7	XIII_1 1792
115	V_1 1027	132	III_1 71	148:8–17	XIII_1 1902
116	XIII_1 367	133	I_2 1212	148:18–20	VI_1 552
117	VI_1 244	134	III_3 3529	148:21–28	I_3 1327
118	VIII 3745	135	VII_2 1237	148:29–42	XII_1 341: 11–24
119	IV_1 979	136	IV_1 567		

COLLECTION LOCALITY INDEX

The customarily used name of the place of collection is given in italics. It is followed by alternative names (in brackets) and a location reference

Akonlahti Kontokki, Archangel Karelia, Russia
9 133 146

Central Finland
78 (cf. also Hankasalmi)

Eräjärvi Häme, Finland
72

Hankasalmi Central Finland
82

Heinola Häme, Finland
111

Hevaa (*Kovashi*) Kaprio (Kaporye), Ingria, Russia
2 11 33 45 55 62 74 76 79 88 94

Hietamäki Ingria, Russia
70

Ilomantsi North Karelia, Finland
1:48–52 14 17 35 103 139

Juva Savo, Finland
114 137

Jyskyjärvi Archangel Karelia, Russia
54 110

Kaavi North Karelia, Finland
46

Kaprio (*Kaporye*) Ingria, Russia
102 (cf. also Hevaa)

Karelian Isthmus Finland (later Russia)
73 148:1–17 (cf. also Metsäpirtti, Sakkola)

Kemi North Ostrobothnia, Finland
6 42 148:29–42

Kiihtelysvaara North Karelia, Finland
81

Kiimaisjärvi Archangel Karelia, Russia
15 34

Kitee North Karelia, Finland
48

Kiuruvesi Savo, Finland
65

Korpiselkä Ladoga Karelia, Finland (later Russia)
7 77

Koski Häme, Finland
63

Kuhmo Kainuu, Finland
64

Kupanitsa (*Gubanits*) Ingria, Russia
106

Latvajärvi Vuokkiniemi, Archangel Karelia, Russia
1:1–14, 23–47 8 12 21 28 37 59 60 148:21–28

Lemi Savo, Finland
117

Liissilä (*Lisino*) Ingria, Russia
70 109

Liperi North Karelia, Finland
144

Metsäpirtti Karelian Isthmus, Finland (later Russia)
130 138

Miikkulainen (*Nikulas*) Ingria, Russia
98

Moloskovitsa (*Moloskovits*) Ingria, Russia
38 119

Narvusi (*Keikino*) Ingria, Russia
36 91 97 105 113 120 132 134 142 147

Nyebelitsa Novgorod District, Russia
126

Ostrobothnia Finland
23 51 (cf. also Kemi, Vaasa)

Paltamo Kainuu, Finland
31

Pyhämaa South-West Finland
118

Repola Olonets Karelia, Russia
29 39 43 61 112

Sakkola Karelian Isthmus, Finland (later Russia)
52 69 71 116 121 122

Savo Finland
148:18–20 (cf. also Juva, Kiuruvesi, Lemi)

Serepetta (*Zherebyat*) Ingria, Russia
96

Skuoritsa (*Skvorits*) Ingria, Russia
107

Soikkola (*Soykino*) Ingria, Russia
18 22 26 32 41 47 49 90 99 101 131 141

Sortavala Ladoga Karelia, Finland (later Russia)
24

South-West Finland
87 (cf. also Koski, Pyhämaa, Turku)

Suistamo Ladoga Karelia, Finland (later Russia)
4 44 53 89 93 123 135 140

Suomussalmi Kainuu, Finland
1:15–22

Sävsen Dalecarlia, Sweden
13

Sääksmäki Häme, Finland
75 85 92

Toksova (*Toksovo*) Ingria, Russia
125

Turku South-West Finland
143

Tuupovaara North Karelia, Finland
95

Tyrö (*Tiris*) Ingria, Russia
38 86 100 108 119 136

Uhtua Archangel Karelia, Russia
40 50 104 129 145

Vaasa South Ostrobothnia, Finland
66

Valkeasaari (*Valki*) Ingria, Russia
3

Venjoki Ingria, Russia
68

Vesilahti Häme, Finland
84

Vuokkiniemi Archangel Karelia, Russia
5 19 57 80 124 (cf. also Latvajärvi, Vuonninen)

Vuole (*Voly*) Ingria, Russia
20 25 83 115 127

Vuonninen Vuokkiniemi, Archangel Karelia, Russia
10 16 30 56 58

Ylöjärvi Häme, Finland
128

COLLECTOR INDEX

Ahlqvist, A. E.
1826–1889, Finno-Ugrist, poet, publicist, university teacher
52 122

Alava, V.
1870–1935, journalist, teacher
36 62 74 79 98 127

Arwidsson, A. I.
1791–1858, historian, publicist, university teacher, director, Royal Library, Stockholm
65 148:10–20

Berner, A.
1843–1892, school inspector
124

Borenius(–Lähteenkorva), A. A.
1846–1931, folklorist, school inspector
1:1–14 3 5 8 15 16 21 29 30 34 40 43 50 54 55 75 138 148:21–28

Cajan (later Kajaani), J. F.
1815–1887, writer on Finnish history, assistant to E. Lönnrot, cleric, publicist
27 60

Castrén, M. A.
1813–1852, linguist, ethnographer, a pioneer of the comparative study of the Uralic languages, university teacher, translator of the *Old Kalevala* into Swedish
9 57 64

Crohns, E. A.
1785–1865, cadet school teacher, cleric
148:18–20

Europaeus, D. E. D.
1820–1884, folklorist, linguist, archeologist, assistant to E. Lönnrot, publicist
1:48–52 7 14 17 35 39 44 70 86 100 132 136 139

Ganander, K.
1741–1790, folklorist, linguist, archeologist, cleric
23 42 51

Gottlund, C. A.
1796–1875, linguist, folklorist, archeologist, publicist, university teacher
13 46 137

Hainari, O. A.
1856–1910, writer on the history of Eastern Finland and Ingria, teacher
4

Heikkilä, A.
fl. 1720–1740
66

Härkönen, I.
1882–1941, writer, teacher, activist in the Karelian movement
123

Juslenius, D.
1676–1752, linguist, cleric, publicist, Bishop of Skara, Sweden
87

Järvinen, N.
1831–1901, cleric
72

Karjalainen, K.
1871–1919, Finno-Ugrist, university teacher
19 145

Karttunen, U.
1874–1959, historian, secondary school teacher
61 112

Killinen, K.
1849–1922, teacher, poet
24

Kohvakka (later Kohvakka-Järvi), T.
1910–, teacher, librarian
117

Koskivaara, A.
1892–1918, forestry student
130

Liipola, J. S.
1868–?, primary school teacher
63

Lorvi, J.
1910s- student
109

Lukkarinen, J.
1884–1963, ethnographer, editor of *Suomen Kansan Vanhat Runot*
134

Länkelä, J.
1833–1916, pedagogue
22 26 49 91 99

Lönnbohm, O. A. F.
1856–1927, pedagogue, journalist, museum curator
48

Lönnrot, E.
1802–1884, folklorist, physician, linguist compiler of the *Kalevala* and *Kanteletar*, university teacher
1:23–47 12 28 37 56 58 59 73 85 92 95 103 104 110 129 144 146 148:1–17

Marttinen, I.
1870–1934, shopkeeper, insurance agent
80

Niemi, A. R.
1869–1931, folklorist, university teacher, editor of *Suomen Kansan Vanhat Runot*
133

Oksanen, J.
1866–?, teacher
82

Pajula, F.
1857–1918, teacher
20, 83, 115

Paldani, B. A.
1823–1860, cleric
128

Petrelius, V.
1869–1963, bank manager
126

Polén, R.
1823–1884, journalist, editor, teacher
77, 93, 135, 140

Porkka, V.
1854–1889, linguist, authority on the Ingrian dialects
2 11 18 32 33 41 45 47 76 90 94 96 97 101 102 108 113 131 141 142 147

Reinholm, H. A.
1819–1883, archeologist, ethnographer, cleric
68, 71, 116

Rothman, A.
1821–1890, postmaster
78

Rudbeck (later Salmelainen), E.
1830–1867, folklorist, teacher
78

Ruotsalainen, J. F.
1877–1951, journalist
106 120

Rytkönen, A.
1870–1930, journalist, author
81

Saxa, K.
1796–1849, cleric
1:15–22

Saxbäck, F. A.
1836–1863, theology student
25

Seppänen (later Itkonen), I.
1904–, technical school teacher
118

Sirelius, S.
1822–1848, theology student
53 89

Sjögren, A. J.
1794–1855, linguist, ethnographer, historian, explorer, academician (St Petersburg)
10

Slöör, K.
1833–1905, journalist, author, school inspector (Finnish schools in St Petersburg)
69 121 125

Stråhlman, K.
1821–1898, cleric, secondary school teacher
107

Tallqvist, T.
1839–1912, railway construction engineer
38 88 119

Tarkiainen, V.
1879–1951, literary scholar, university teacher
114

Topelius, Z.

1781–1831, folklorist, physician
6 148:29–42

Toppola, J.

1869–1928, secondary school teacher
111

Törneroos, A.

1835–1896, poet, journalist, primary school teacher
38 88 119

Unknown

23 31 42 67 84

SELECT BIBLIOGRAPHY

The wealth of material written about Kalevala epic and closely related subjects made the compilation of a bibliography especially difficult, all the more so as the editors had to consider the very different interests of the general reader and the specialist, and of readers both with and without a knowledge of Finnish. With these various requirements in mind, the editors based their choice on two main criteria: they restricted their selection to works that provide a starting-point for further reading and are likely to be readily available in major libraries.

The Bibliography is divided into four sections. The first (Collections of folk poetry) was compiled primarily with the Finnish reader in mind, while Section II (Translations of the *Kalevala*) is intended for both Finnish and other readers. Section III (Introductory works) assumes a knowledge of Finnish. In view of the huge amount of material, both general and specialist, in Finnish, the editors thought it wisest to limit their choice to four basic works which include important bibliographies and to other major bibliographical sources, thus allowing the reader to decide for himself which particular aspects of Finnish folk poetry he wishes to pursue. The final Section comprises monographs and articles, mainly in English, French, German and Russian, all of which provide additional references to works in languages other than Finnish.

Abbreviations:

FFC	Folklore Fellows Communications, Helsinki, 1910–.
FUF	Finnisch-Ugrische Forschungen, Helsinki, 1901–.
JSF	Arv. Journal of Scandinavian Folklore, Stockholm, 1945–.
JSFOu	Journal de la Société Finno-Ougrienne, Helsinki, 1886–.
MSFOu	Mémoires de la Société Finno-Ougrienne, Helsinki, 1890–.
SF	Studia Fennica, Helsinki, 1933–.

I. COLLECTIONS OF FOLK POETRY

Primary:

Suomen Kansan Vanhat Runot ('Ancient Poems of the Finnish People'), 33 vols, Helsinki, 1908–1948 (cf. above pp. 11, 13, 38, 596).

Karel'skie epicheskie pesni ('Karelian epic poetry'), ed. V. Ya. Yevseyev, Moskva-Leningrad, 1950 (contains 188 Karelian epic poems with Russian translations, introduction and commentary).

Karjalan Kansan Runot ('The poems of the Karelian people'), ed. V. Jevsejev, Tallinn, 1976 (contains 160 Karelian epic poems arranged to illustrate the themes of the *Kalevala*; introduction in Finnish, Russian and German).

Narodnie pesni Ingermanlandii ('The poetry of the Ingrian people'), ed. Eino Kiuru, Terttu Koski, Elina Kylmäsuu, Leningrad, 1974 (includes 29 Ingrian epic poems with Russian translations and introduction).

Suomen kansan kannel. Vanhaa kansanrunoutta julkaistuna alkuperäisten kirjaanpanojen mukaan ('The *kantele* of the Finnish people. Old folk poetry published according to the original sources'), selected and ed. V. Tarkiainen, Hertta Harmas (= *Suomen Kansalliskirjallisuus*, Vol. III), Helsinki, 1943 (includes 57 epic poems selected from *Suomen Kansan Vanhat Runot*, with introduction and notes).

Secondary:

Kirjokansi. Suomen kansan kertomarunoutta ('The brightly-worked cover. Narrative poetry of the Finnish people'), selected and ed. Martti Haavio, Helsinki, 1952 (includes the most important poems, a detailed commentary and numerous bibliographical references. The language of the poems has been standardized according to the norms of Modern Literary Finnish and the materials have been arranged to illustrate the editor's view of the archetypal structure of the poems).

Suomen muinaisrunoja, kertovaisia ('Ancient poems of Finland – narrative'), selected and ed. Kaarle Krohn, Helsinki, 1930 (contains 82 narrative poems and incantations. The editor provides notes and attempts to reconstruct the possible archetypal form of the poems).

II. TRANSLATIONS OF THE KALEVALA

34 verse translations of the complete 1849 edition of the *Kalevala* have appeared in 22 languages. The selection below is limited to readily available editions in English, French, German, Russian, Spanish (the first translations appearing in 1888, 1931, 1852, 1888, 1953 respectively) and, where applicable, in the Nordic languages.

Kalevala. The Land of the Heroes, 2 vols, tr. W. F. Kirby, London and New York, 1907.

The Kalevala or Poems of the Kaleva District, tr. Francis Peabody Magoun, Jr., Cambridge, Massachusetts, 1963 (prose).

Le Kalevala. Épopée populaire finnoise, tr. Jean-Louis Perret, Paris, 1931.

Kalevala, das finnische Epos des Elias Lönnrot, tr. Lore and Hans Fromm, München, 1967.

Kalevala, tr. Albert Lange Fliflet, Oslo, 1967.

Kalevala. Finskaya narodnaya epopeya, tr. L. P. Bel'skii, S.-Peterburg, 1888.

Kalevala, tr. María Dolores Arroyo, Barcelona, 1953.

Kalevala, tr. Björn Collinder, Stockholm, 1948.

III. INTRODUCTORY WORKS

MARTTI HAAVIO, *Suomalainen mytologia* ('Finnish mythology'), Helsinki, 1967.

Karjalan laulajat ('Singers of Karelia'), ed. Pertti Virtaranta, Väinö Kaukonen, Matti Kuusi, Leea Virtanen, Helsinki, 1968.

MATTI KUUSI et alii, *Kirjoittamaton kirjallisuus* ('Unwritten literature' = *Suomen kirjallisuus*, Vol. 1), Helsinki, 1963.

AIMO TURUNEN, *Kalevalan sanakirja* ('Kalevala dictionary'), Helsinki, 1949.

Bibliography

Biographical and subject:

SULO HALTSONEN, 'Finnische linguistische und volkskundliche Bibliographie für die Jahre 1935–1970', *SF* 3–7, 9, 10, 12–14, 16, 1938–1971.
- 'Verzeichnis der Veröffentlichungen Uno Holmberg-Harva's', *FFC* 112, 1934.

LAILA HÄNNINEN, *Luettelo ennen v. 1927 painetusta Kalevalaa koskevasta kirjallisuudesta. Bibliographie du Kalevala jusqu'en 1926*, Helsinki, 1928.

H. LAIDVEE, *'Kalevipoja' bibliograafia 1836–1961*, Tallinn, 1964.

RAUNI PURANEN, 'Kaarle Krohn. Bibliography', *SF* 11, 1964.
- 'Martti Haavio. Bibliographie', *SF* 8, 17, 1959, 1974.

KAIJA VIRTANEN, 'Jouko Hautala. Bibliography', *JSF* 27, 1971.

Periodicals:

Kalevalaseuran Vuosikirja ('Yearbook of the Kalevala Society'), Helsinki, 1921–. Ethnological Index in Vol. 40 (1960), Author Index in Vol. 50 (1970).

Kotiseutu (Periodical of the Society for Local Studies), Helsinki, 1909–. Indexes compiled by Eeva Mäkelä-Henriksson (1953), Kirsti Kuisma (1962), and Henni Ilomäki (1977).

Suomi (Periodical of the Finnish Literature Society), Helsinki, 1841–. Indexes in Vols IV: 20 (1927) and V: 20 (1938).

Virittäjä (Periodical of the Mother Tongue Society), Helsinki, 1883–. Indexes compiled by Erkki Itkonen & Pertti Virtaranta (1952), Reino Peltola (1961), Irja Leena Suhonen (1973), and Eeva Mäkelä-Henriksson (ethnological, 1963).

IV. BACKGROUND WORKS

ANTTI AARNE, *Das estnisch-ingermanländische Maie-Lied. Eine vergleichende Untersuchung* (= FFC 47), 1922.
- *Das Lied vom Angeln der Jungfrau Vellamos. Eine vergleichende Untersuchung* (= FFC 48), 1923.

JOHN ABERCROMBY, *The Pre- and Proto-historic Finns both Eastern and Western with the Magic Songs of the West Finns*, 2 vols, London, 1898.

WALTER ANDERSON, 'Geographisch-historische Methode', *Handwörterbuch des deutschen Märchens*, Vol. 2, Berlin, 1934/1940.

OTTO ANDERSSON, *The Bowed-Harp. A Study in the History of Early Musical Instruments*, London, 1930.

K. V. CHISTOV, *"Kalevala" – velikii epos karelo-finskogo naroda*, Petrozavodsk, 1949.

REIDAR TH. CHRISTIANSEN, *Die finnischen und nordischen Varianten des zweiten Merseburgerspruches* (= FFC 18), 1914.

BJÖRN COLLINDER, 'The Kalevala and its Background', JSF 20, 1964.

DOMENICO COMPARETTI, *Der Kalewala oder die traditionelle Poesie der Finnen. Historisch-kritische Studie über den Ursprung der grossen nationalen Epopäen*, Halle, 1892.

ELSA ENÄJÄRVI-HAAVIO, 'On the Performance of the Finnish Folk Runes. Two-part Singing', *Folk-liv*, 1951, Stockholm.

HANS FROMM, *Kalevala. Das finnische Epos des Elias Lönnrot*. Vol 2. *Kommentar*, München, 1967.

MARTTI HAAVIO, 'Das Seelengericht', SF 9, 1961.
- 'Der Charakter der finnischen Heldendichtung', *Nordische Rundschau*, VIII Jahrg. Leipzig & Berlin, 1935.
- 'Elias Lönnrot', JSF 25–26, 1970.
- *Essais folkloriques* (= SF 8), 1959.
- *Heilige Haine in Ingermanland* (= FFC 189), 1963.
- *Väinämöinen. Eternal Sage* (= FFC 144), 1952.

UNO HARVA [formerly HOLMBERG], 'Antero Vipunen', FUF 24, 1937.
- 'Der Bacchus der Altfinnen', *Sitzungsberichte der Finnischen Akademie der Wissenschaften 1944*, Helsinki, 1945.
- 'Ilmarinen', FUF 29, 1946.
- 'Sämpsä Pellervoinen', *Sitzungsberichte der Finnischen Akademie der Wissenschaften 1946*, Helsinki, 1947.

Jouko Hautala, 'Die folkloristische Forschung in Finland', JSFOu 60, 1958.
- *Finnish Folklore Research 1828–1918* (= The History of Learning and Science in Finland 1828–1918, Vol. 12), Helsinki, 1969.
- 'Vicissitudes in Publishing the Ancient Poetry of the Finnish People', SF 7, 1957.
- 'Über Arbeitsweise und Möglichkeiten bei der Erforschung altfinnischer Runendichtung', SF 5, 1947.

Uno Holmberg [later Harva], *Der Baum des Lebens*, Helsinki, 1922.
- 'Finno-Ugric Mythology', *The Mythology of All Races*, Vol. 4, Boston, 1927.

Lauri Honko, 'Finnische Mythologie', *Wörterbuch der Mythologie* (herausg. von H. W. Haussig), Teil II: *Das alte Europa*, Stuttgart, 1965.
- 'Uno Harva', JSF 25–26, 1970.

Oskar Kallas, *Die Wiederholungslieder der estnischen Volkspoesie*, Vol. 1 (= MSFOu 16), 1901.

Väinö Kaukonen, 'Die Entstehung des Kalevala-Epos', *Wissenschaftliche Zeitschrift der Ernst Moritz Arndt Universität Greifswald*, 8, Gesellschaft- und sprachwissenschaftliche Reihe 3, 1958–1959.
- 'Elias Lönnrot als Förderer der Kenntnis der nahe verwandten Völker Finnlands', *Acta Ethnographica*, 11, Budapest, 1963.
- 'Elias Lönnrot, velikii uchenyy karelo-finskogo naroda', *Izvestiya Ak. Nauk SSSR, otd. lit. i yazyka* 11, Leningrad, 1952.
- 'Jacob Grimm und das Kalevala-Epos', *Deutsches Jahrbuch für Volkskunde*, 9, Berlin, 1963.
- 'Kalevala-Dichtung im heutigen Viena', *Mitteilungen des Vereins für finnische Volkskunde*, 2: 1–2, Helsinki, 1944.
- 'Sozdanie eposa "Kalevala" ', *Finno-ugorskaya filologiya*, Leningrad, 1962.
- 'The Kalevala and the Kalevipoeg', *Ancient Cultures of the Uralian Peoples* (ed. Péter Hajdú), Budapest, 1976.

Iivar Kemppinen, *The Ballad of Lady Isabel and the False Knight*, Helsinki, 1954.

A. Khurmevaara, *"Kalevala" v Rossii. K istorii perevoda*, Petrozavodsk, 1972.

John I. Kolehmainen, *Epic of the North. The Story of Finland's Kalevala*, New York Mills, 1973.

Wolfgang Krause, 'Zur Herkunft von finn. *runo* 'Lied", FUF 37, 1969.

Julius Krohn, 'Das Lied vom Mädchen, welches erlöst werden soll', JSFOu 10, 1892.

Kaarle Krohn, 'Das Lazarusthema in der finnisch-estnischen Volksdichtung', MSFOu 52, 1924.
- 'Der gefangene Unhold', FUF 7, 1907.
- 'Der Hansakaufmann in der finnischen Volksdichtung', FUF 16, 1923.
- *Die folkloristische Arbeitsmethode, begründet von Julius Krohn und weitergeführt von nordischen Forschern*, Oslo, 1926.
- 'Die Freierei der Himmelslichter', FUF 3, 1903.
- 'Die Fundorte der epischen Gesänge des Kalevala (mit einer Karte)', FUF 4, 1904.
- *Folklore Methodology, Formulated by* Julius Krohn *and Expanded by Nordic Researchers* (= Publications of the American Folklore Society, Bibliographical and Special Series, Vol. 21), Austin & London, 1971.
- 'Kaleva und seine Sippe', JSFOu 30, 1918.
- *Kalevalastudien* I–VI (= FFC 53, 67, 71, 72, 75, 76), 1924–1928.
- 'Lemminkäinens Tod < Christi > Balders Tod', FUF 5, 1905.
- 'Sampsa Pellervoinen > Njordr, Freyr?', FUF 4, 1904.
- 'Über Ortsnamen in den Gesängen des archangelschen Karelien I–III', FUF 16, 1923.
- *Zur finnischen Mythologie*, Vol. I (= FFC 104), 1932.

Kulturhistoriskt Lexikon för nordisk medeltid från vikingatid till reformationstid, Vols. 1–19, Helsingfors, 1956–1975 (sub e.g. *Ahti, Annikainen, Antero Vipunen, Anterus från Pyhäjoki, Balladdiktning, Ilmarinen, Kaleva, Kalevala, Kantele, Kaukomieli, Kullervo, Legendvisor, Lemminkäinen, Mariadigtning, Maria Magdalena, Mytiske dikt, Naturmytiska visor, Osmo, Reiser, Sampo, Skjemteviser, Sämpsä Pellervoinen, Trolldom, Untamo, Väinämöinen*).

Erich Kunze, 'Goethes "Finnisches Lied" ', SF 6, 1952.

Anna-Leena Kuusi, 'Finnish Mythology', *Ancient Cultures of the Uralian Peoples* (ed. Péter Hajdú), Budapest, 1976.

Matti Kuusi, 'Beiträge zur Feuermythologie', *Miscellanea K. C. Peeters*, Antwerpen, 1975.
- 'Le discours direct comme critère de datation de la poésie épique ancienne', *Mélanges offerts à Aurélien Sauvageot pour son soixantequinzième anniversaire* (= Études Finno-Ougriennes 8), Paris, 1971.
- *Sampo-eepos. Typologinen analyysi* (= MSFOu 96), 1949 (Deutsches Referat).
- ' 'The Bridge and the Church', an Anti-church Legend', SF 18, 1975.
- 'Über Wiederholungstypen in der Volksepik unter besonderer Berücksichtigung der Edda, der Bylinen und der finnisch-estnischen Volksdichtung', SF 6, 1952.

Armas Launis, 'Über Art, Entstehung und Verbreitung der estnisch-finnischen Runenmelodien. Eine Studie aus dem Gebiet der vergleichenden Volksmelodienforschung', MSFOu 31, 1913.

Outi Lehtipuro, 'Trends in Finnish Folkloristics', SF 18, 1975.

Pentti Leino, *Strukturaalinen alkusointu suomessa*, Helsinki, 1970 (Summary: Structural alliteration in Finnish).

NILS LID, 'Kring Kalevala-miljøet', *Syn og Segn*, Oslo, 1943.
- 'The Mythical Realm of the Far North as it appears in the National Finnish Epic Kalevala and the Scandinavian Fornalder-Saga Tradition', *Laos*, 1, *Comparative Studies of Folklore and Regional Ethnology*, Stockholm, 1951.

OSKAR LOORITS, *Grundzüge des estnischen Volksglaubens*, 3 vols, Lund, 1949–1957 (cf. Namen- und Stichwortregister, Vol. 3, sub e.g. *Ballade, Eiche, Finnen, finnisch-ugrisch, Heldenepik, Ingermanland, Kalevala, Karelien, Legende, Maie-Lied, Schmied, Wasserjungfrau, Welteimythe, Wiederholungslieder*).

V. J. MANSIKKA, 'Alesha Popovich i Ivan Godinovich v Finlyandii', *Etnograficheskiye Obozreniye*, Moskva, 1907.
- 'Der "blaue Stein" in der finnischen Volkstradition', FUF 11, 1911.
- 'Kleinere Beiträge zur Balder-Lemminkäinenfrage', FUF 8, 1908.

E. M. MELETINSKII, 'K voprosu o genezise karelofinskogo eposa', *Sovetskaya etnografiya*, Moskva, 1960 (English summary).

RUDOLF MEYER, *Kalewala. Der finnische Mythos und das Geisteserbe Finnlands*, Stuttgart, 1964.

ERNEST J. MOYNE, *Hiawatha and Kalevala. A Study of the Relationship between Longfellow's "Indian Edda" and the Finnish Epic* (= FFC 192), 1963.

EINO NIEMINEN, 'Finnisch *kantele* und die damit verbundenen Namen baltischer Musikinstrumente', SF 10, 1963.

FELIX J. OINAS, 'Folk Epic', *Folklore and Folklife* (ed. Richard M. Dorson), Chicago, 1972.
- *Studies in Finnic-Slavic Folklore Relations* (= FFC 205), 1969.

ISTVÁN PAPP, 'Die Rhythmusprobleme des Kalevala', JSFOu 58, 1956.

JUHA PENTIKÄINEN, 'Julius and Kaarle Krohn', JSF 25–26, 1970.

ERICH POHL, *Die deutsche Volksballade von der "Losgekauften". Ein Versuch zur Erforschung des Ursprungs und Werdeganges einer Volksballade von europäischer Verbreitung* (= FFC 105), 1934.

PIRKKO-LIISA RAUSMAA, 'Antti Aarne', JSF 25–26, 1970.

W. EDSON RICHMOND, 'The Study of Folklore in Finland', *Journal of American Folklore*, Vol. 74, Philadelphia, 1961.

MATTI SADENIEMI, *Die Metrik des Kalevala-Verses* (= FFC 139), 1951.

VÄINÖ SALMINEN, 'Die alten Lieder des finnischen Volkes', *Mitteilungen des Vereins für finnische Volkskunde*, I: 1–2, Helsinki, 1943.

AURELIEN SAUVAGEOT. *Les anciens Finnois*, Paris, 1961.

INGRID SCHELLBACH, 'Die Bahuvrihi-Komposita in der alten finnischen Volksdichtung', JSFOu 65, 1964.

E. N. SETÄLÄ, 'Das Rätsel vom Sampo', FUF 22, 1934.
- 'Die Übersetzungen und Übersetzer des Kalevalas. Kleine Nachträge zu der Bibliographie der Kalevala-Übersetzungen', FUF 10, 11, 1910, 1911.
- 'Kullervo-Hamlet. Ein sagenvergleichender Versuch', FUF 3, 7, 10, 1907–1910.
- 'Zur Etymologie von Sampo', FUF 2, 1902.

WOLFGANG STEINITZ, *Der Parallelismus in der finnisch-karelischen Volksdichtung untersucht an den Liedern des karelischen Sängers Arhippa Perttunen* (= FFC 115), 1934.

Studia Fennica, Vol. 11. Dédié à la mémoire de Kaarle Krohn à l'occasion de son centenaire, par la Société de la Littérature Finnoise, 1964 (Articles on Kaarle Krohn in English, German and French by Martti Haavio, Irja-Leena Evijärvi, Jouko Hautala, Matti Kuusi and Bertalan Korompay).

STITH THOMPSON and JONAS BALYS, 'Finnish Folklore', *Standard Dictionary of Folklore, Mythology and Legend*, Vol. 1, New York, 1949.

Y. H. TOIVONEN, 'Le gros chêne des chants populaires finnois', JSFOu 53, 1947.

ASKO VILKUNA, *Das Verhalten der Finnen in "Heiligen" Situationen* (= FFC 164), 1956.

WILLIAM A. WILSON, *Folklore and Nationalism in Modern Finland*, Bloomington and London, 1976.

LEEA VIRTANEN, 'Väinö Salminen', JSF 25–26, 1970.

V. YA. YEVSEYEV, *Istoricheskie osnovy karelo-finskogo eposa*, 2 vols, Moskva-Leningrad, 1957, 1960.